PACO ROCA

*The Winter of
the Cartoonist*

TRANSLATED BY
Andrea Rosenberg

Other Fantagraphics Titles by Paco Roca

The House
La Casa (Spanish Edition)
Twists of Fate
Wrinkles

Translator: Andrea Rosenberg
Editor: RJ Casey
Supervising Editor: Gary Groth
Designer: Chelsea Wirtz
Production: Paul Baresh
Editorial Assistance: Sora Hong
Promotion: Jacq Cohen
Associate Publisher: Eric Reynolds
Publisher: Gary Groth

Fantagraphics Books, Inc.
7563 Lake City Way NE
Seattle, WA 98115
www.fantagraphics.com

First Printing: 2020
ISBN 978-1-68396-324-0
Library of Congress Control Number: 2019953938
Printed in Malaysia

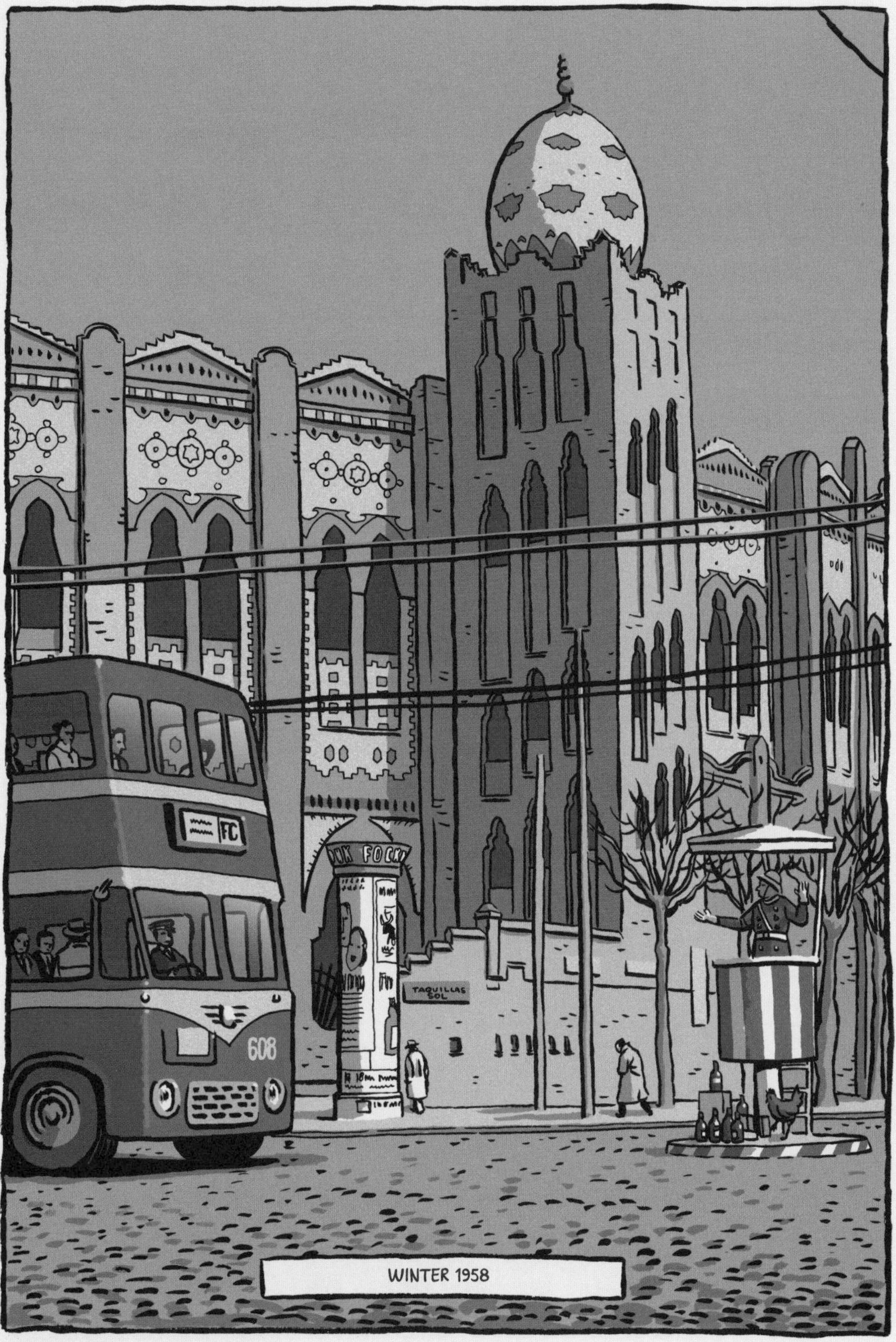
FC
608
TAQUILLAS
SOL
WINTER 1958

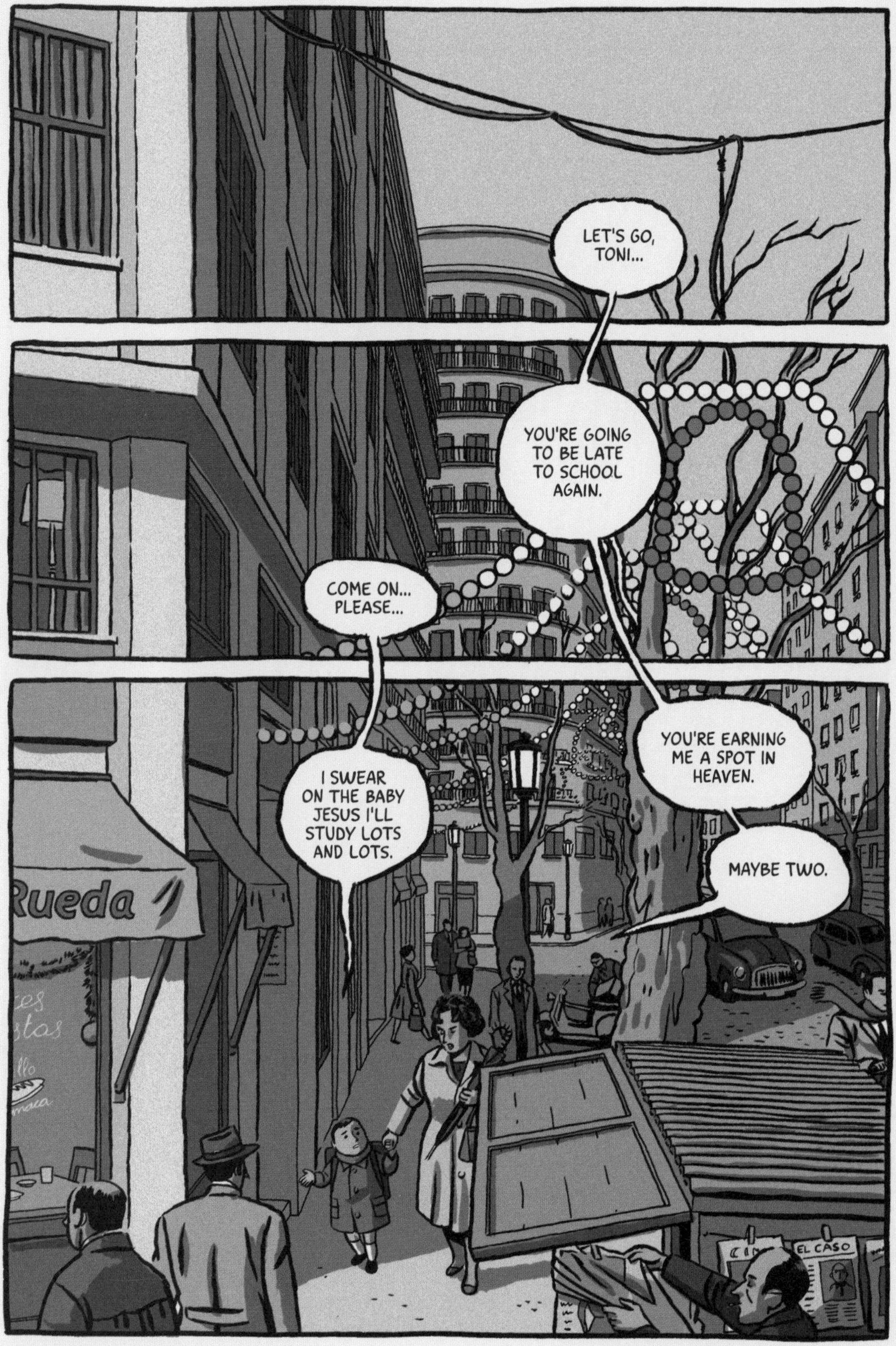
LET'S GO, TONI...
YOU'RE GOING TO BE LATE TO SCHOOL AGAIN.
COME ON... PLEASE...
I SWEAR ON THE BABY JESUS I'LL STUDY LOTS AND LOTS.
YOU'RE EARNING ME A SPOT IN HEAVEN.
MAYBE TWO.
Rueda
EL CASO

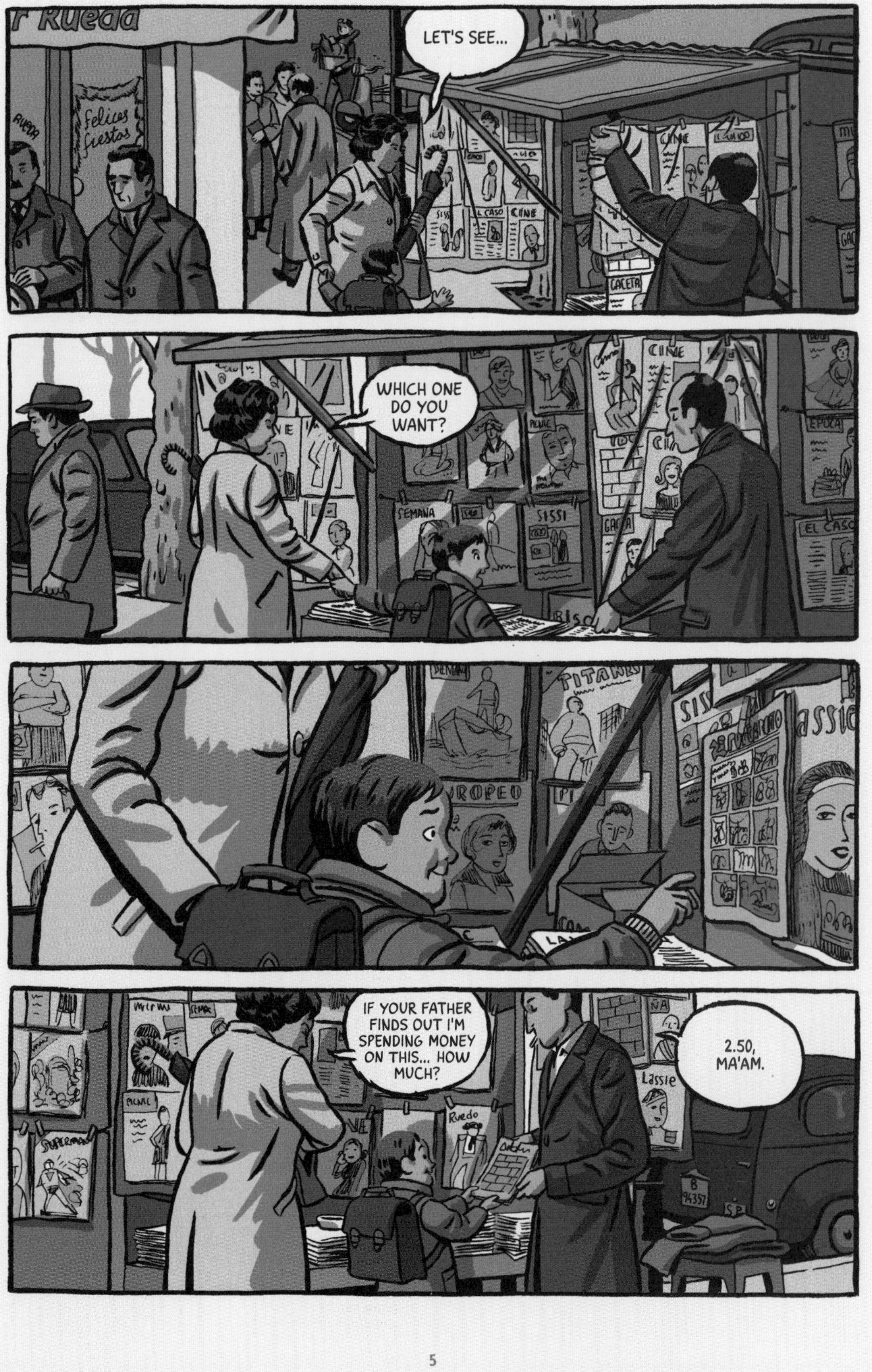
LET'S SEE...
WHICH ONE DO YOU WANT?
IF YOUR FATHER FINDS OUT I'M SPENDING MONEY ON THIS... HOW MUCH?
2.50, MA'AM.

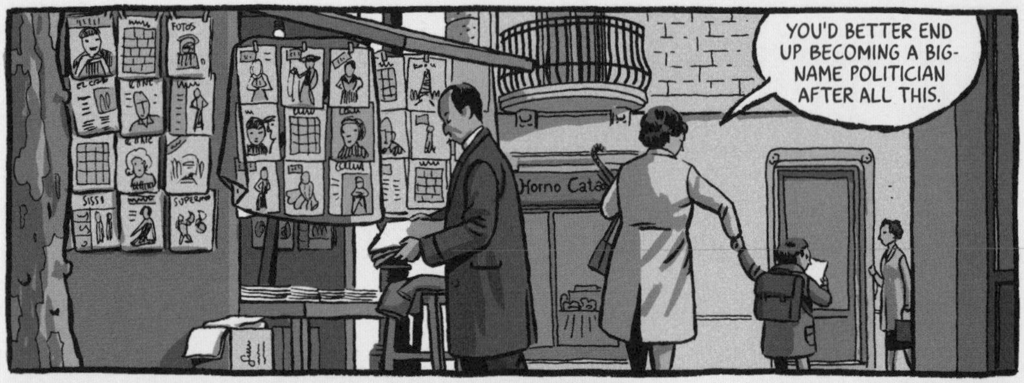
YOU'D BETTER END UP BECOMING A BIG-NAME POLITICIAN AFTER ALL THIS.

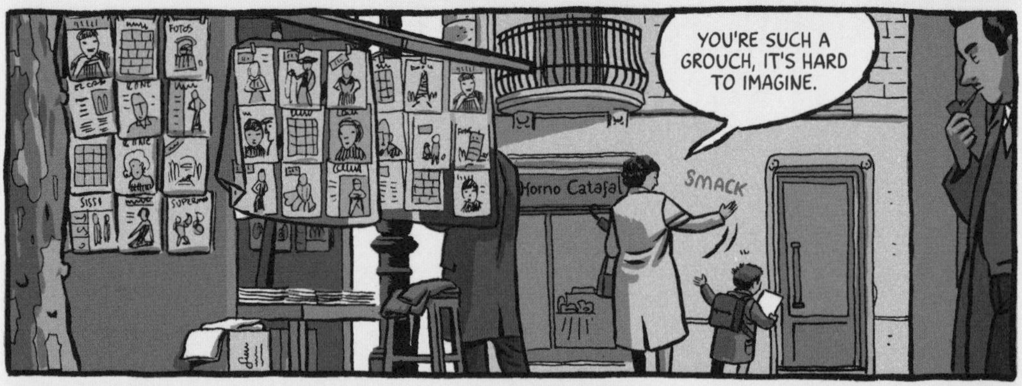
YOU'RE SUCH A GROUCH, IT'S HARD TO IMAGINE.
SMACK
Horno Catafal

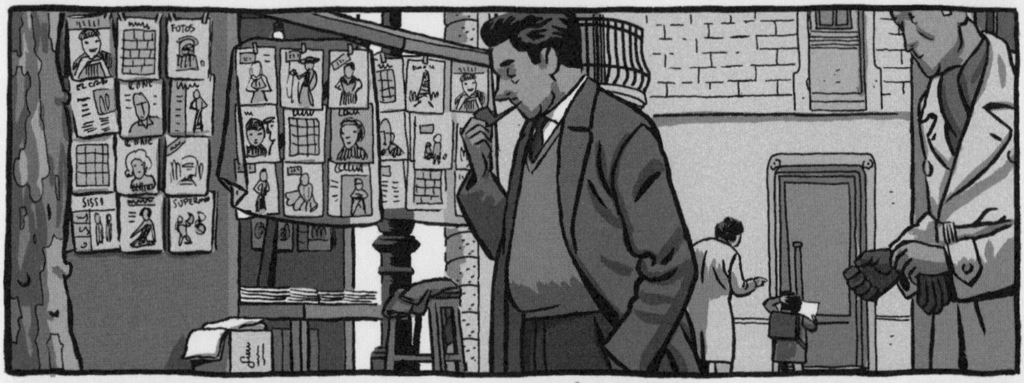

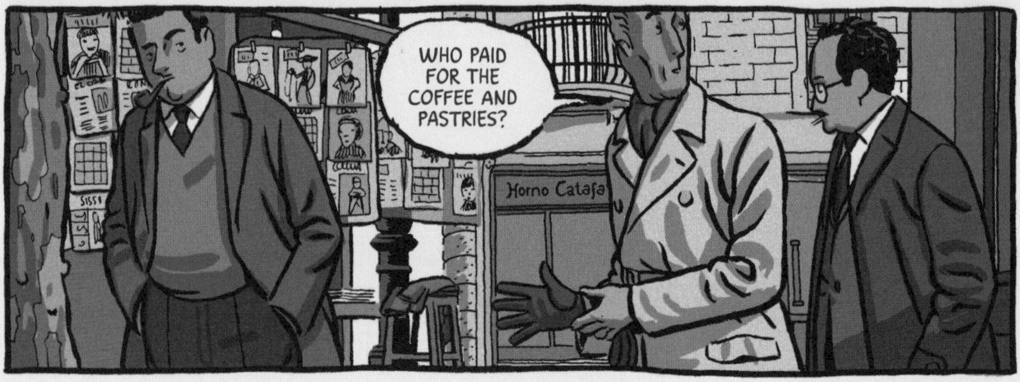
WHO PAID FOR THE COFFEE AND PASTRIES?

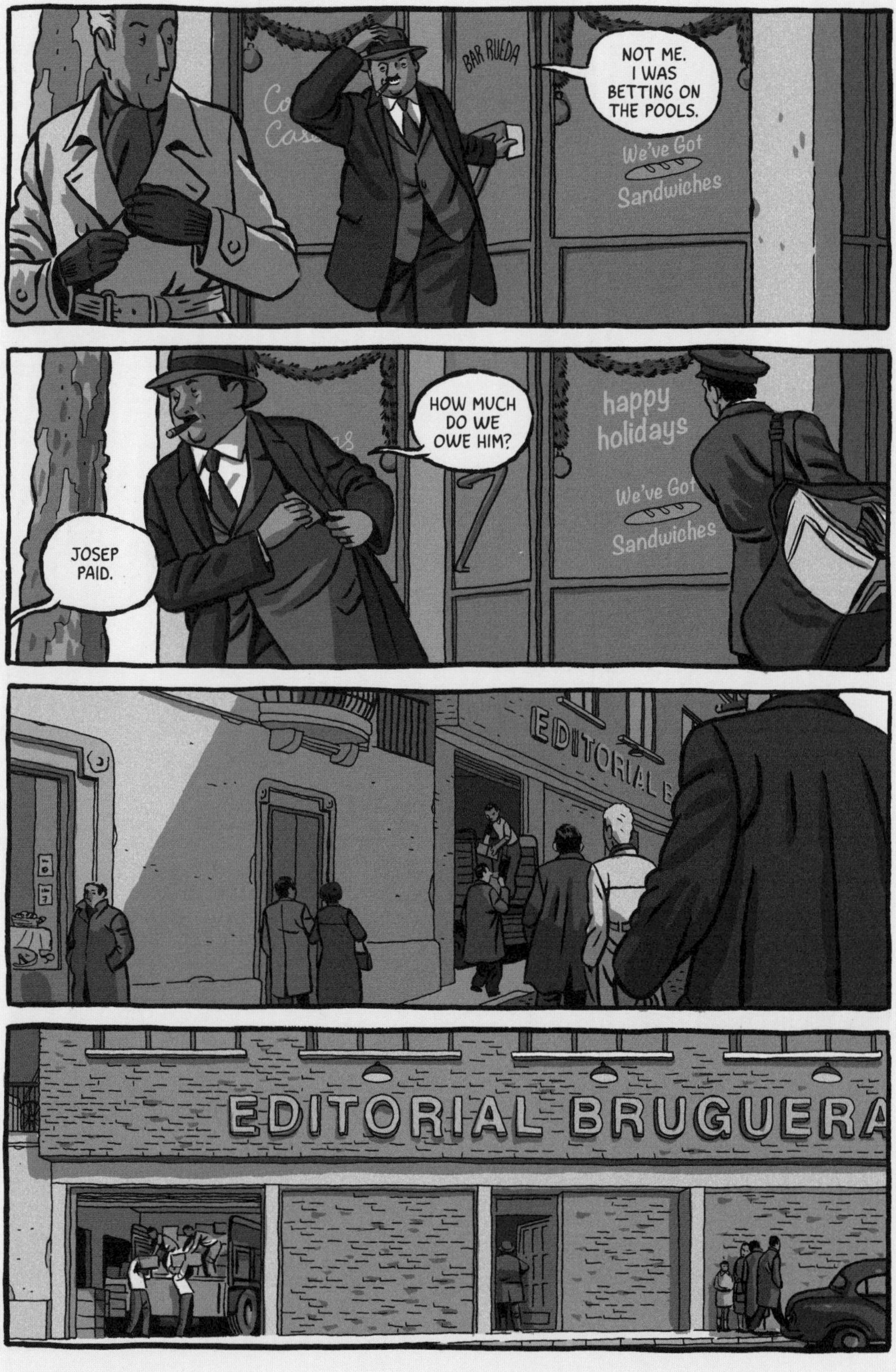
BAR RUEDA
NOT ME. I WAS BETTING ON THE POOLS.
We've Got Sandwiches
happy holidays
HOW MUCH DO WE OWE HIM?
JOSEP PAID.
We've Got Sandwiches
EDITORIAL BRUGUERA

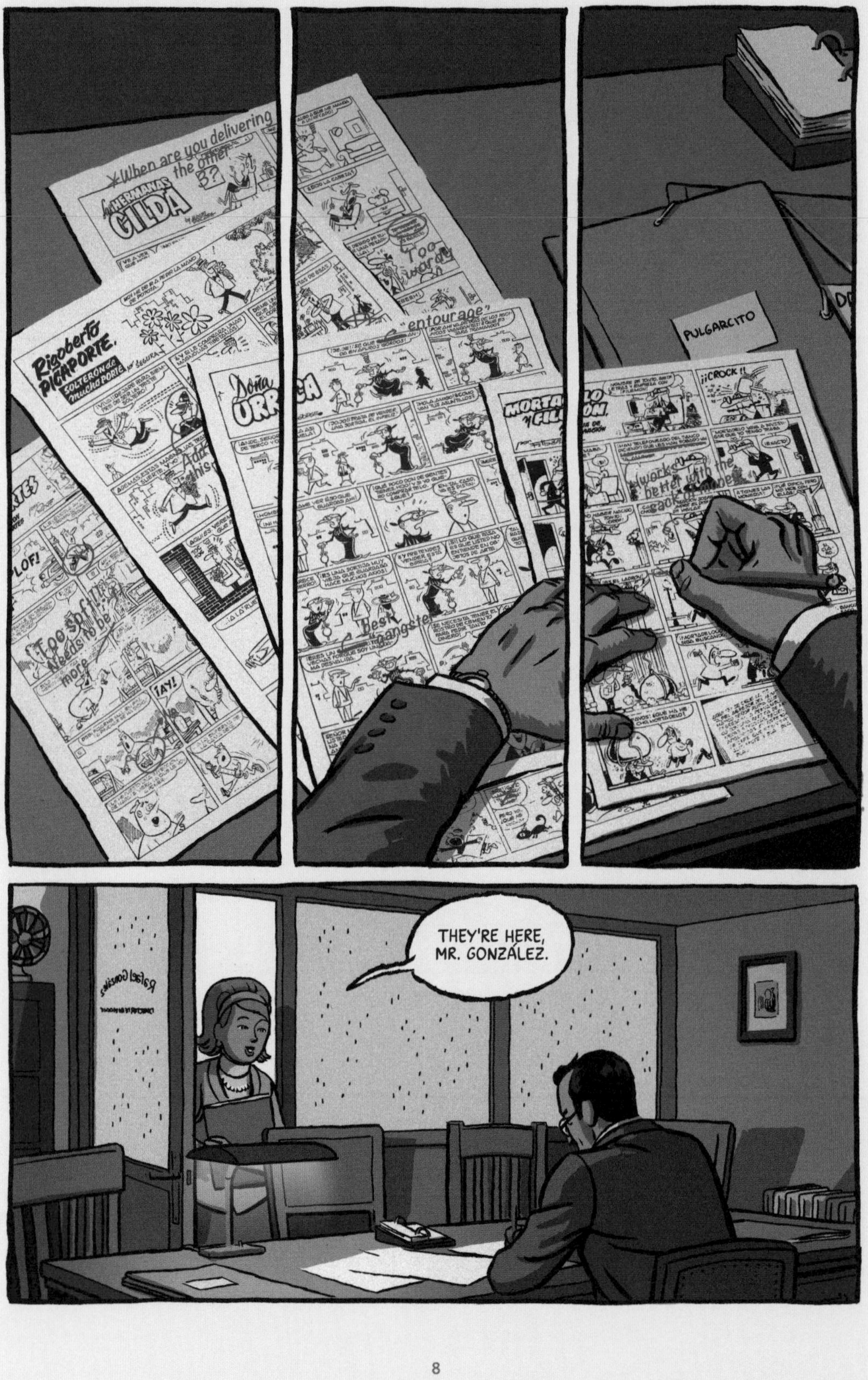
When are you delivering the other 3?
Las Hermanas Gilda
Too wordy
Rigoberto Picaporte. Solterón de mucho porte
Doña Urraca
"entourage"
Too soft! Needs to be more
¡AY!
Best gangster
Mortadelo y Filemón
¡¡CROCK!!
works better with the
PULGARCITO
THEY'RE HERE, MR. GONZÁLEZ.

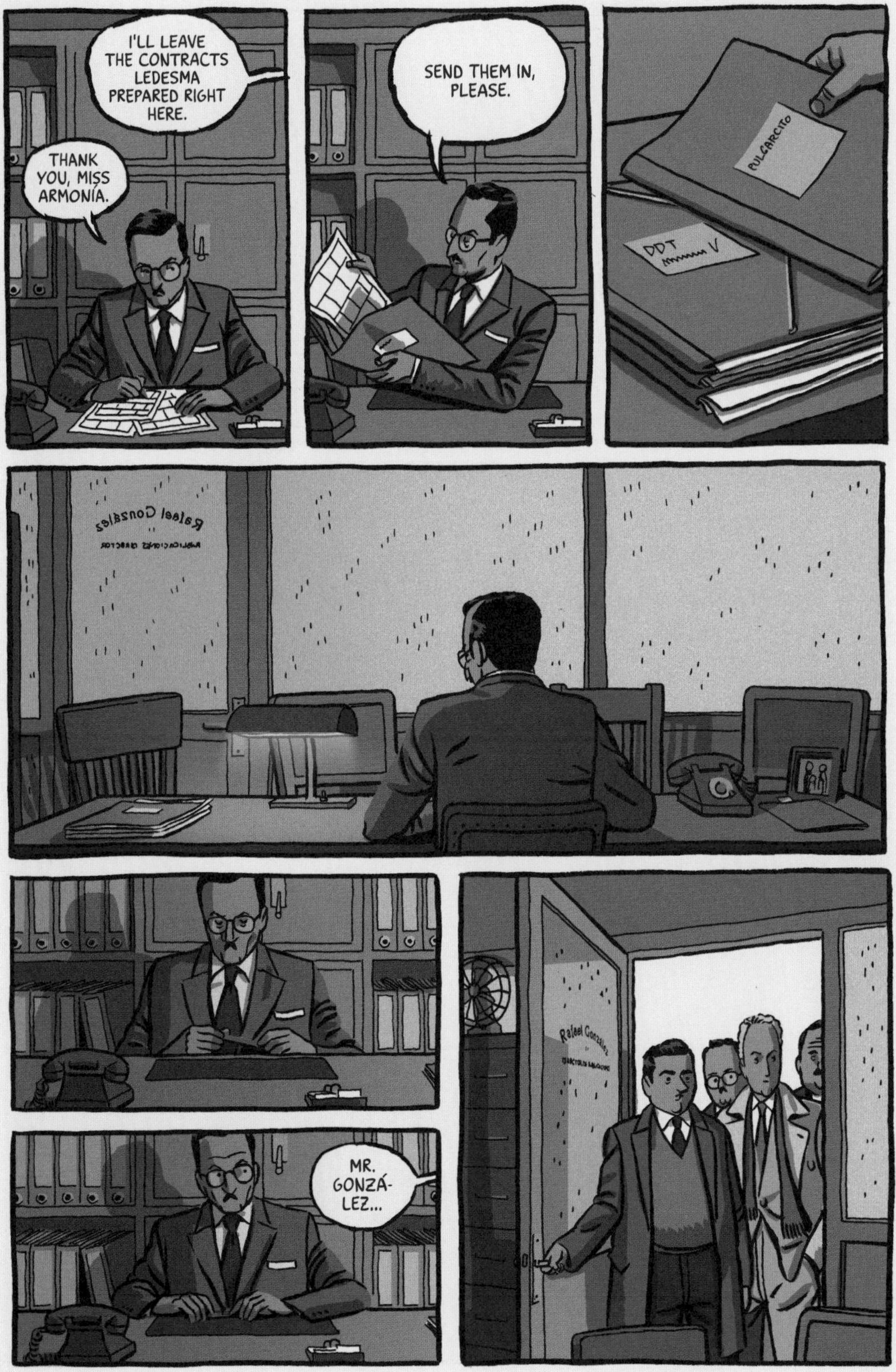
I'LL LEAVE THE CONTRACTS LEDESMA PREPARED RIGHT HERE.
THANK YOU, MISS ARMONÍA.
SEND THEM IN, PLEASE.
PULGARCITO
DDT
MR. GONZÁ-LEZ...

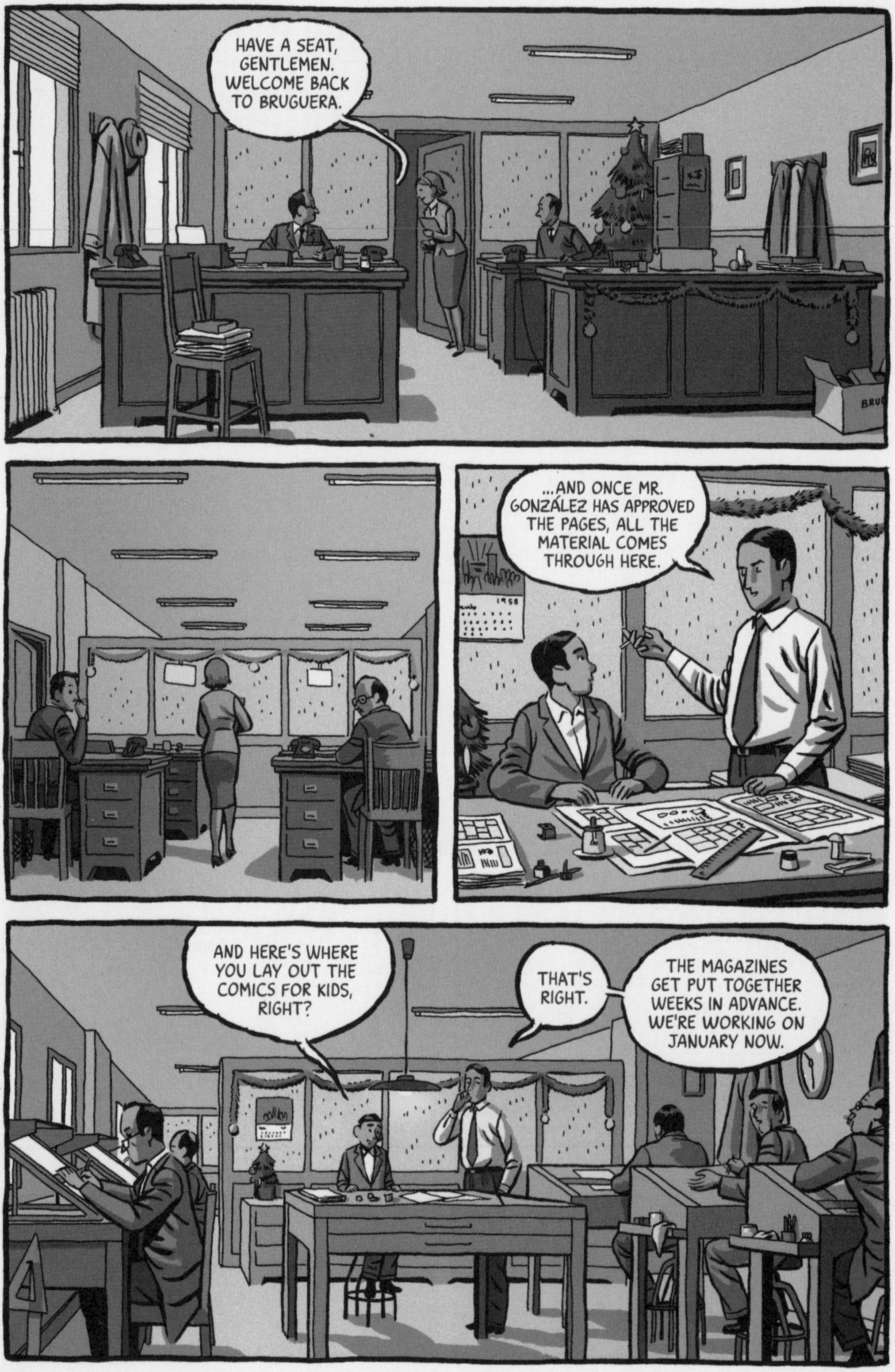
HAVE A SEAT, GENTLEMEN. WELCOME BACK TO BRUGUERA.
...AND ONCE MR. GONZÁLEZ HAS APPROVED THE PAGES, ALL THE MATERIAL COMES THROUGH HERE.
AND HERE'S WHERE YOU LAY OUT THE COMICS FOR KIDS, RIGHT?
THAT'S RIGHT.
THE MAGAZINES GET PUT TOGETHER WEEKS IN ADVANCE. WE'RE WORKING ON JANUARY NOW.

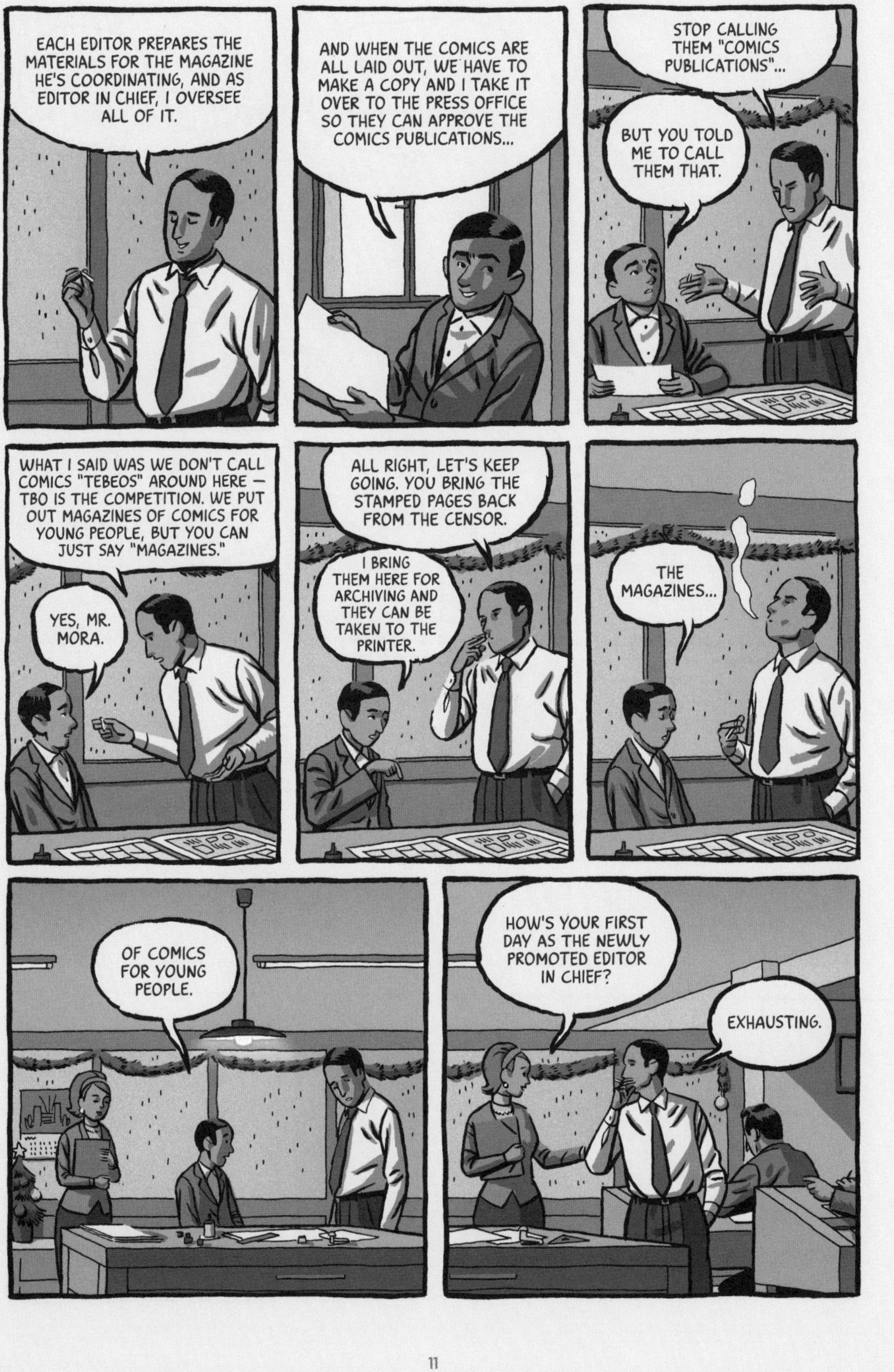
EACH EDITOR PREPARES THE MATERIALS FOR THE MAGAZINE HE'S COORDINATING, AND AS EDITOR IN CHIEF, I OVERSEE ALL OF IT.
AND WHEN THE COMICS ARE ALL LAID OUT, WE HAVE TO MAKE A COPY AND I TAKE IT OVER TO THE PRESS OFFICE SO THEY CAN APPROVE THE COMICS PUBLICATIONS...
STOP CALLING THEM "COMICS PUBLICATIONS"...
BUT YOU TOLD ME TO CALL THEM THAT.
WHAT I SAID WAS WE DON'T CALL COMICS "TEBEOS" AROUND HERE — TBO IS THE COMPETITION. WE PUT OUT MAGAZINES OF COMICS FOR YOUNG PEOPLE, BUT YOU CAN JUST SAY "MAGAZINES."
YES, MR. MORA.
ALL RIGHT, LET'S KEEP GOING. YOU BRING THE STAMPED PAGES BACK FROM THE CENSOR.
I BRING THEM HERE FOR ARCHIVING AND THEY CAN BE TAKEN TO THE PRINTER.
THE MAGAZINES...
OF COMICS FOR YOUNG PEOPLE.
HOW'S YOUR FIRST DAY AS THE NEWLY PROMOTED EDITOR IN CHIEF?
EXHAUSTING.

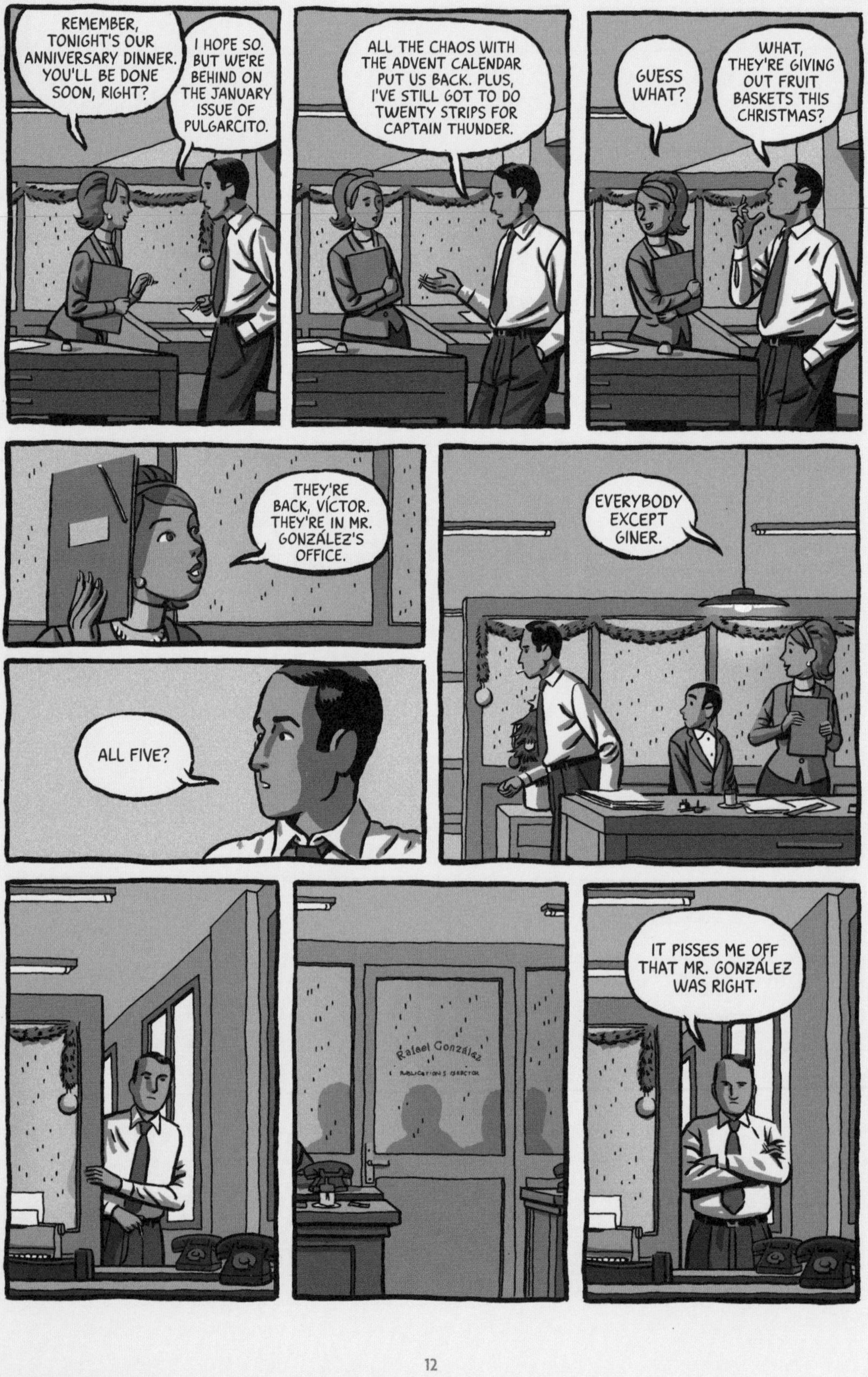
REMEMBER, TONIGHT'S OUR ANNIVERSARY DINNER. YOU'LL BE DONE SOON, RIGHT?
I HOPE SO. BUT WE'RE BEHIND ON THE JANUARY ISSUE OF PULGARCITO.
ALL THE CHAOS WITH THE ADVENT CALENDAR PUT US BACK. PLUS, I'VE STILL GOT TO DO TWENTY STRIPS FOR CAPTAIN THUNDER.
GUESS WHAT?
WHAT, THEY'RE GIVING OUT FRUIT BASKETS THIS CHRISTMAS?
THEY'RE BACK, VÍCTOR. THEY'RE IN MR. GONZÁLEZ'S OFFICE.
ALL FIVE?
EVERYBODY EXCEPT GINER.
Rafael González
IT PISSES ME OFF THAT MR. GONZÁLEZ WAS RIGHT.

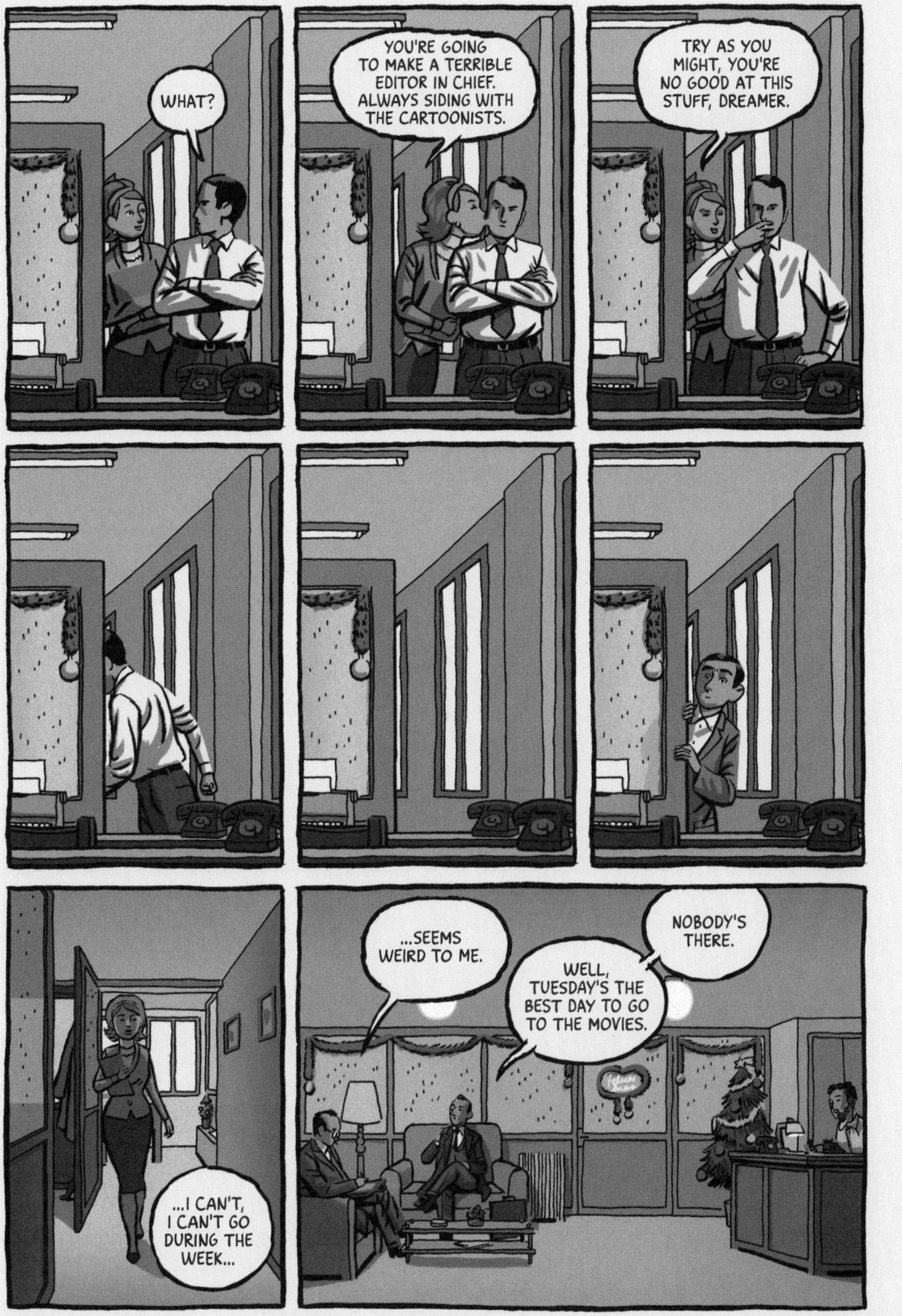
WHAT?
YOU'RE GOING TO MAKE A TERRIBLE EDITOR IN CHIEF. ALWAYS SIDING WITH THE CARTOONISTS.
TRY AS YOU MIGHT, YOU'RE NO GOOD AT THIS STUFF, DREAMER.
...I CAN'T, I CAN'T GO DURING THE WEEK...
...SEEMS WEIRD TO ME.
NOBODY'S THERE.
WELL, TUESDAY'S THE BEST DAY TO GO TO THE MOVIES.

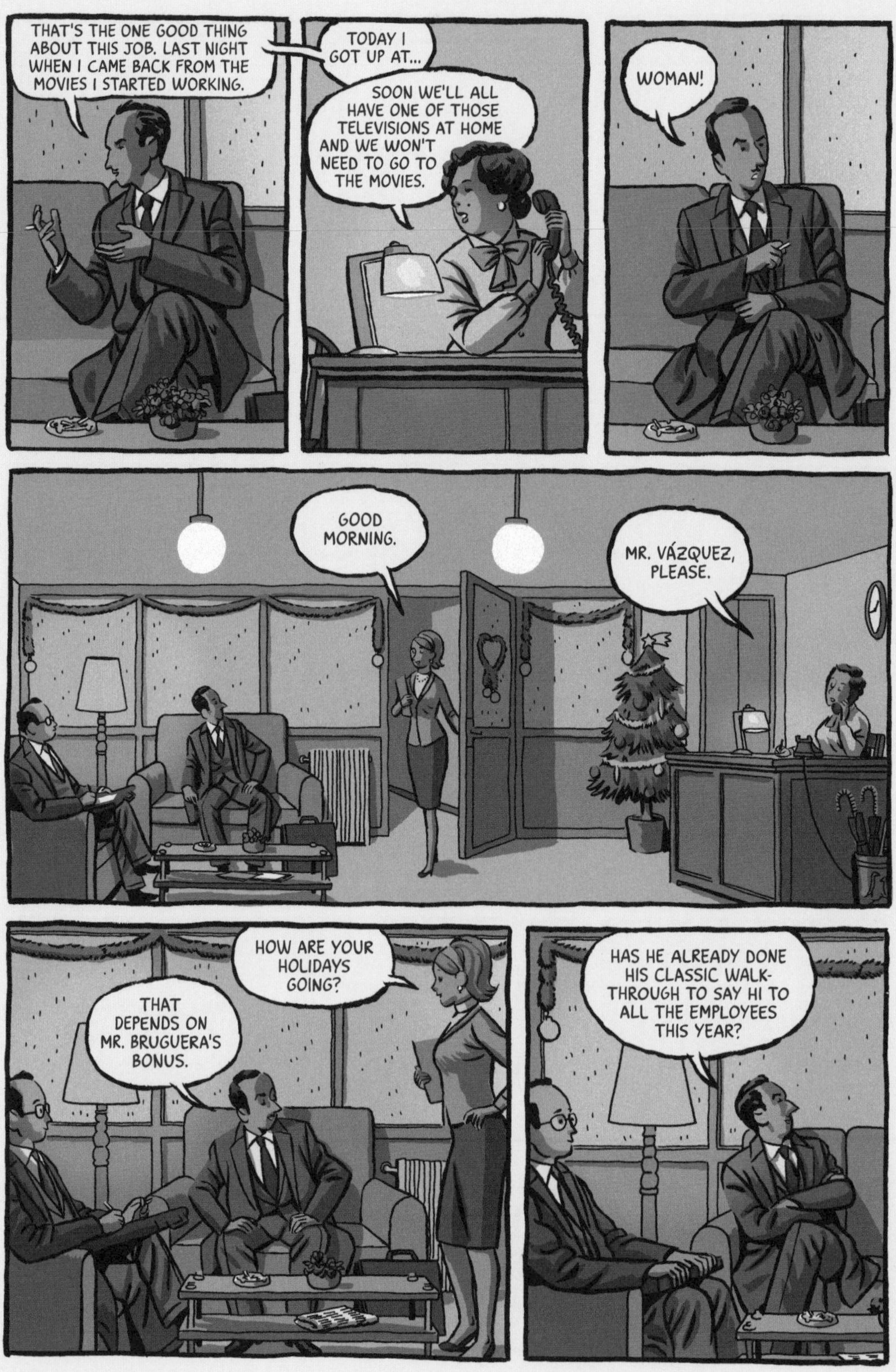

THAT'S THE ONE GOOD THING ABOUT THIS JOB. LAST NIGHT WHEN I CAME BACK FROM THE MOVIES I STARTED WORKING.
TODAY I GOT UP AT...
SOON WE'LL ALL HAVE ONE OF THOSE TELEVISIONS AT HOME AND WE WON'T NEED TO GO TO THE MOVIES.
WOMAN!
GOOD MORNING.
MR. VÁZQUEZ, PLEASE.
HOW ARE YOUR HOLIDAYS GOING?
THAT DEPENDS ON MR. BRUGUERA'S BONUS.
HAS HE ALREADY DONE HIS CLASSIC WALK-THROUGH TO SAY HI TO ALL THE EMPLOYEES THIS YEAR?

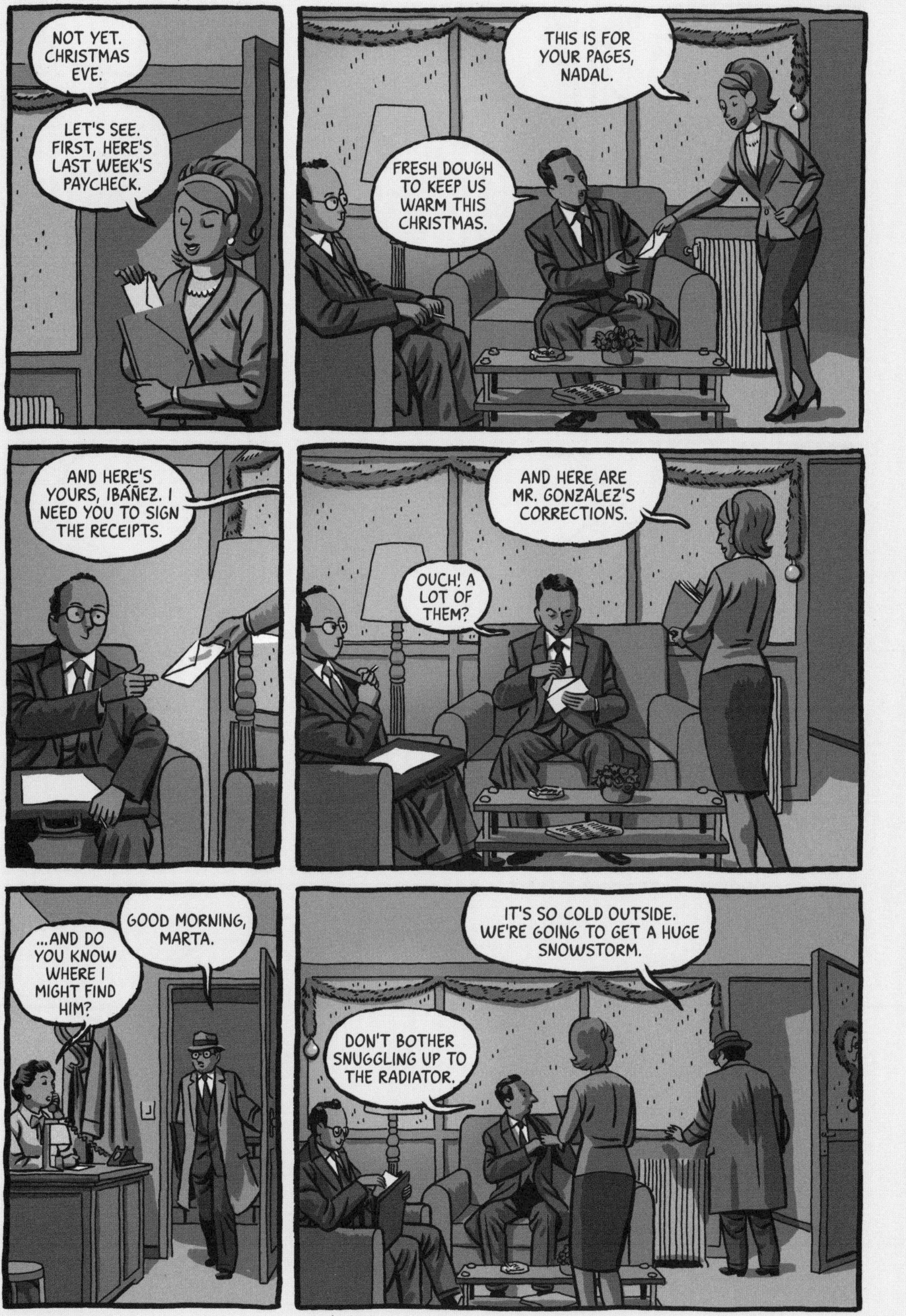
NOT YET. CHRISTMAS EVE.
LET'S SEE. FIRST, HERE'S LAST WEEK'S PAYCHECK.
THIS IS FOR YOUR PAGES, NADAL.
FRESH DOUGH TO KEEP US WARM THIS CHRISTMAS.
AND HERE'S YOURS, IBÁÑEZ. I NEED YOU TO SIGN THE RECEIPTS.
AND HERE ARE MR. GONZÁLEZ'S CORRECTIONS.
OUCH! A LOT OF THEM?
GOOD MORNING, MARTA.
...AND DO YOU KNOW WHERE I MIGHT FIND HIM?
IT'S SO COLD OUTSIDE. WE'RE GOING TO GET A HUGE SNOWSTORM.
DON'T BOTHER SNUGGLING UP TO THE RADIATOR.

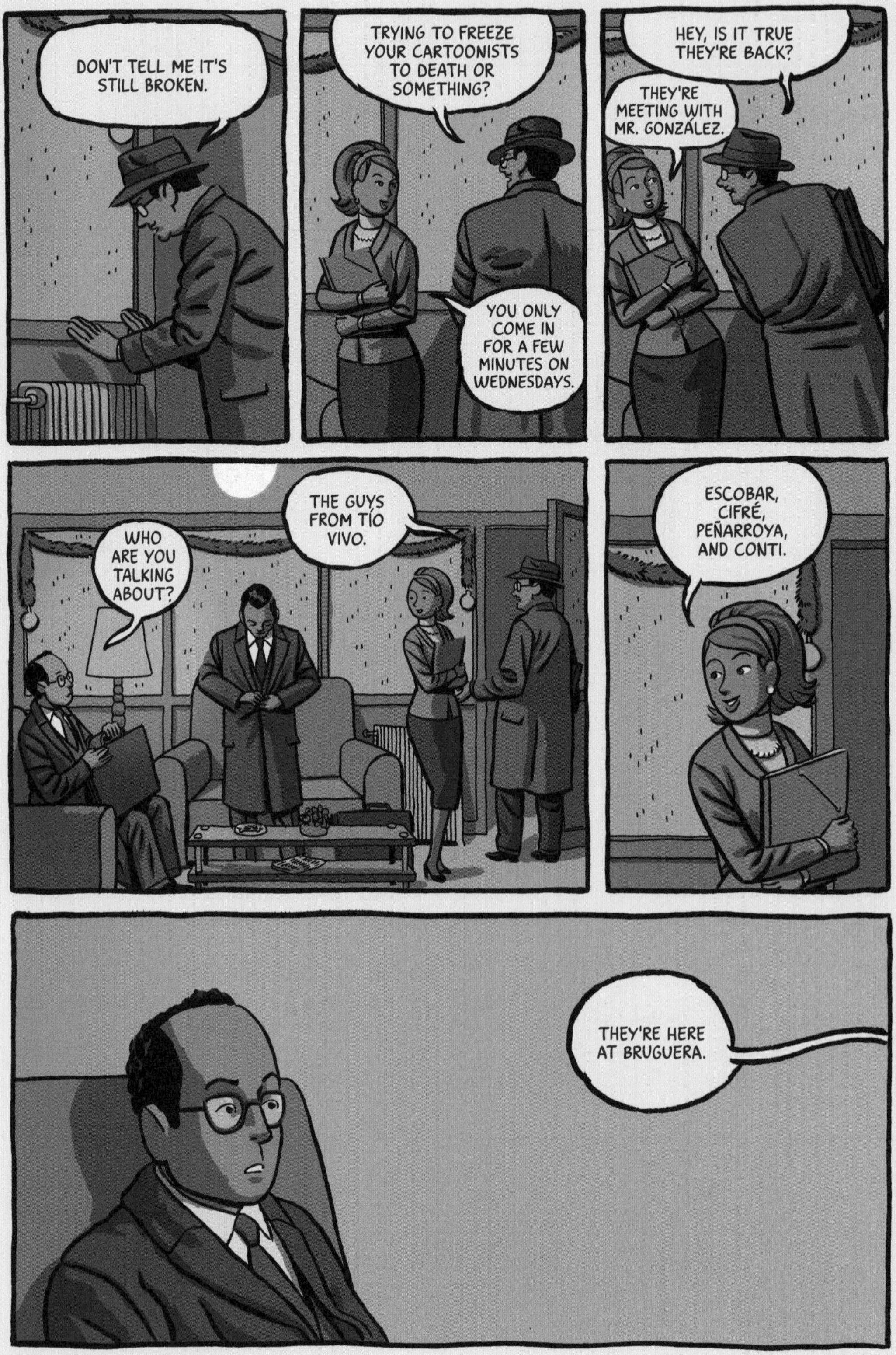
DON'T TELL ME IT'S STILL BROKEN.
TRYING TO FREEZE YOUR CARTOONISTS TO DEATH OR SOMETHING?
YOU ONLY COME IN FOR A FEW MINUTES ON WEDNESDAYS.
HEY, IS IT TRUE THEY'RE BACK?
THEY'RE MEETING WITH MR. GONZÁLEZ.
WHO ARE YOU TALKING ABOUT?
THE GUYS FROM TÍO VIVO.
ESCOBAR, CIFRÉ, PEÑARROYA, AND CONTI.
THEY'RE HERE AT BRUGUERA.

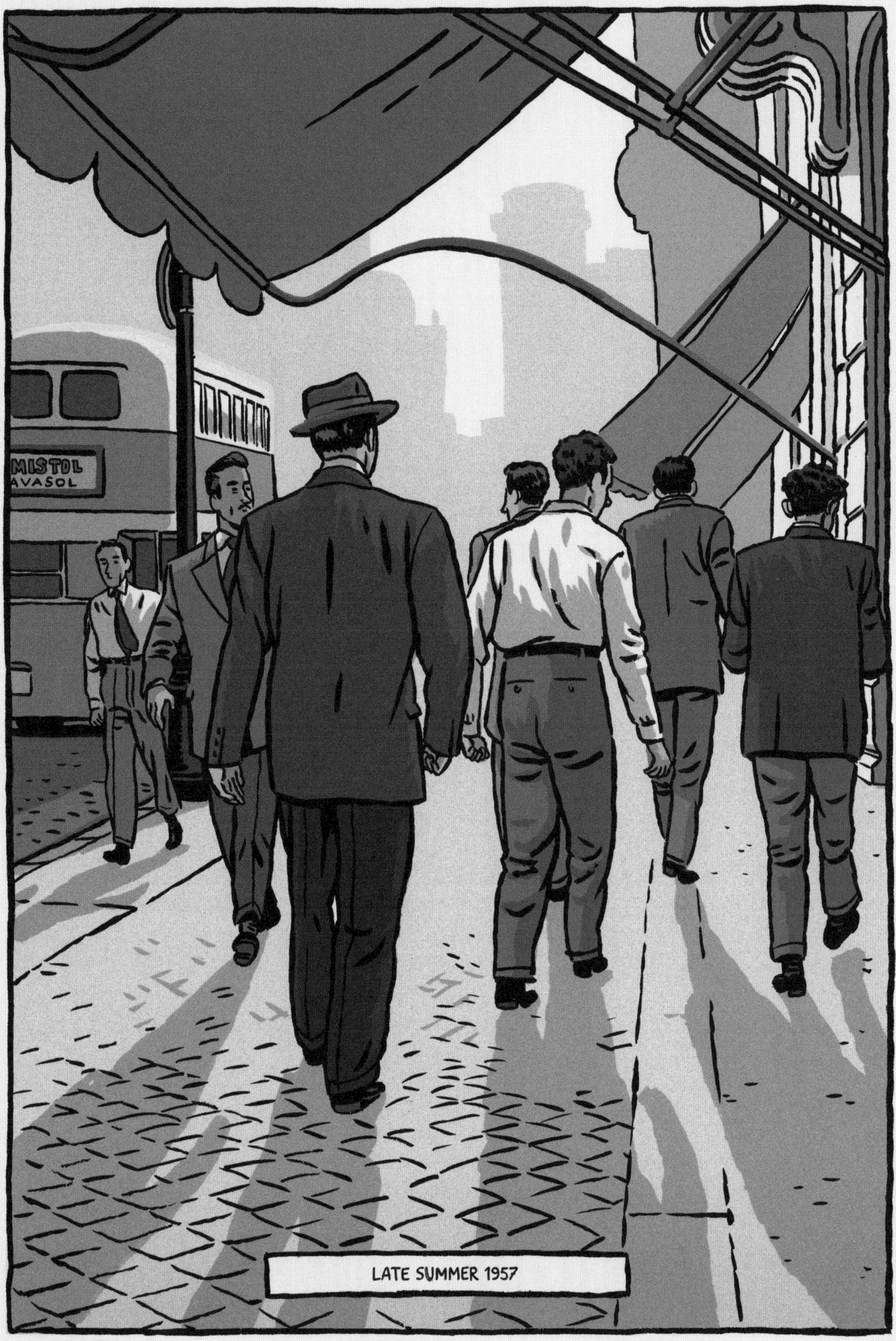
MISTOL
AVASOL
LATE SUMMER 1957

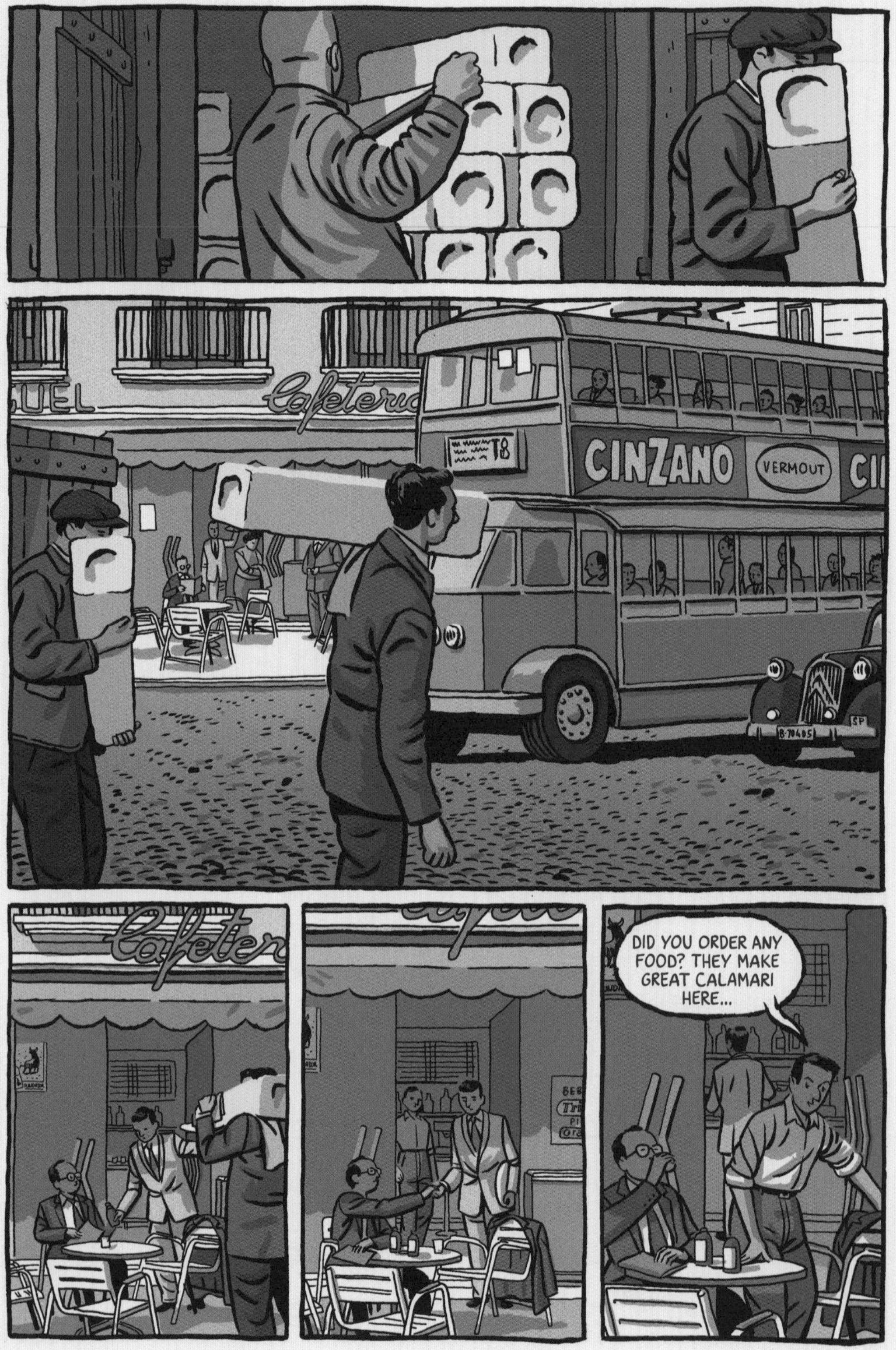
CINZANO
VERMOUT
DID YOU ORDER ANY FOOD? THEY MAKE GREAT CALAMARI HERE...

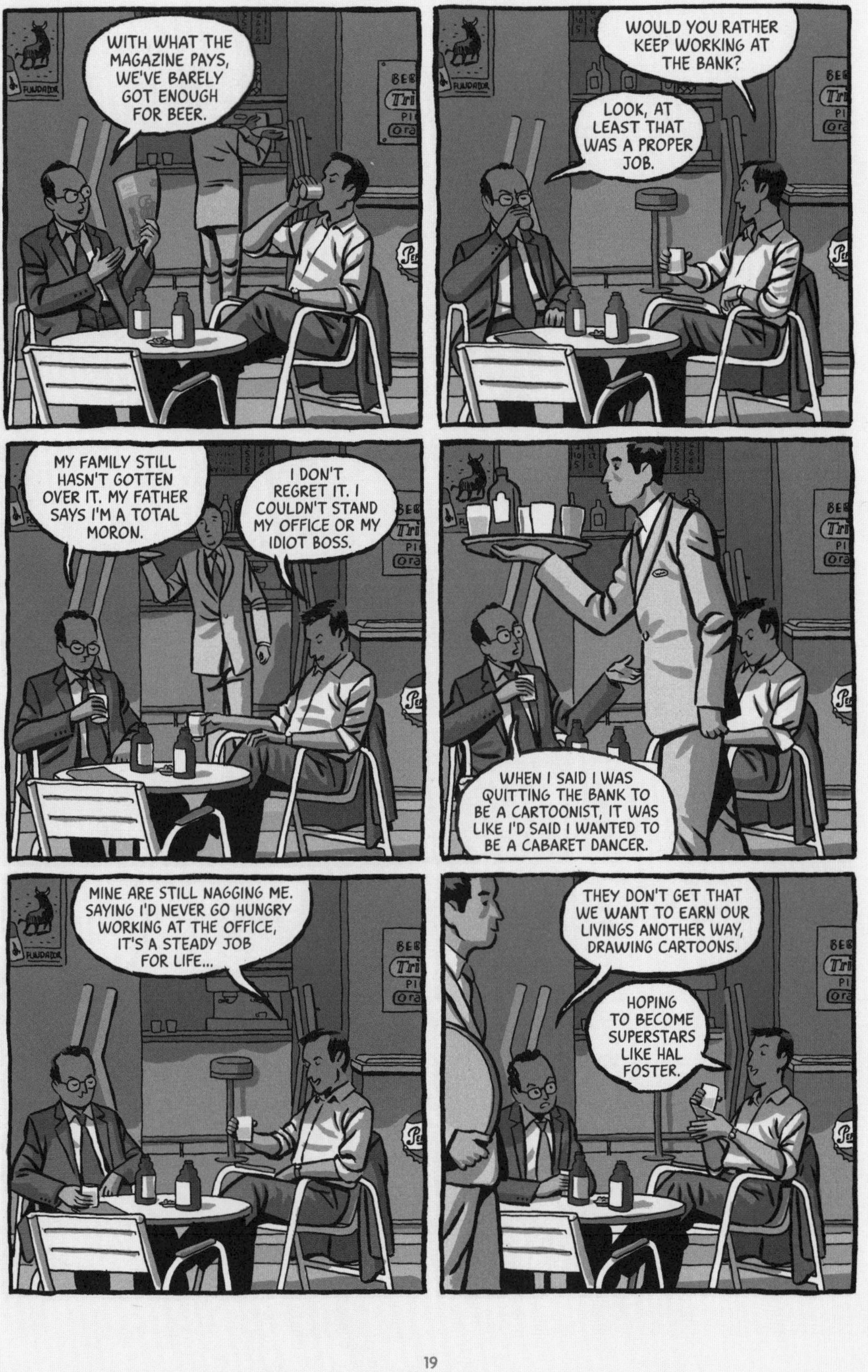
WITH WHAT THE MAGAZINE PAYS, WE'VE BARELY GOT ENOUGH FOR BEER.
FUNDADOR
WOULD YOU RATHER KEEP WORKING AT THE BANK?
LOOK, AT LEAST THAT WAS A PROPER JOB.
MY FAMILY STILL HASN'T GOTTEN OVER IT. MY FATHER SAYS I'M A TOTAL MORON.
I DON'T REGRET IT. I COULDN'T STAND MY OFFICE OR MY IDIOT BOSS.
WHEN I SAID I WAS QUITTING THE BANK TO BE A CARTOONIST, IT WAS LIKE I'D SAID I WANTED TO BE A CABARET DANCER.
MINE ARE STILL NAGGING ME. SAYING I'D NEVER GO HUNGRY WORKING AT THE OFFICE, IT'S A STEADY JOB FOR LIFE...
FUNDADOR
THEY DON'T GET THAT WE WANT TO EARN OUR LIVINGS ANOTHER WAY, DRAWING CARTOONS.
HOPING TO BECOME SUPERSTARS LIKE HAL FOSTER.

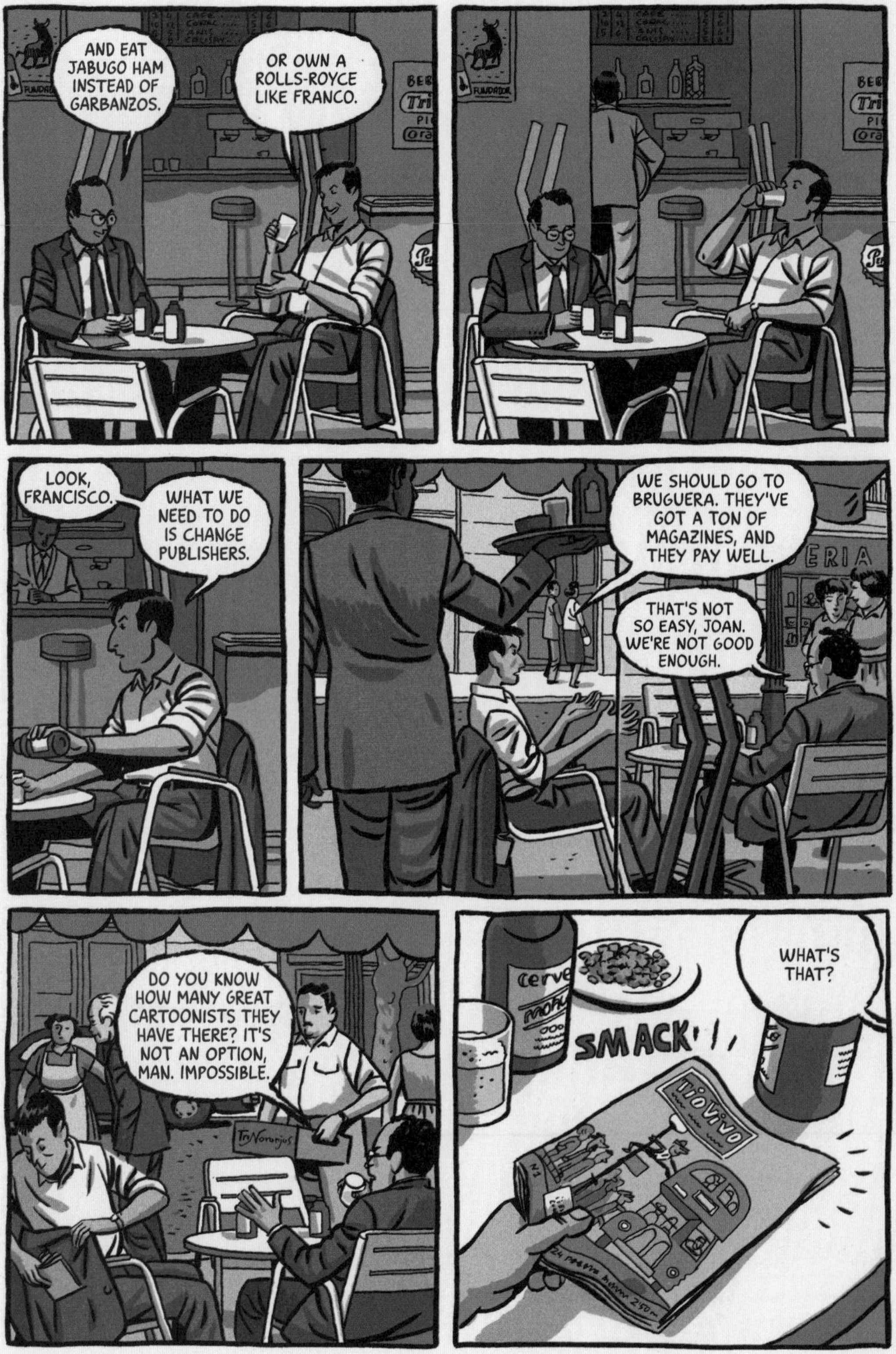
AND EAT JABUGO HAM INSTEAD OF GARBANZOS.
OR OWN A ROLLS-ROYCE LIKE FRANCO.
LOOK, FRANCISCO.
WHAT WE NEED TO DO IS CHANGE PUBLISHERS.
WE SHOULD GO TO BRUGUERA. THEY'VE GOT A TON OF MAGAZINES, AND THEY PAY WELL.
THAT'S NOT SO EASY, JOAN. WE'RE NOT GOOD ENOUGH.
DO YOU KNOW HOW MANY GREAT CARTOONISTS THEY HAVE THERE? IT'S NOT AN OPTION, MAN. IMPOSSIBLE.
WHAT'S THAT?
SMACK
TíoVivo

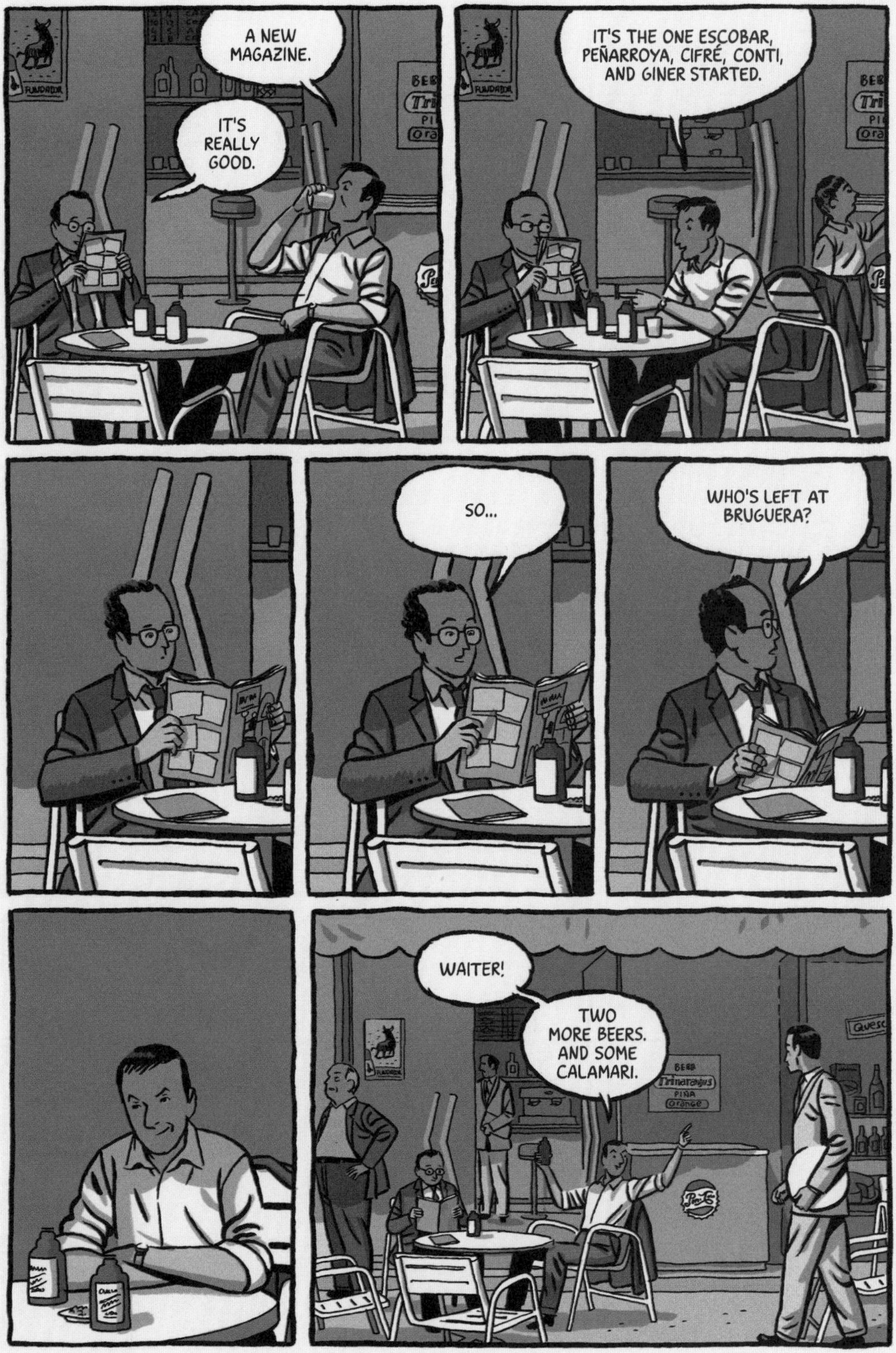
A NEW MAGAZINE.
IT'S REALLY GOOD.
IT'S THE ONE ESCOBAR, PEÑARROYA, CIFRÉ, CONTI, AND GINER STARTED.
SO...
WHO'S LEFT AT BRUGUERA?
WAITER!
TWO MORE BEERS. AND SOME CALAMARI.

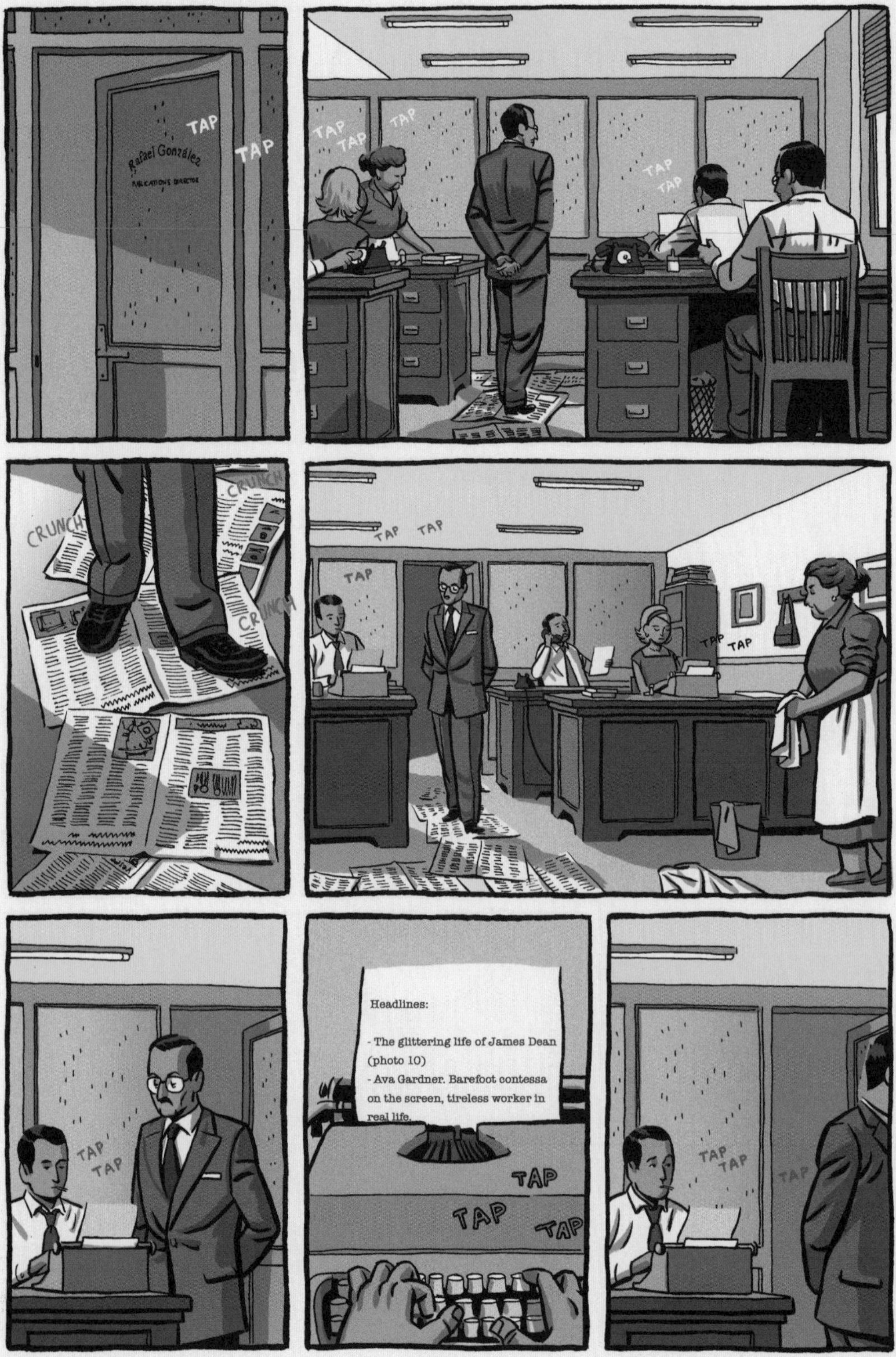
Rafael González
PUBLICATIONS DIRECTOR
TAP
TAP
TAP
TAP
TAP
TAP
TAP
CRUNCH
CRUNCH
CRUNCH
TAP TAP
TAP
TAP
TAP
TAP
TAP
Headlines:
- The glittering life of James Dean (photo 10)
- Ava Gardner. Barefoot contessa on the screen, tireless worker in real life.
TAP
TAP
TAP
TAP
TAP
TAP

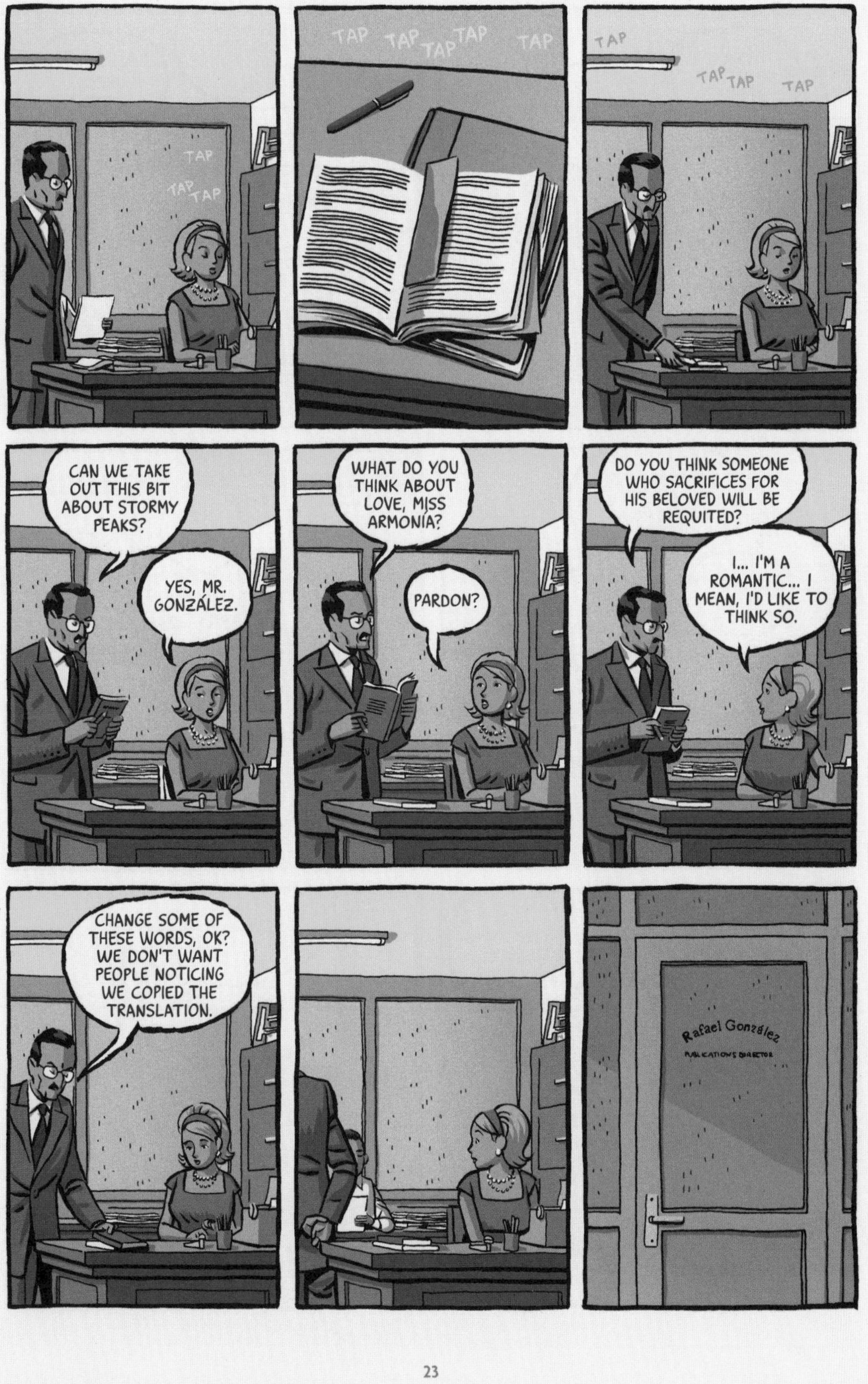
TAP
TAP TAP
TAP TAP TAP TAP TAP
TAP
TAP TAP TAP
CAN WE TAKE OUT THIS BIT ABOUT STORMY PEAKS?
YES, MR. GONZÁLEZ.
WHAT DO YOU THINK ABOUT LOVE, MISS ARMONÍA?
PARDON?
DO YOU THINK SOMEONE WHO SACRIFICES FOR HIS BELOVED WILL BE REQUITED?
I... I'M A ROMANTIC... I MEAN, I'D LIKE TO THINK SO.
CHANGE SOME OF THESE WORDS, OK? WE DON'T WANT PEOPLE NOTICING WE COPIED THE TRANSLATION.
Rafael González
PUBLICATIONS DIRECTOR

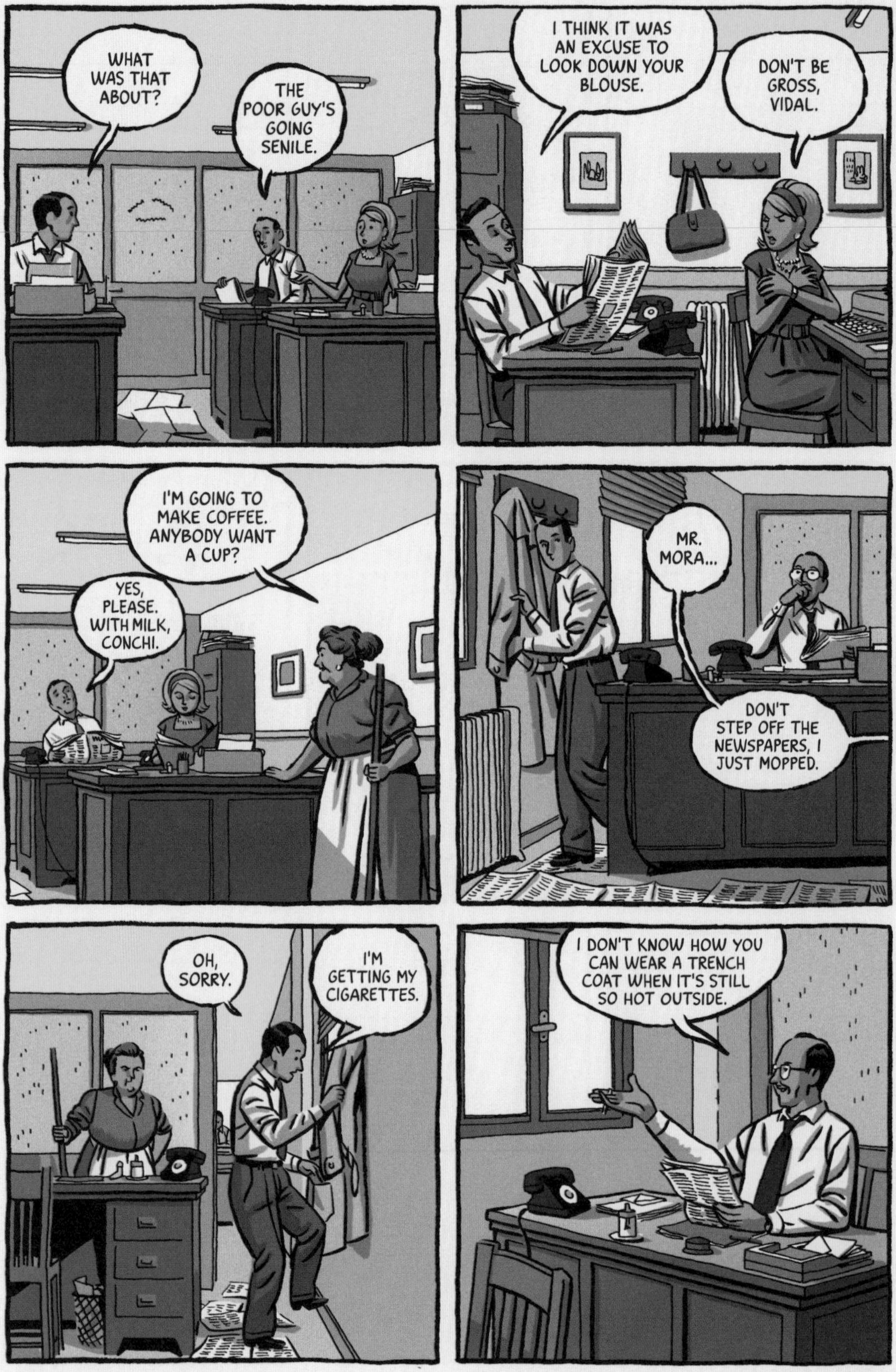
WHAT WAS THAT ABOUT?
THE POOR GUY'S GOING SENILE.
I THINK IT WAS AN EXCUSE TO LOOK DOWN YOUR BLOUSE.
DON'T BE GROSS, VIDAL.
I'M GOING TO MAKE COFFEE. ANYBODY WANT A CUP?
YES, PLEASE. WITH MILK, CONCHI.
MR. MORA...
DON'T STEP OFF THE NEWSPAPERS, I JUST MOPPED.
OH, SORRY.
I'M GETTING MY CIGARETTES.
I DON'T KNOW HOW YOU CAN WEAR A TRENCH COAT WHEN IT'S STILL SO HOT OUTSIDE.

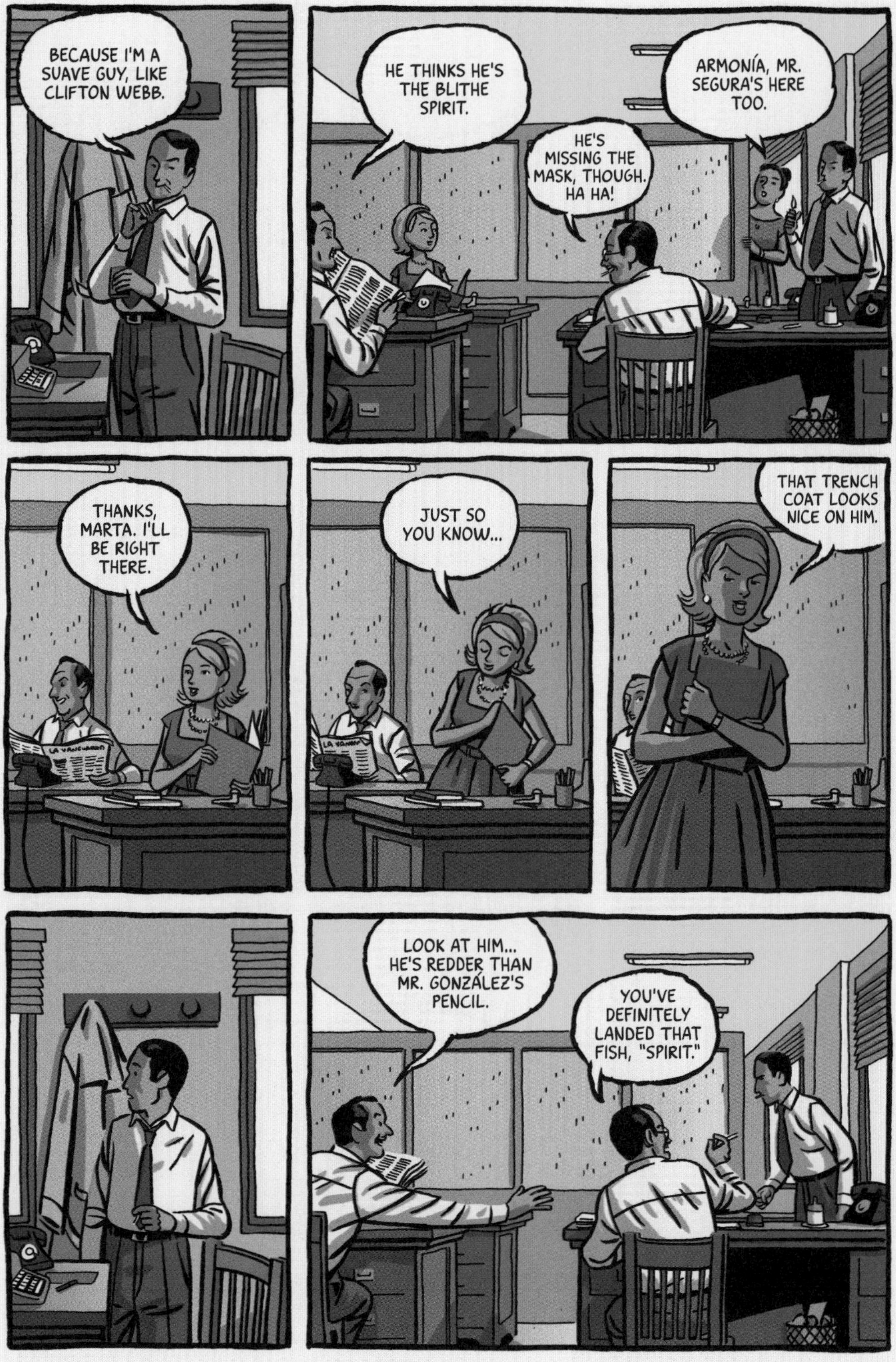
BECAUSE I'M A SUAVE GUY, LIKE CLIFTON WEBB.
HE THINKS HE'S THE BLITHE SPIRIT.
HE'S MISSING THE MASK, THOUGH. HA HA!
ARMONÍA, MR. SEGURA'S HERE TOO.
THANKS, MARTA. I'LL BE RIGHT THERE.
JUST SO YOU KNOW...
THAT TRENCH COAT LOOKS NICE ON HIM.
LOOK AT HIM... HE'S REDDER THAN MR. GONZÁLEZ'S PENCIL.
YOU'VE DEFINITELY LANDED THAT FISH, "SPIRIT."

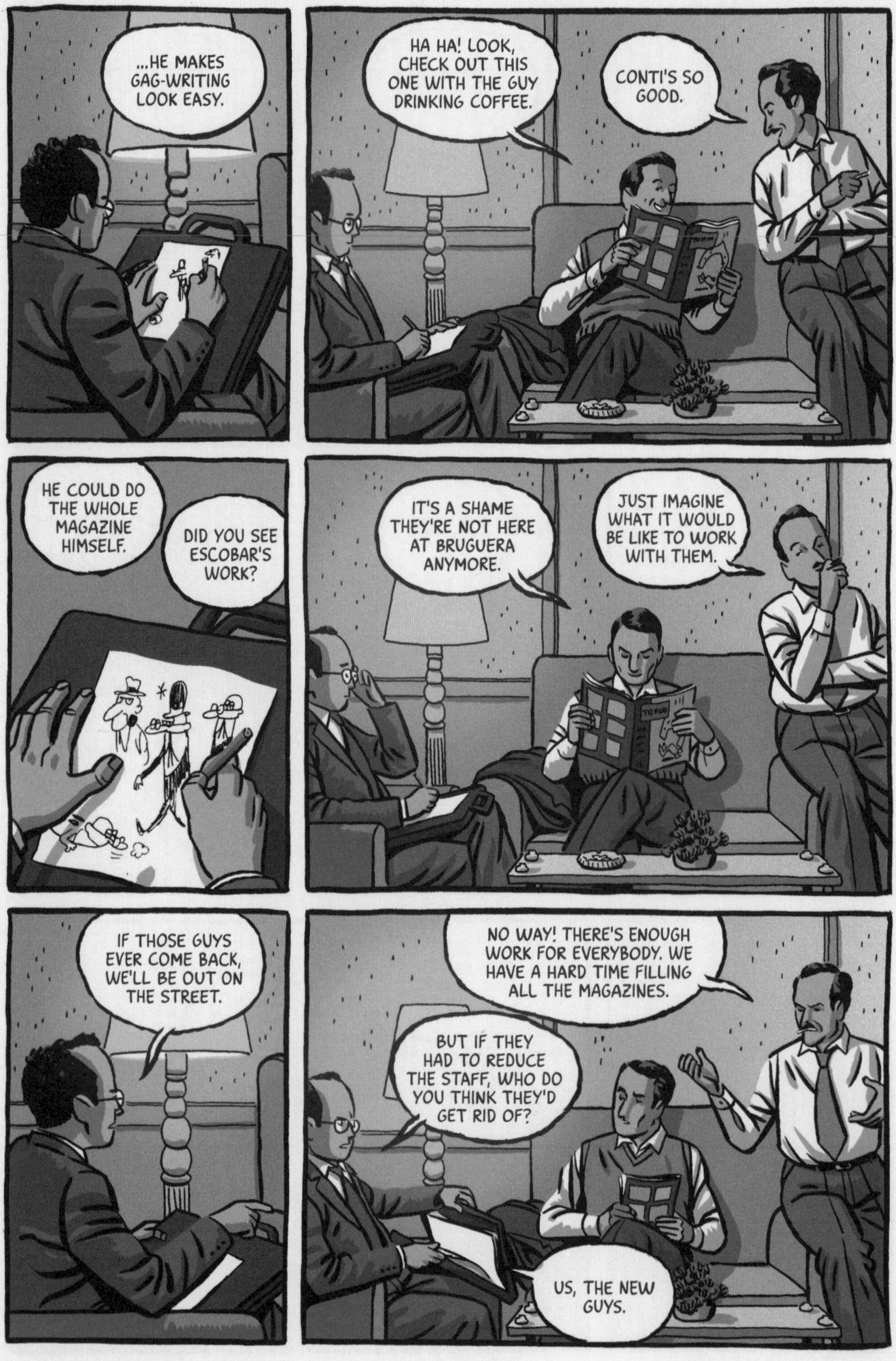
...HE MAKES GAG-WRITING LOOK EASY.
HA HA! LOOK, CHECK OUT THIS ONE WITH THE GUY DRINKING COFFEE.
CONTI'S SO GOOD.
HE COULD DO THE WHOLE MAGAZINE HIMSELF.
DID YOU SEE ESCOBAR'S WORK?
IT'S A SHAME THEY'RE NOT HERE AT BRUGUERA ANYMORE.
JUST IMAGINE WHAT IT WOULD BE LIKE TO WORK WITH THEM.
IF THOSE GUYS EVER COME BACK, WE'LL BE OUT ON THE STREET.
NO WAY! THERE'S ENOUGH WORK FOR EVERYBODY. WE HAVE A HARD TIME FILLING ALL THE MAGAZINES.
BUT IF THEY HAD TO REDUCE THE STAFF, WHO DO YOU THINK THEY'D GET RID OF?
US, THE NEW GUYS.

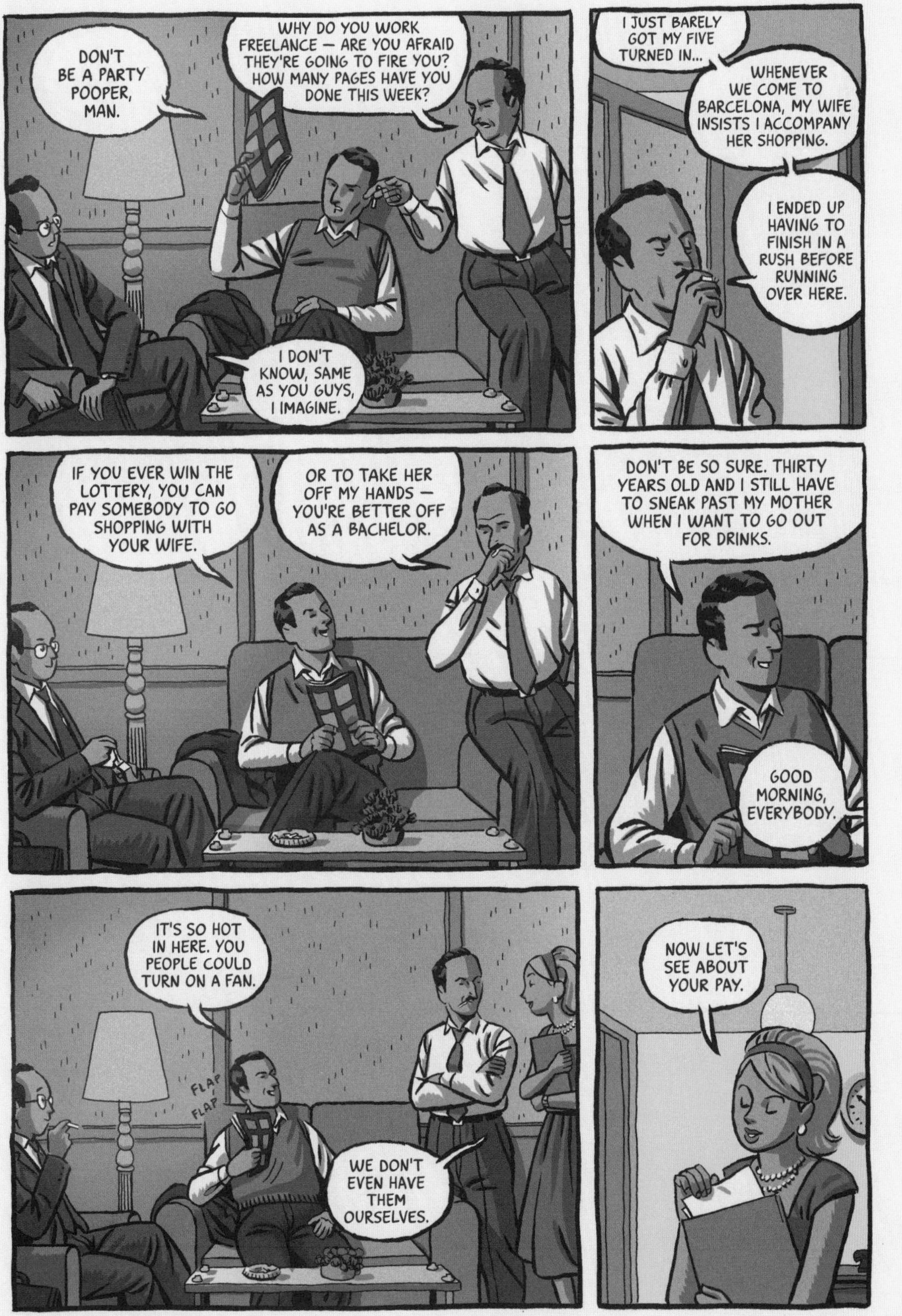
DON'T BE A PARTY POOPER, MAN.
WHY DO YOU WORK FREELANCE — ARE YOU AFRAID THEY'RE GOING TO FIRE YOU? HOW MANY PAGES HAVE YOU DONE THIS WEEK?
I DON'T KNOW, SAME AS YOU GUYS, I IMAGINE.
I JUST BARELY GOT MY FIVE TURNED IN...
WHENEVER WE COME TO BARCELONA, MY WIFE INSISTS I ACCOMPANY HER SHOPPING.
I ENDED UP HAVING TO FINISH IN A RUSH BEFORE RUNNING OVER HERE.
IF YOU EVER WIN THE LOTTERY, YOU CAN PAY SOMEBODY TO GO SHOPPING WITH YOUR WIFE.
OR TO TAKE HER OFF MY HANDS — YOU'RE BETTER OFF AS A BACHELOR.
DON'T BE SO SURE. THIRTY YEARS OLD AND I STILL HAVE TO SNEAK PAST MY MOTHER WHEN I WANT TO GO OUT FOR DRINKS.
GOOD MORNING, EVERYBODY.
IT'S SO HOT IN HERE. YOU PEOPLE COULD TURN ON A FAN.
FLAP FLAP
WE DON'T EVEN HAVE THEM OURSELVES.
NOW LET'S SEE ABOUT YOUR PAY.

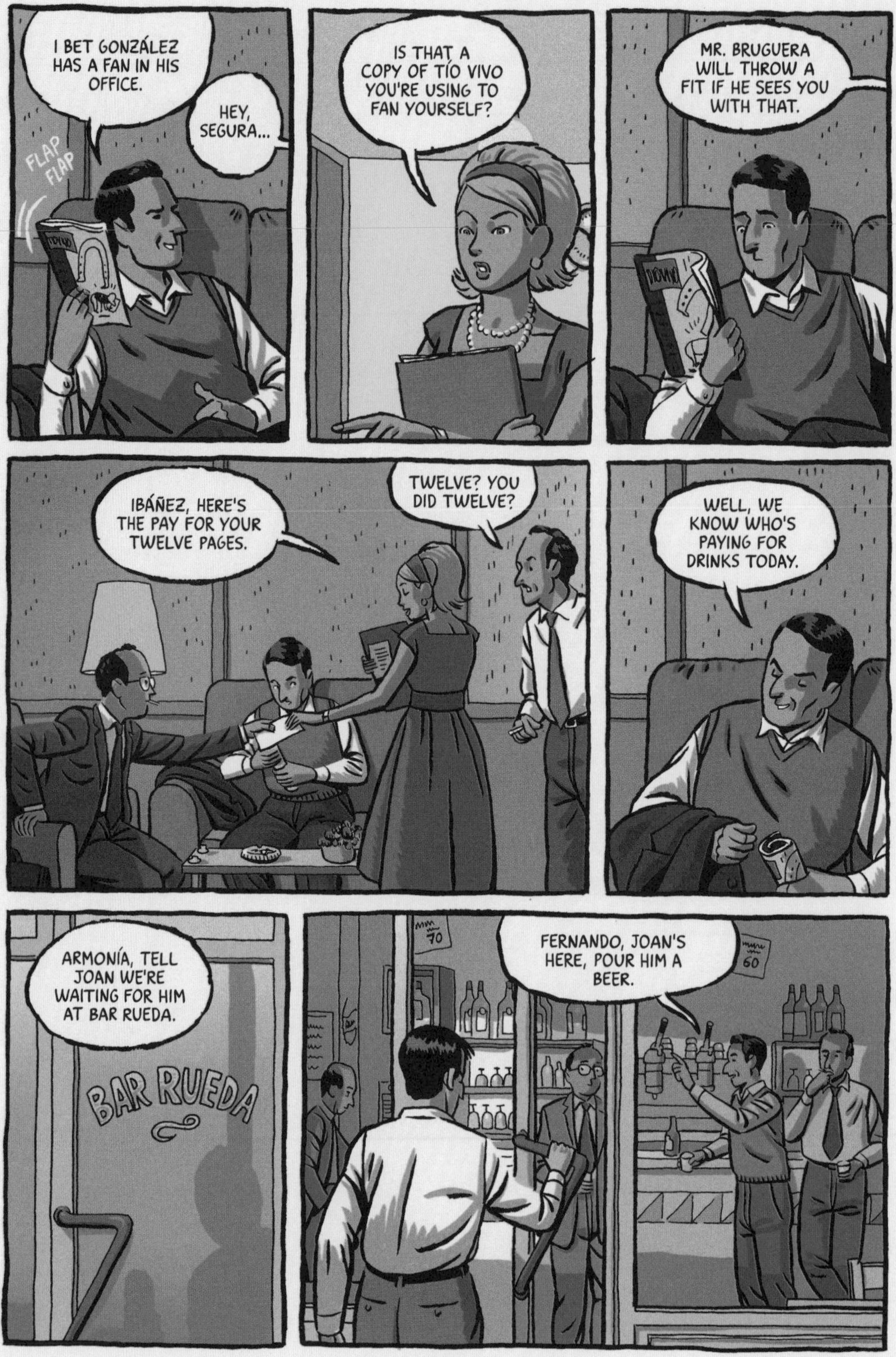
I BET GONZÁLEZ HAS A FAN IN HIS OFFICE.
FLAP FLAP
HEY, SEGURA...
IS THAT A COPY OF TÍO VIVO YOU'RE USING TO FAN YOURSELF?
MR. BRUGUERA WILL THROW A FIT IF HE SEES YOU WITH THAT.
IBÁÑEZ, HERE'S THE PAY FOR YOUR TWELVE PAGES.
TWELVE? YOU DID TWELVE?
WELL, WE KNOW WHO'S PAYING FOR DRINKS TODAY.
ARMONÍA, TELL JOAN WE'RE WAITING FOR HIM AT BAR RUEDA.
BAR RUEDA
FERNANDO, JOAN'S HERE, POUR HIM A BEER.

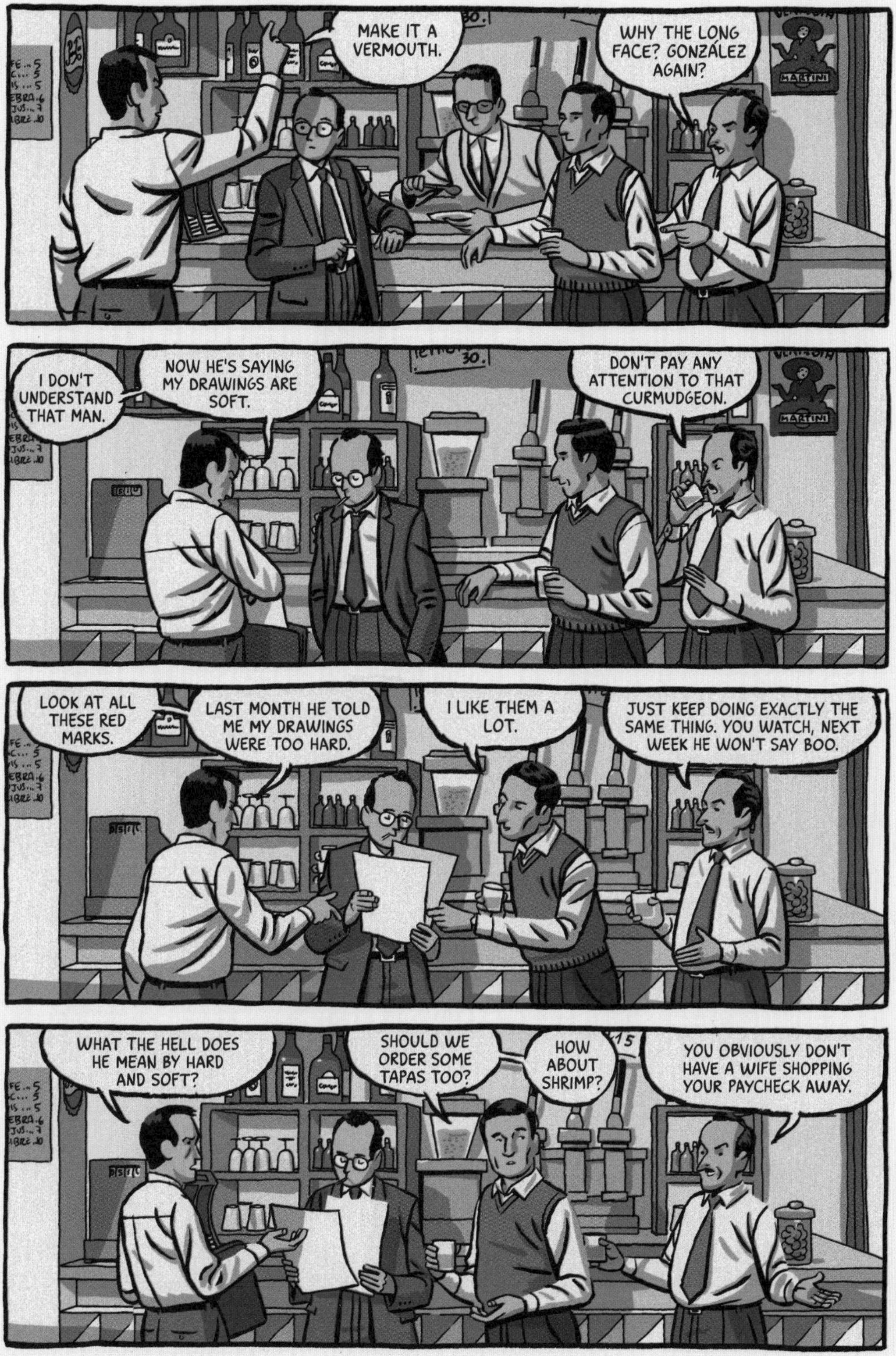
MAKE IT A VERMOUTH.
WHY THE LONG FACE? GONZÁLEZ AGAIN?
MARTINI
I DON'T UNDERSTAND THAT MAN.
NOW HE'S SAYING MY DRAWINGS ARE SOFT.
DON'T PAY ANY ATTENTION TO THAT CURMUDGEON.
LOOK AT ALL THESE RED MARKS.
LAST MONTH HE TOLD ME MY DRAWINGS WERE TOO HARD.
I LIKE THEM A LOT.
JUST KEEP DOING EXACTLY THE SAME THING. YOU WATCH, NEXT WEEK HE WON'T SAY BOO.
WHAT THE HELL DOES HE MEAN BY HARD AND SOFT?
SHOULD WE ORDER SOME TAPAS TOO?
HOW ABOUT SHRIMP?
YOU OBVIOUSLY DON'T HAVE A WIFE SHOPPING YOUR PAYCHECK AWAY.

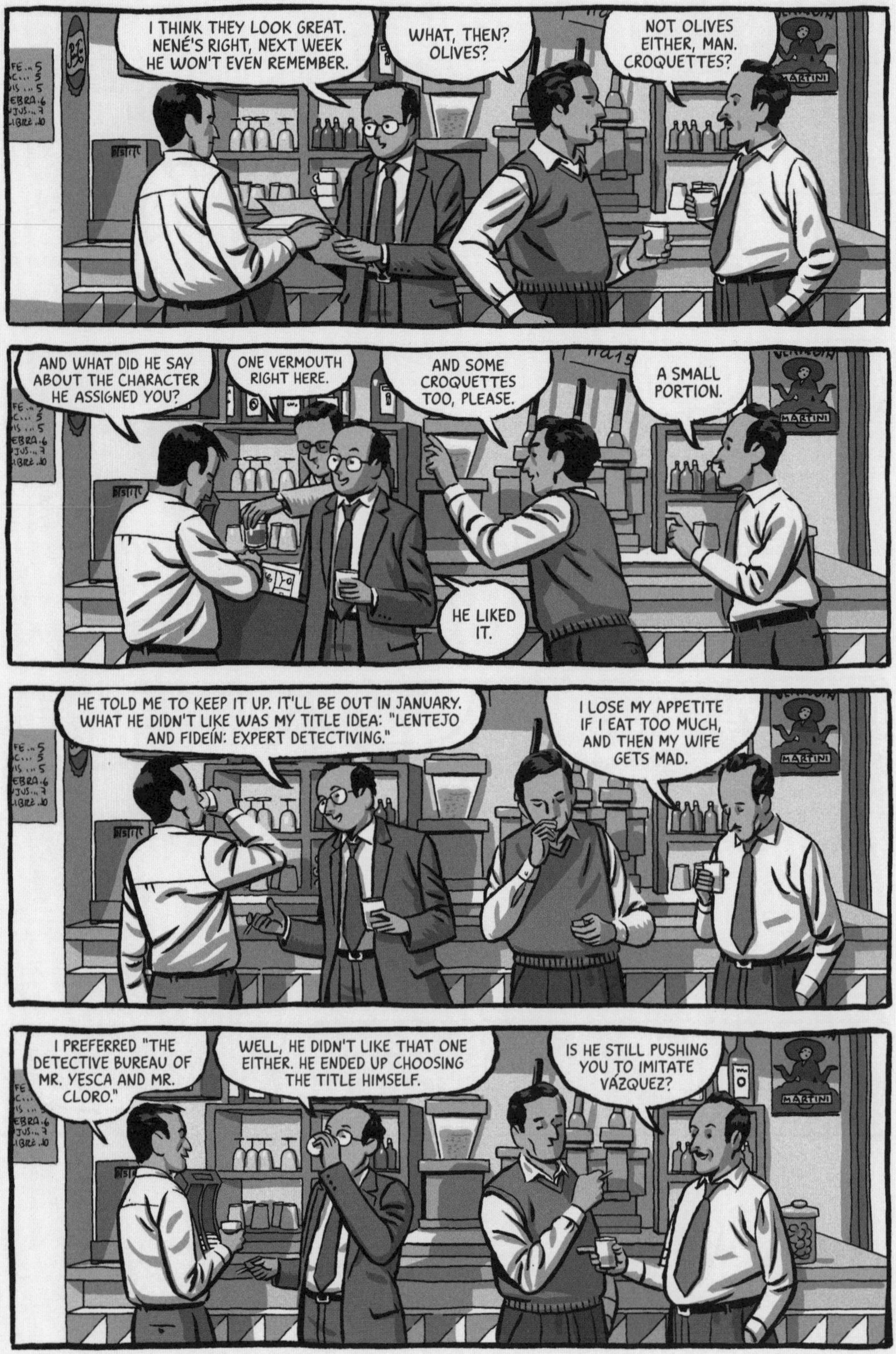
I THINK THEY LOOK GREAT. NENÉ'S RIGHT, NEXT WEEK HE WON'T EVEN REMEMBER.
WHAT, THEN? OLIVES?
NOT OLIVES EITHER, MAN. CROQUETTES?
MARTINI
AND WHAT DID HE SAY ABOUT THE CHARACTER HE ASSIGNED YOU?
ONE VERMOUTH RIGHT HERE.
AND SOME CROQUETTES TOO, PLEASE.
A SMALL PORTION.
HE LIKED IT.
HE TOLD ME TO KEEP IT UP. IT'LL BE OUT IN JANUARY. WHAT HE DIDN'T LIKE WAS MY TITLE IDEA: "LENTEJO AND FIDEÍN: EXPERT DETECTIVING."
I LOSE MY APPETITE IF I EAT TOO MUCH, AND THEN MY WIFE GETS MAD.
I PREFERRED "THE DETECTIVE BUREAU OF MR. YESCA AND MR. CLORO."
WELL, HE DIDN'T LIKE THAT ONE EITHER. HE ENDED UP CHOOSING THE TITLE HIMSELF.
IS HE STILL PUSHING YOU TO IMITATE VÁZQUEZ?

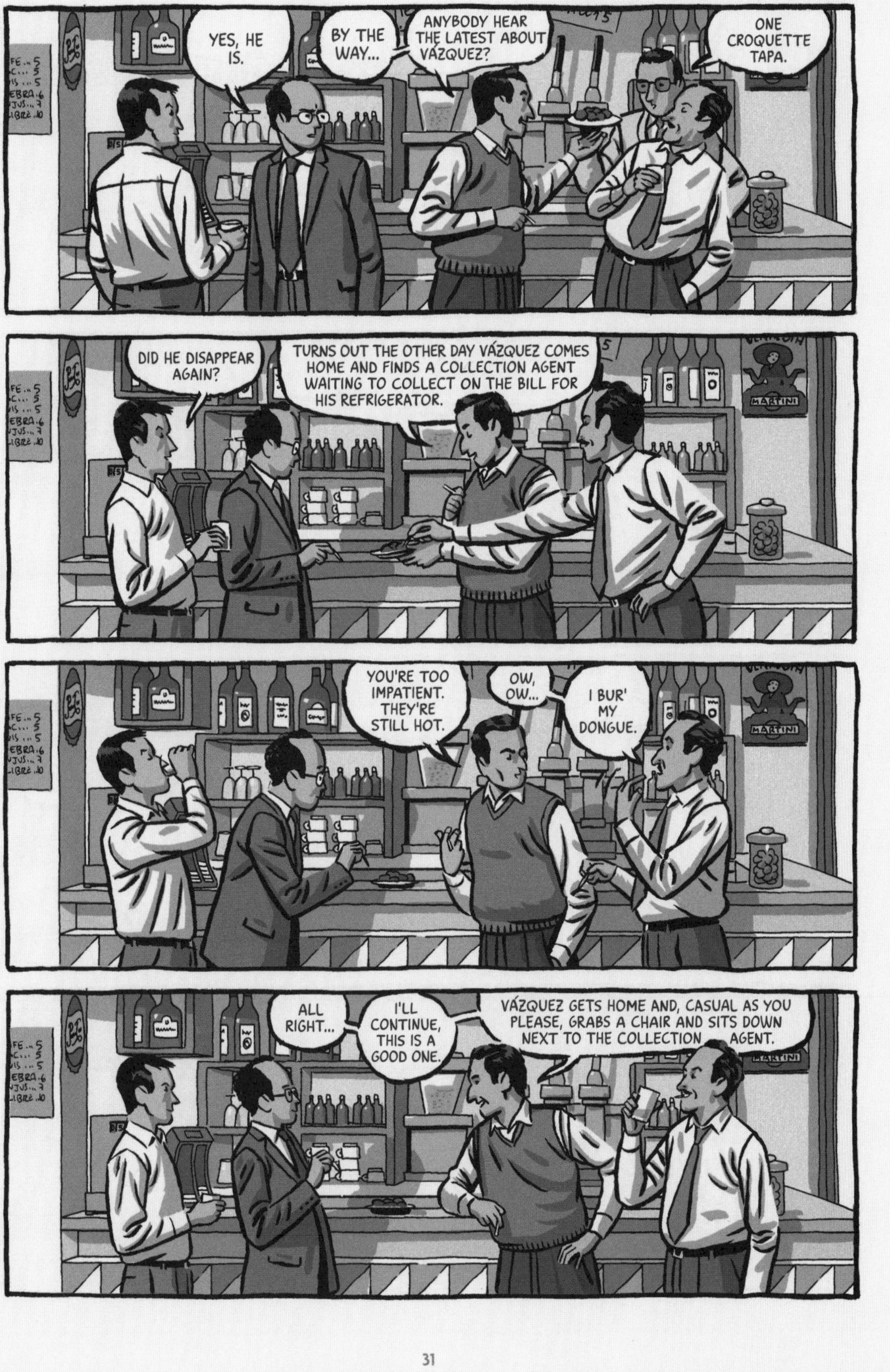
YES, HE IS.
BY THE WAY...
ANYBODY HEAR THE LATEST ABOUT VÁZQUEZ?
ONE CROQUETTE TAPA.
DID HE DISAPPEAR AGAIN?
TURNS OUT THE OTHER DAY VÁZQUEZ COMES HOME AND FINDS A COLLECTION AGENT WAITING TO COLLECT ON THE BILL FOR HIS REFRIGERATOR.
MARTINI
YOU'RE TOO IMPATIENT. THEY'RE STILL HOT.
OW, OW...
I BUR' MY DONGUE.
MARTINI
ALL RIGHT...
I'LL CONTINUE, THIS IS A GOOD ONE.
VÁZQUEZ GETS HOME AND, CASUAL AS YOU PLEASE, GRABS A CHAIR AND SITS DOWN NEXT TO THE COLLECTION AGENT.

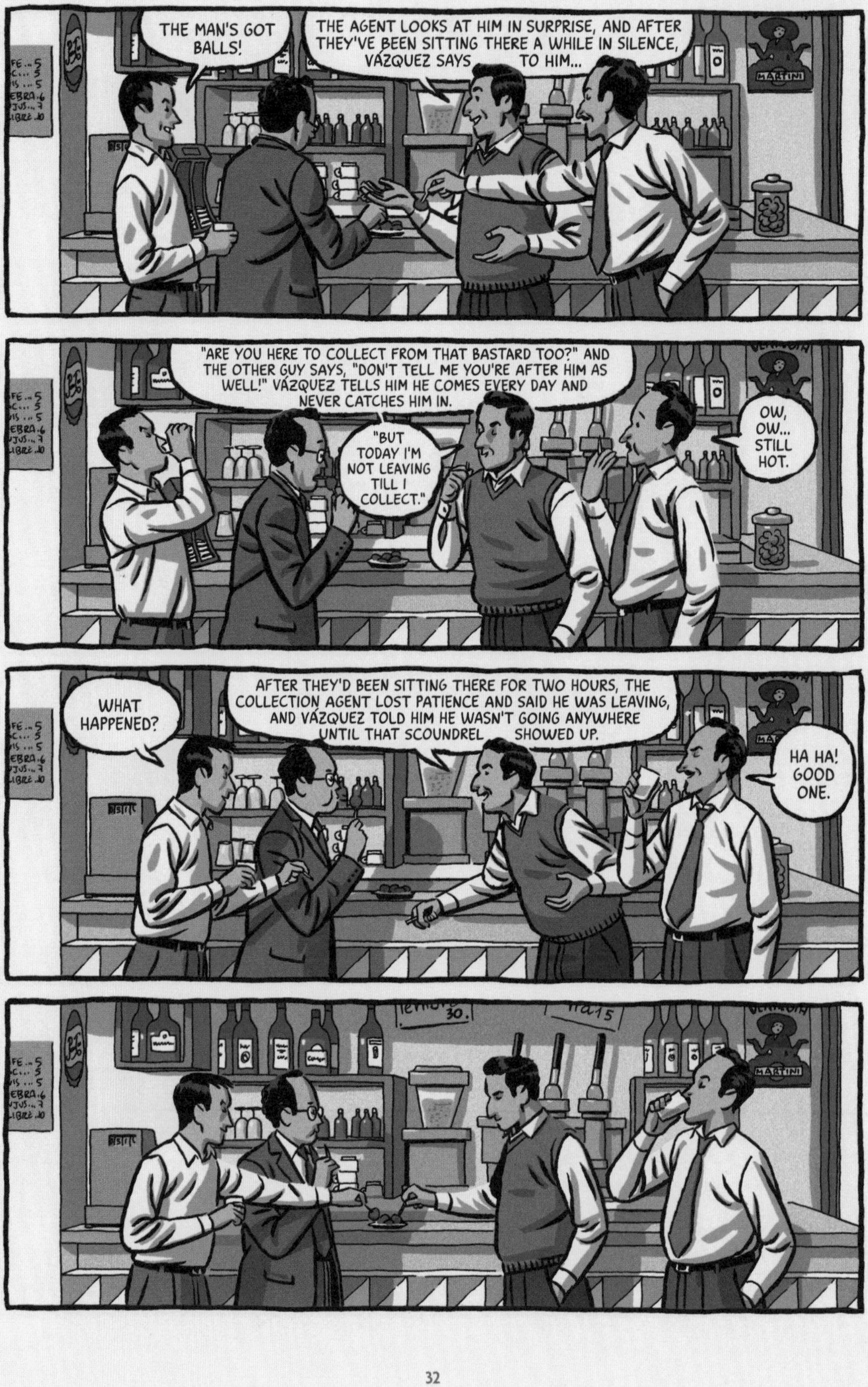
THE MAN'S GOT BALLS!
THE AGENT LOOKS AT HIM IN SURPRISE, AND AFTER THEY'VE BEEN SITTING THERE A WHILE IN SILENCE, VÁZQUEZ SAYS TO HIM...
MARTINI
"ARE YOU HERE TO COLLECT FROM THAT BASTARD TOO?" AND THE OTHER GUY SAYS, "DON'T TELL ME YOU'RE AFTER HIM AS WELL!" VÁZQUEZ TELLS HIM HE COMES EVERY DAY AND NEVER CATCHES HIM IN.
"BUT TODAY I'M NOT LEAVING TILL I COLLECT."
OW, OW... STILL HOT.
WHAT HAPPENED?
AFTER THEY'D BEEN SITTING THERE FOR TWO HOURS, THE COLLECTION AGENT LOST PATIENCE AND SAID HE WAS LEAVING, AND VÁZQUEZ TOLD HIM HE WASN'T GOING ANYWHERE UNTIL THAT SCOUNDREL SHOWED UP.
HA HA! GOOD ONE.
MARTINI

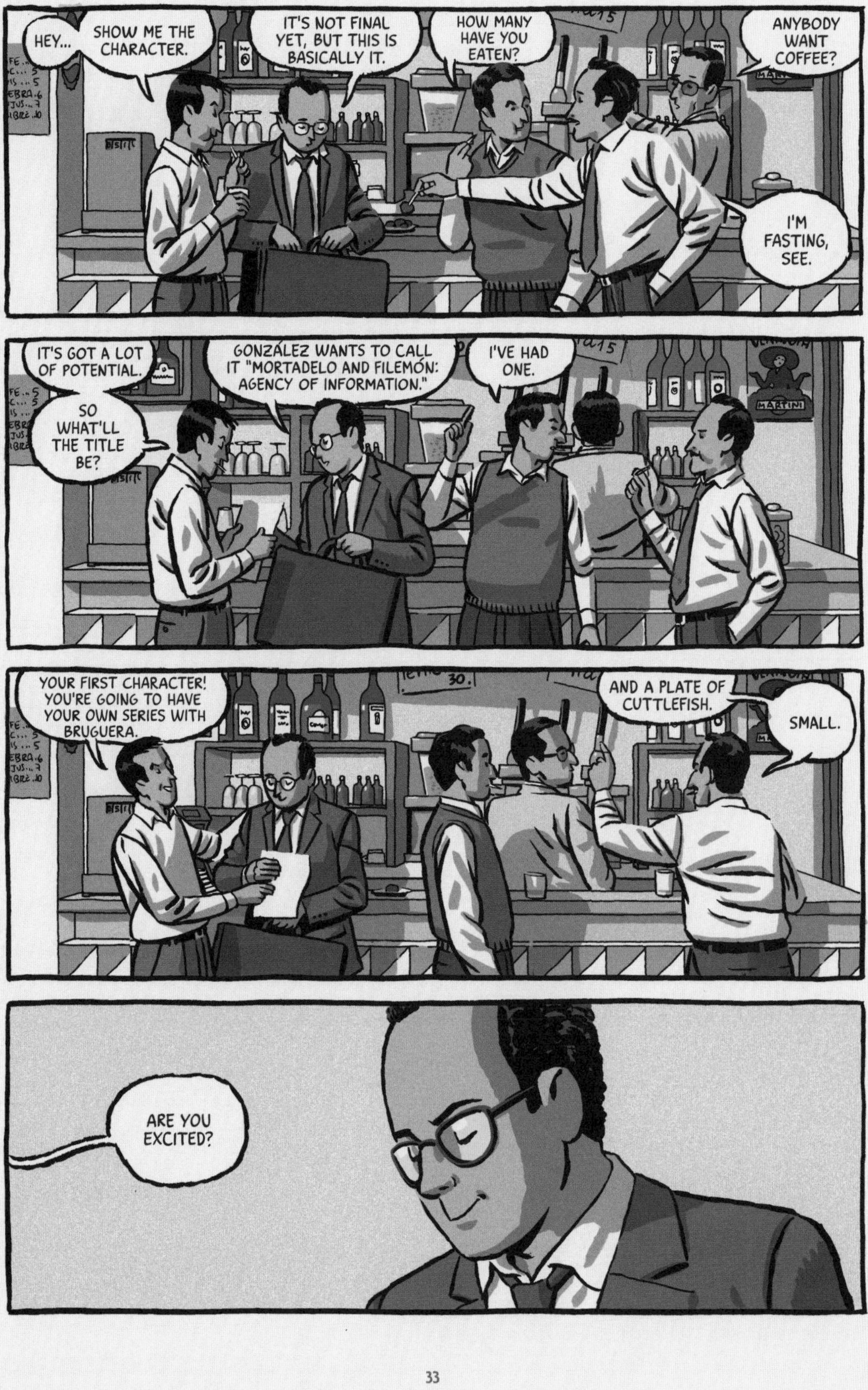

HEY...
SHOW ME THE CHARACTER.
IT'S NOT FINAL YET, BUT THIS IS BASICALLY IT.
HOW MANY HAVE YOU EATEN?
ANYBODY WANT COFFEE?
I'M FASTING, SEE.
IT'S GOT A LOT OF POTENTIAL.
SO WHAT'LL THE TITLE BE?
GONZÁLEZ WANTS TO CALL IT "MORTADELO AND FILEMÓN: AGENCY OF INFORMATION."
I'VE HAD ONE.
MARTINI
YOUR FIRST CHARACTER! YOU'RE GOING TO HAVE YOUR OWN SERIES WITH BRUGUERA.
AND A PLATE OF CUTTLEFISH.
SMALL.
ARE YOU EXCITED?

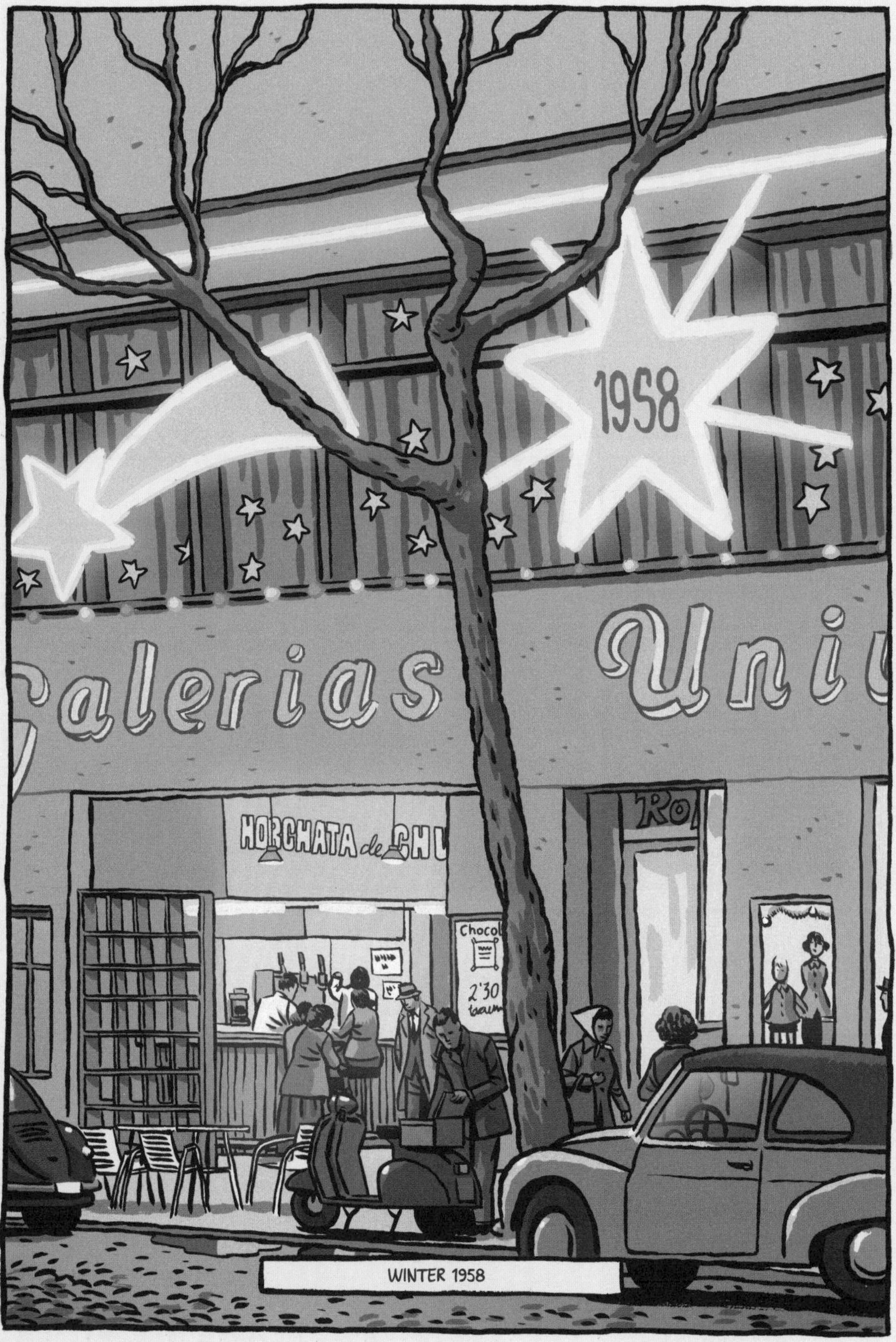
1958
WINTER 1958

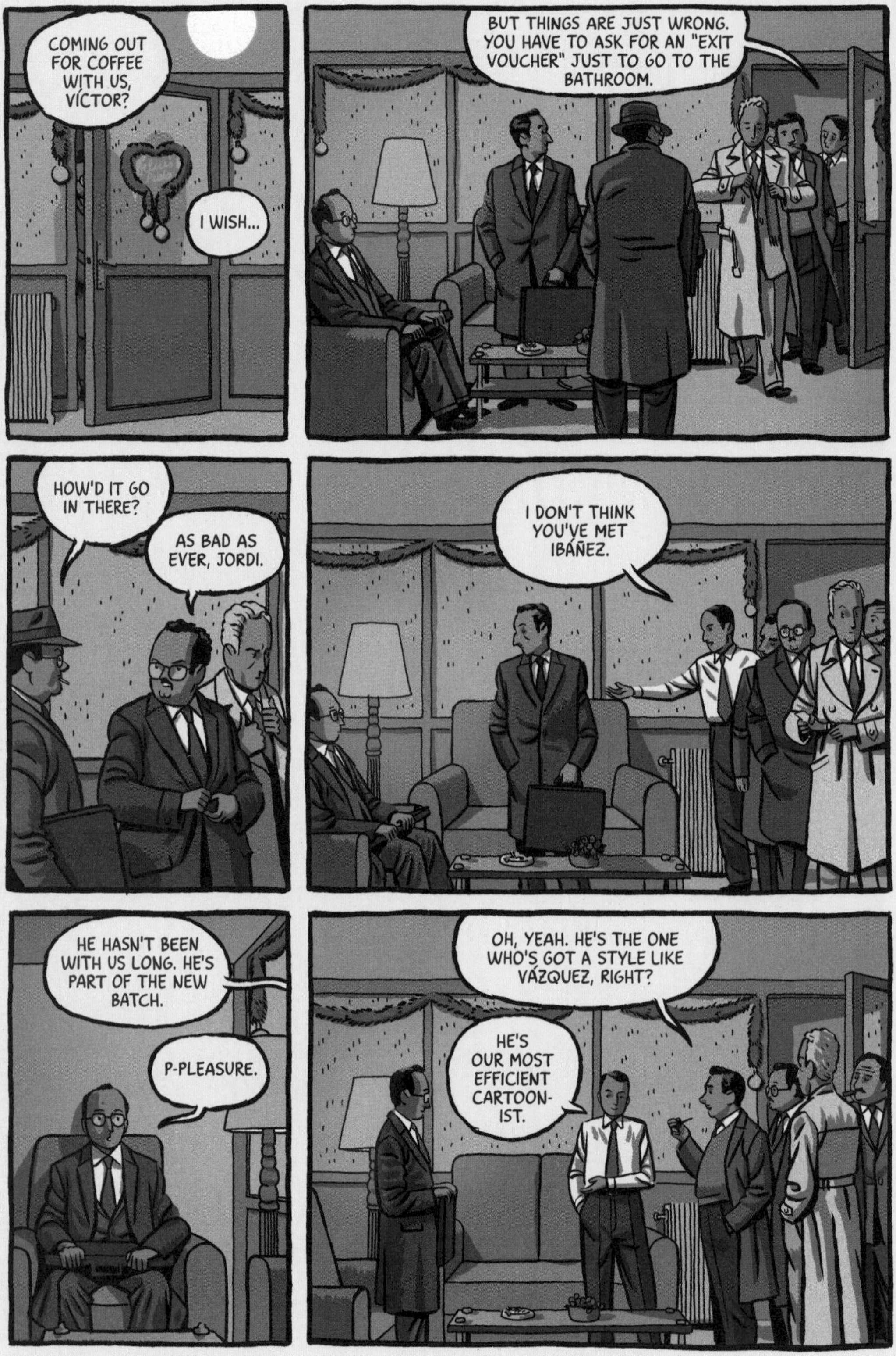
COMING OUT FOR COFFEE WITH US, VÍCTOR?
I WISH...
BUT THINGS ARE JUST WRONG. YOU HAVE TO ASK FOR AN "EXIT VOUCHER" JUST TO GO TO THE BATHROOM.
HOW'D IT GO IN THERE?
AS BAD AS EVER, JORDI.
I DON'T THINK YOU'VE MET IBÁÑEZ.
HE HASN'T BEEN WITH US LONG. HE'S PART OF THE NEW BATCH.
P-PLEASURE.
OH, YEAH. HE'S THE ONE WHO'S GOT A STYLE LIKE VÁZQUEZ, RIGHT?
HE'S OUR MOST EFFICIENT CARTOON-IST.

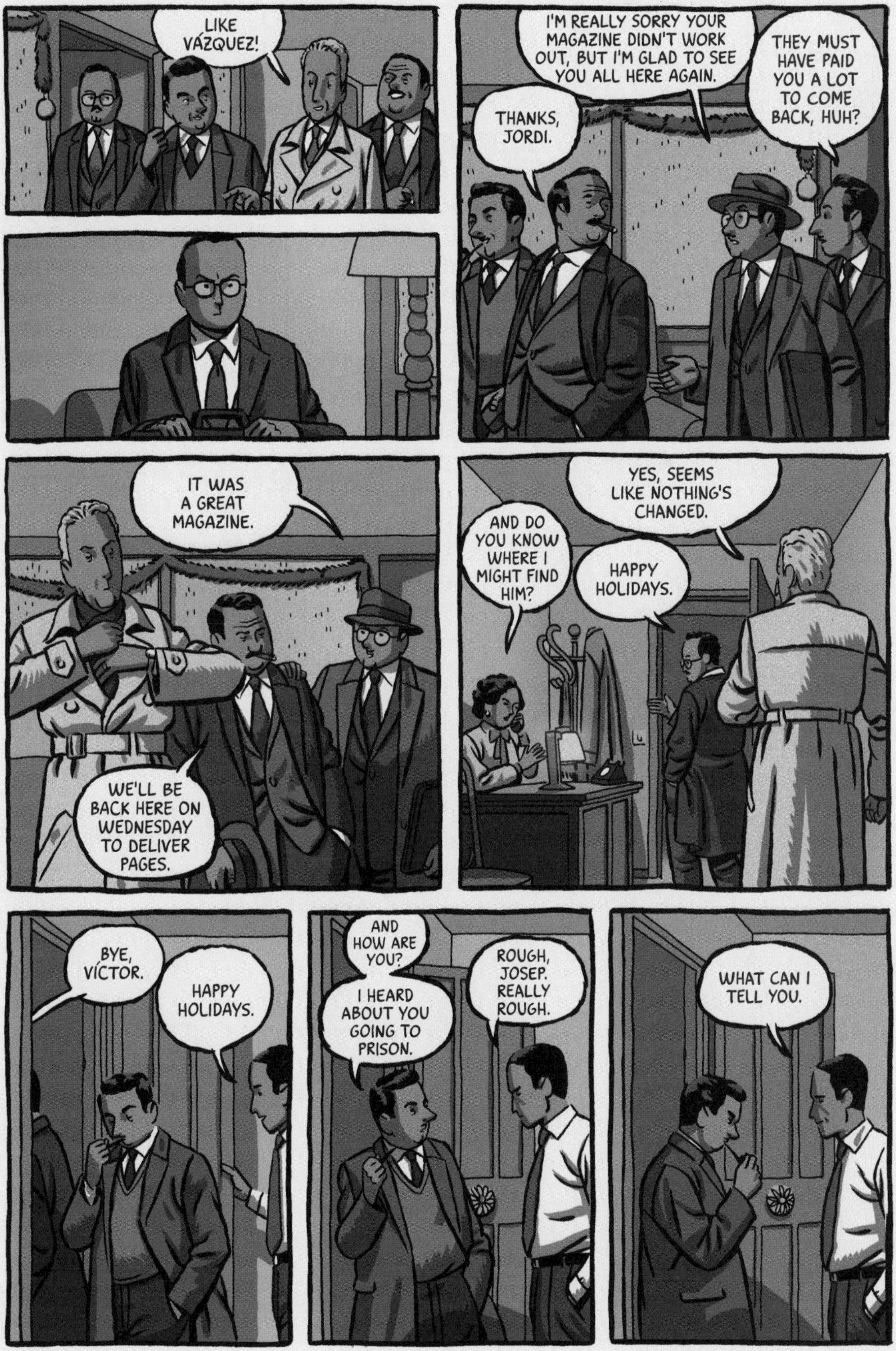
LIKE VÁZQUEZ!
I'M REALLY SORRY YOUR MAGAZINE DIDN'T WORK OUT, BUT I'M GLAD TO SEE YOU ALL HERE AGAIN.
THANKS, JORDI.
THEY MUST HAVE PAID YOU A LOT TO COME BACK, HUH?
IT WAS A GREAT MAGAZINE.
WE'LL BE BACK HERE ON WEDNESDAY TO DELIVER PAGES.
YES, SEEMS LIKE NOTHING'S CHANGED.
AND DO YOU KNOW WHERE I MIGHT FIND HIM?
HAPPY HOLIDAYS.
BYE, VÍCTOR.
HAPPY HOLIDAYS.
AND HOW ARE YOU?
I HEARD ABOUT YOU GOING TO PRISON.
ROUGH, JOSEP. REALLY ROUGH.
WHAT CAN I TELL YOU.

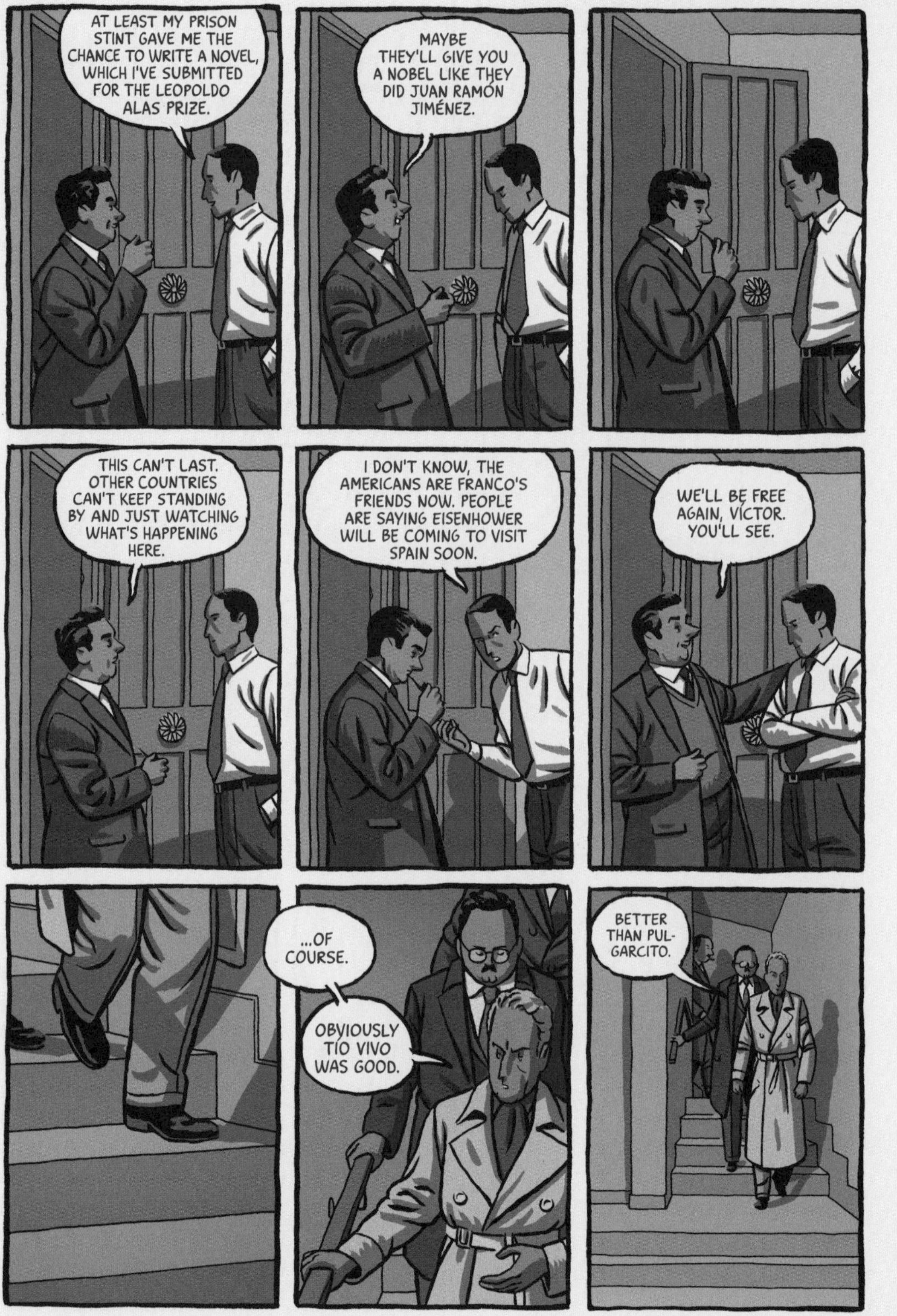
AT LEAST MY PRISON STINT GAVE ME THE CHANCE TO WRITE A NOVEL, WHICH I'VE SUBMITTED FOR THE LEOPOLDO ALAS PRIZE.
MAYBE THEY'LL GIVE YOU A NOBEL LIKE THEY DID JUAN RAMÓN JIMÉNEZ.
THIS CAN'T LAST. OTHER COUNTRIES CAN'T KEEP STANDING BY AND JUST WATCHING WHAT'S HAPPENING HERE.
I DON'T KNOW, THE AMERICANS ARE FRANCO'S FRIENDS NOW. PEOPLE ARE SAYING EISENHOWER WILL BE COMING TO VISIT SPAIN SOON.
WE'LL BE FREE AGAIN, VÍCTOR. YOU'LL SEE.
...OF COURSE.
OBVIOUSLY TÍO VIVO WAS GOOD.
BETTER THAN PUL-GARCITO.

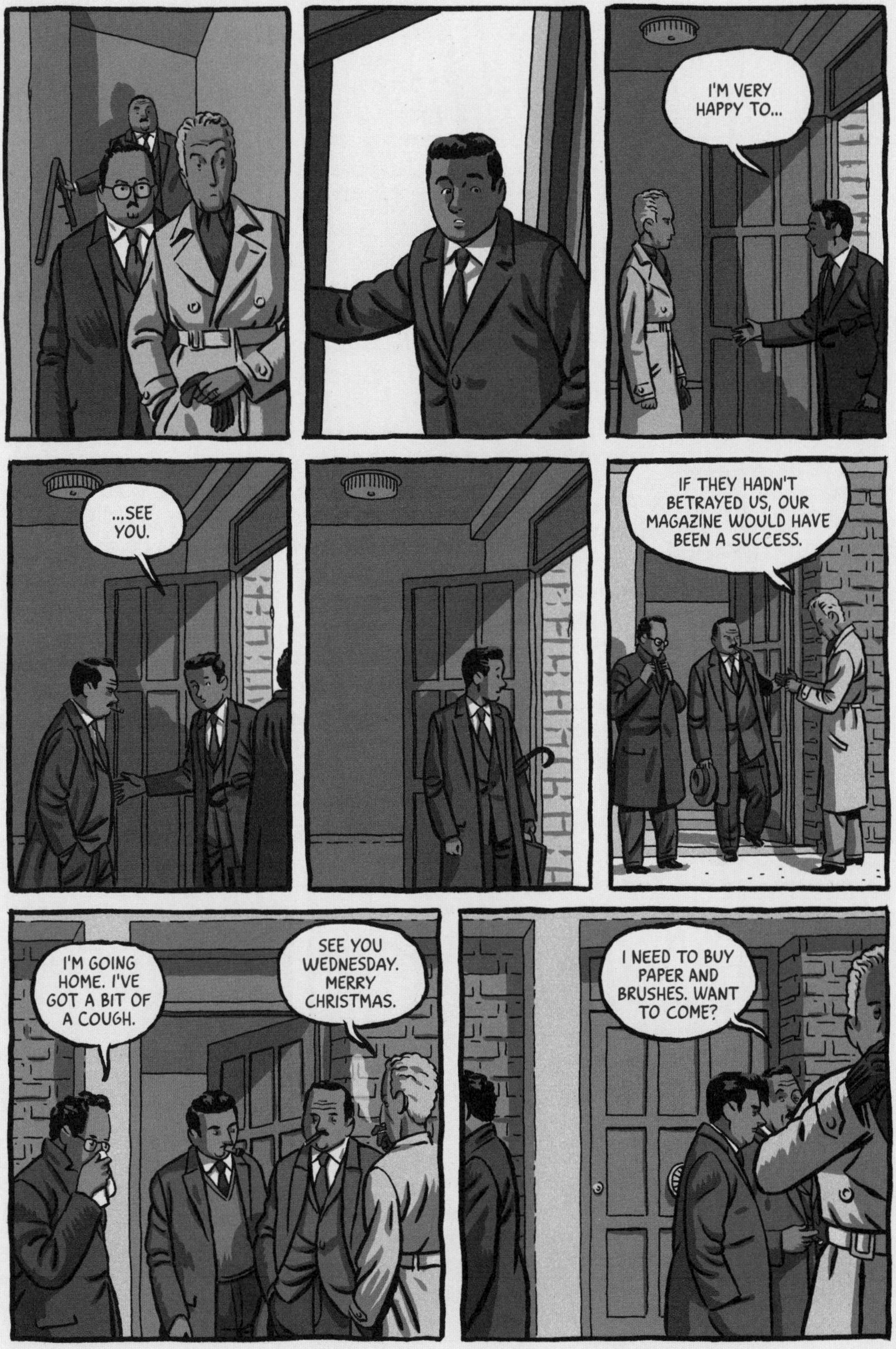
I'M VERY HAPPY TO...
...SEE YOU.
IF THEY HADN'T BETRAYED US, OUR MAGAZINE WOULD HAVE BEEN A SUCCESS.
I'M GOING HOME. I'VE GOT A BIT OF A COUGH.
SEE YOU WEDNESDAY. MERRY CHRISTMAS.
I NEED TO BUY PAPER AND BRUSHES. WANT TO COME?

LEGAL DEPT.
LEDESMA...
HERE ARE THE CONTRACTS YOU PREPARED. THEY'VE BEEN SIGNED.
THEY'RE COMING BACK TO WORK FOR BRUGUERA.
UNDER THE SAME CONTRACT AS BEFORE.
THEY JUST LEFT. DID YOU SEE THEM?
YES, I SAW THEM.

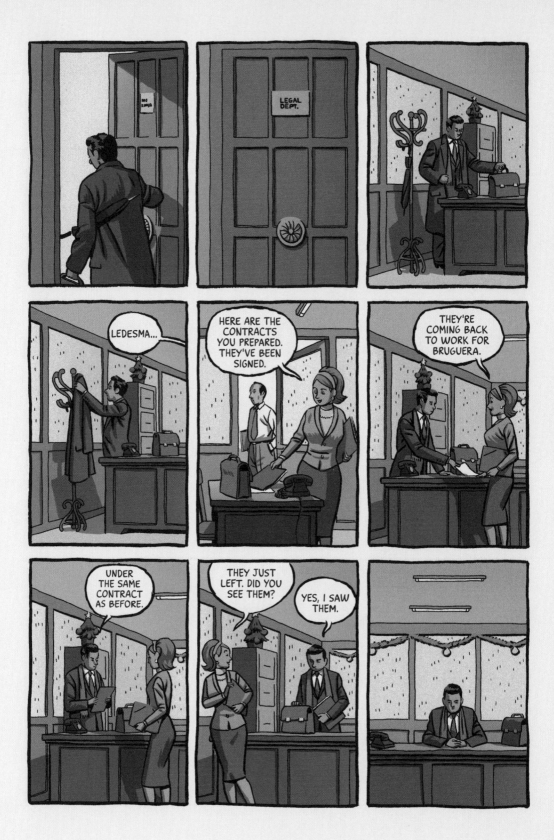

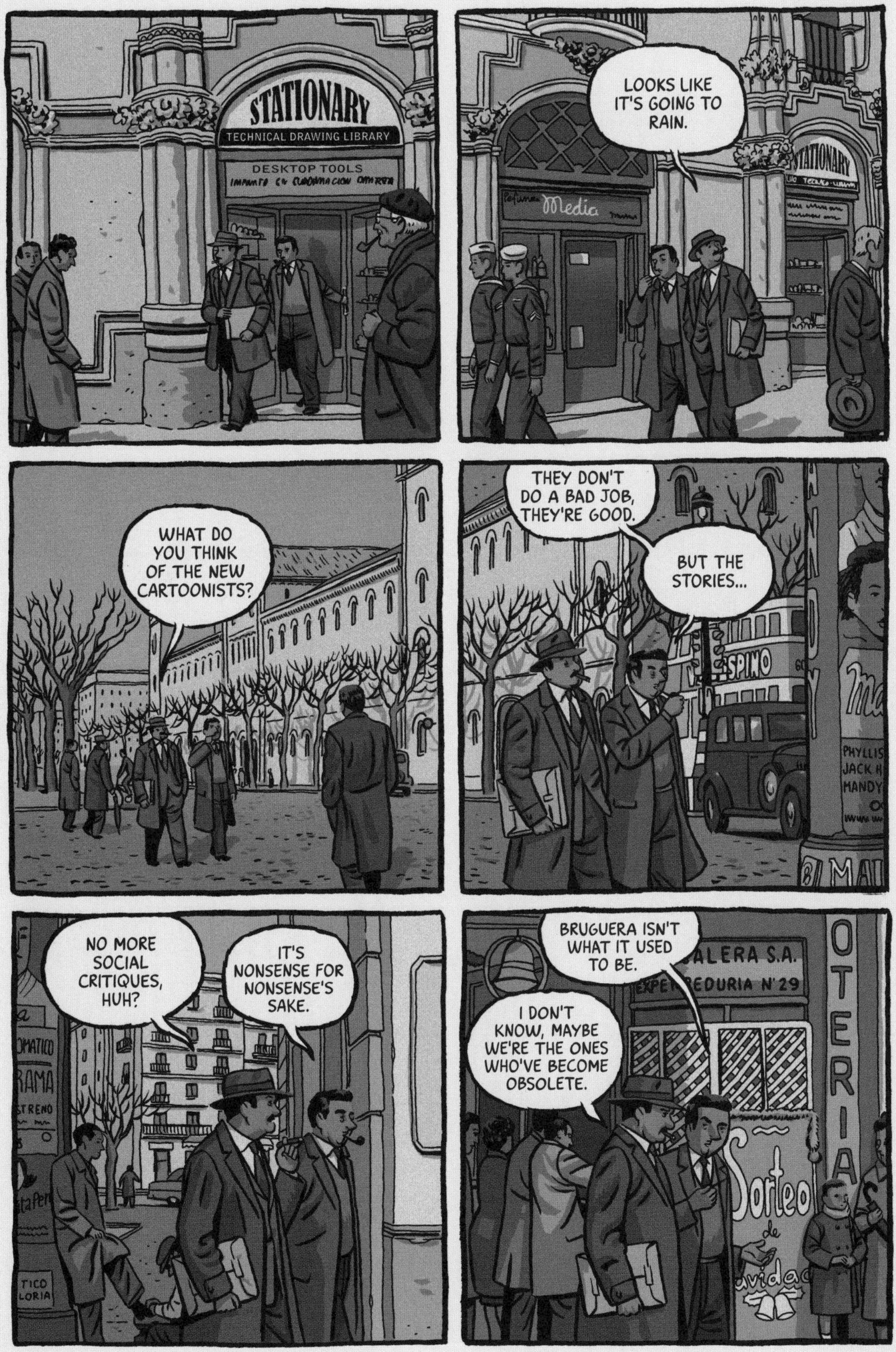
STATIONARY
TECHNICAL DRAWING LIBRARY
DESKTOP TOOLS
LOOKS LIKE IT'S GOING TO RAIN.
Media
STATIONARY
WHAT DO YOU THINK OF THE NEW CARTOONISTS?
THEY DON'T DO A BAD JOB, THEY'RE GOOD.
BUT THE STORIES...
SPINO
PHYLLIS
MANDY
NO MORE SOCIAL CRITIQUES, HUH?
IT'S NONSENSE FOR NONSENSE'S SAKE.
BRUGUERA ISN'T WHAT IT USED TO BE.
I DON'T KNOW, MAYBE WE'RE THE ONES WHO'VE BECOME OBSOLETE.
Sorteo
de

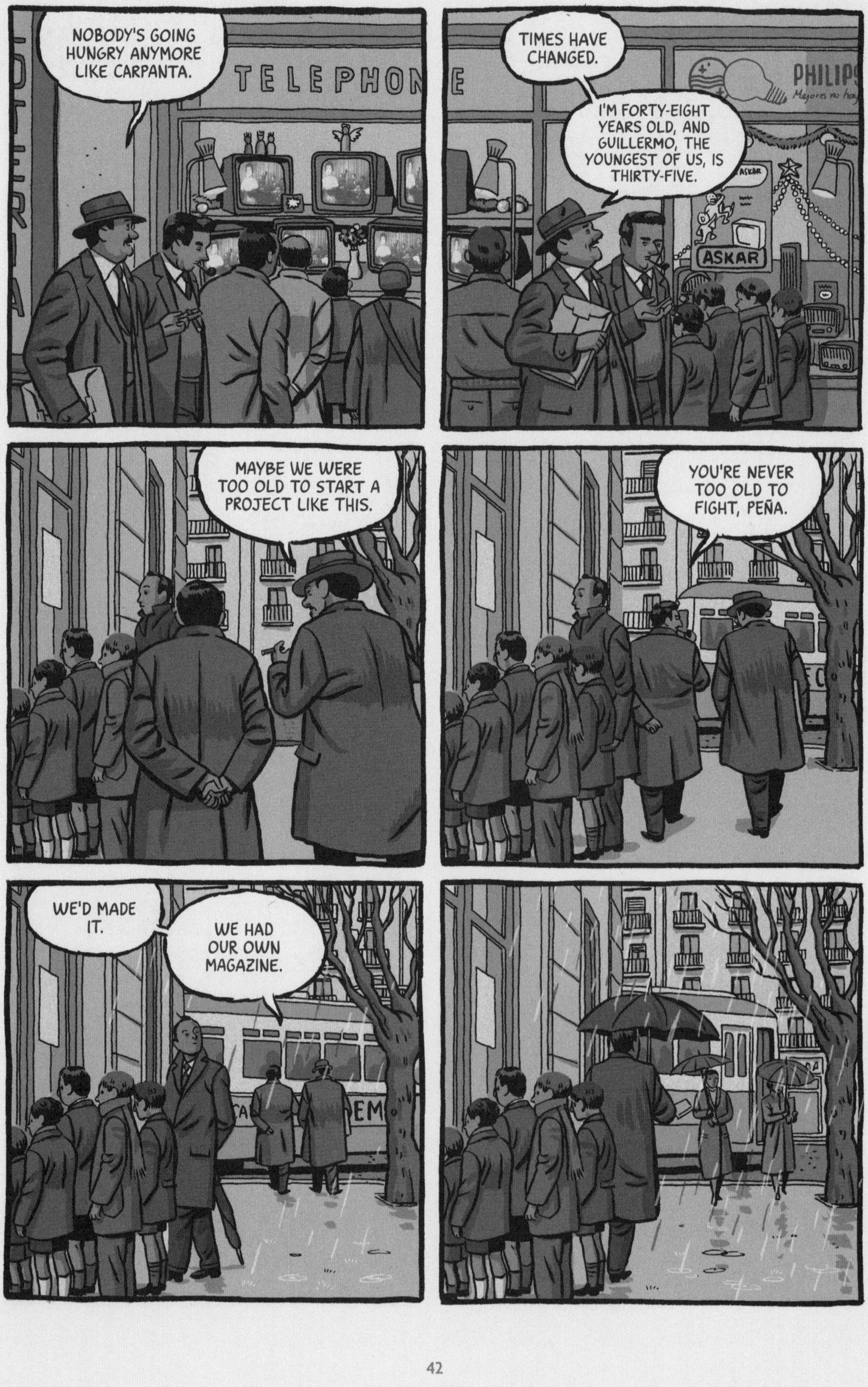
NOBODY'S GOING HUNGRY ANYMORE LIKE CARPANTA.
TELEPHONE
TIMES HAVE CHANGED.
PHILIPS
I'M FORTY-EIGHT YEARS OLD, AND GUILLERMO, THE YOUNGEST OF US, IS THIRTY-FIVE.
ASKAR
MAYBE WE WERE TOO OLD TO START A PROJECT LIKE THIS.
YOU'RE NEVER TOO OLD TO FIGHT, PEÑA.
WE'D MADE IT.
WE HAD OUR OWN MAGAZINE.

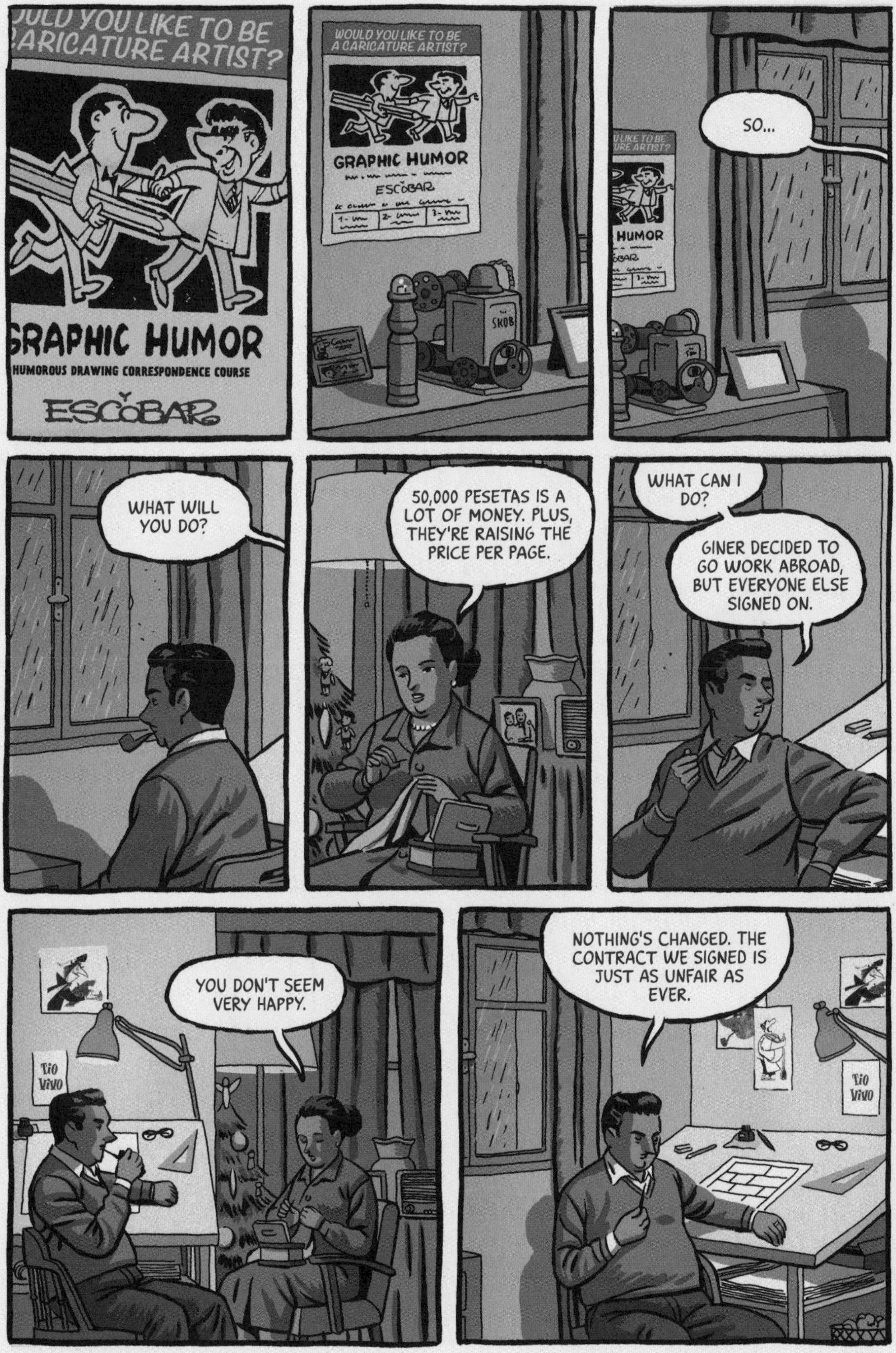

OULD YOU LIKE TO BE
ARICATURE ARTIST?
GRAPHIC HUMOR
HUMOROUS DRAWING CORRESPONDENCE COURSE
ESCOBAR
WOULD YOU LIKE TO BE
A CARICATURE ARTIST?
GRAPHIC HUMOR
ESCOBAR
SKOB
SO...
WHAT WILL YOU DO?
50,000 PESETAS IS A LOT OF MONEY. PLUS, THEY'RE RAISING THE PRICE PER PAGE.
WHAT CAN I DO?
GINER DECIDED TO GO WORK ABROAD, BUT EVERYONE ELSE SIGNED ON.
TIO VIVO
YOU DON'T SEEM VERY HAPPY.
NOTHING'S CHANGED. THE CONTRACT WE SIGNED IS JUST AS UNFAIR AS EVER.
TIO VIVO

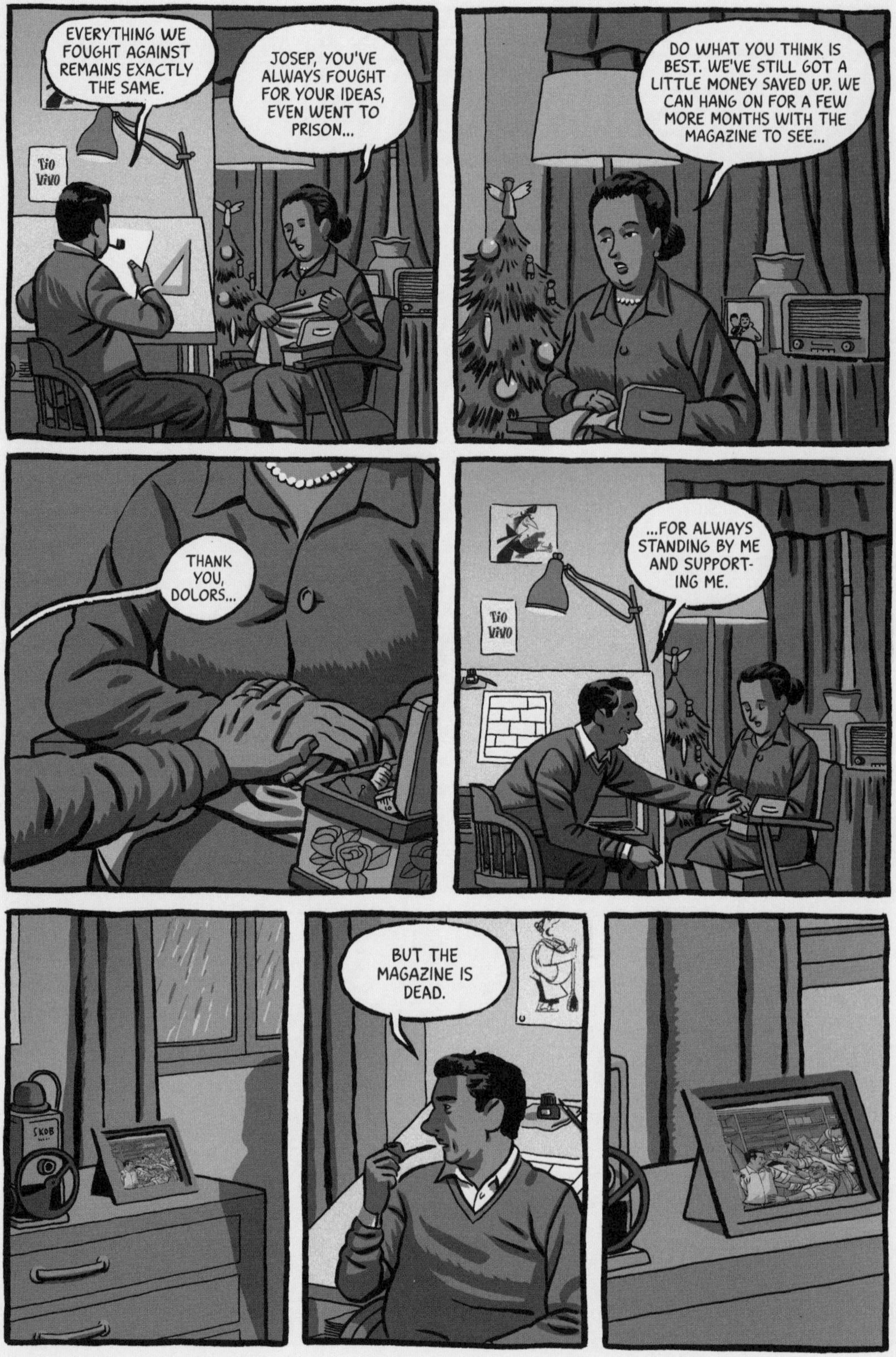
EVERYTHING WE FOUGHT AGAINST REMAINS EXACTLY THE SAME.
JOSEP, YOU'VE ALWAYS FOUGHT FOR YOUR IDEAS, EVEN WENT TO PRISON...
TIO VIVO
DO WHAT YOU THINK IS BEST. WE'VE STILL GOT A LITTLE MONEY SAVED UP. WE CAN HANG ON FOR A FEW MORE MONTHS WITH THE MAGAZINE TO SEE...
THANK YOU, DOLORS...
...FOR ALWAYS STANDING BY ME AND SUPPORTING ME.
TIO VIVO
SKOB
BUT THE MAGAZINE IS DEAD.

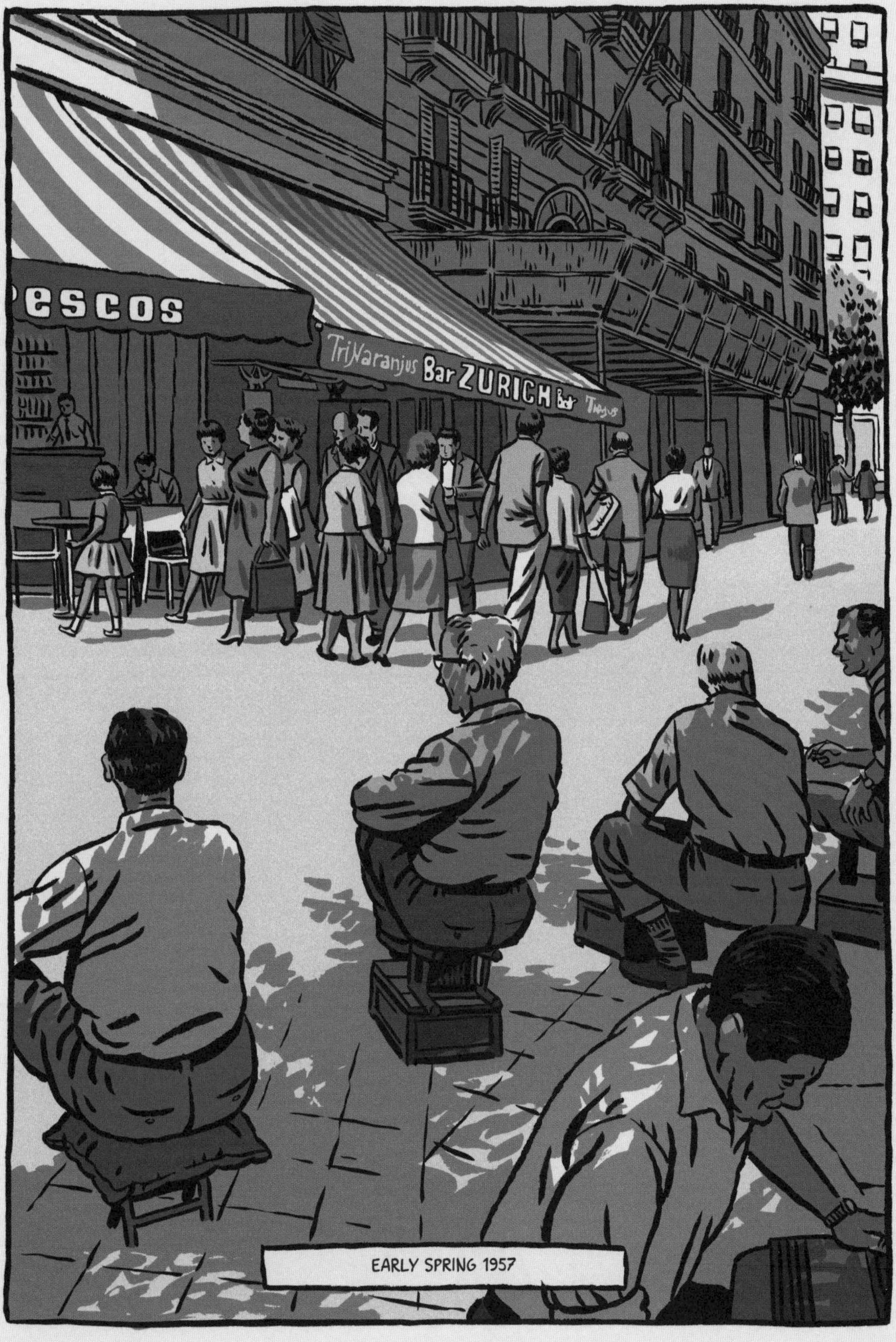

pescos
TriNaranjus Bar ZURICH Bar
EARLY SPRING 1957

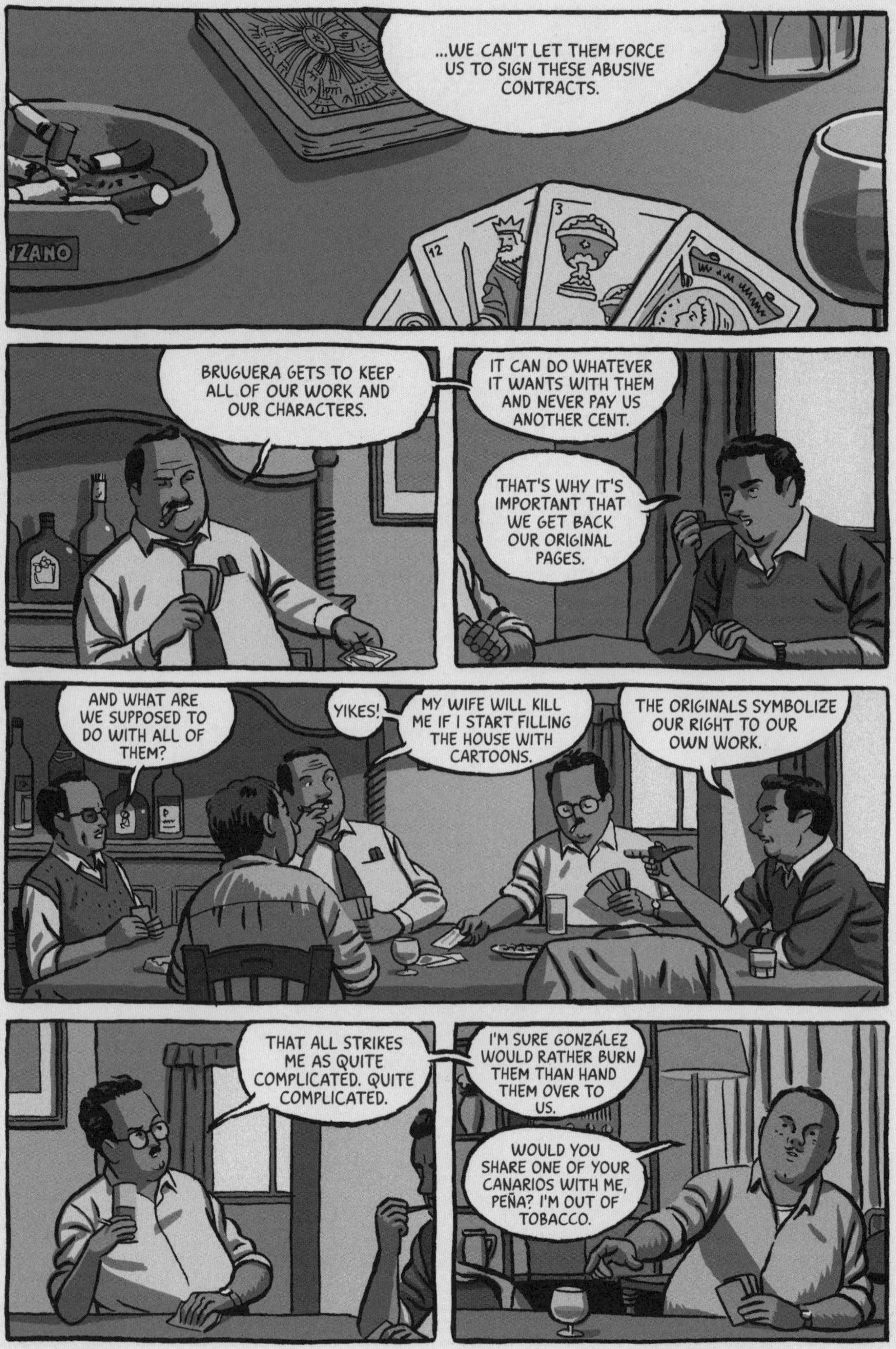
...WE CAN'T LET THEM FORCE US TO SIGN THESE ABUSIVE CONTRACTS.
NZANO
BRUGUERA GETS TO KEEP ALL OF OUR WORK AND OUR CHARACTERS.
IT CAN DO WHATEVER IT WANTS WITH THEM AND NEVER PAY US ANOTHER CENT.
THAT'S WHY IT'S IMPORTANT THAT WE GET BACK OUR ORIGINAL PAGES.
AND WHAT ARE WE SUPPOSED TO DO WITH ALL OF THEM?
YIKES!
MY WIFE WILL KILL ME IF I START FILLING THE HOUSE WITH CARTOONS.
THE ORIGINALS SYMBOLIZE OUR RIGHT TO OUR OWN WORK.
THAT ALL STRIKES ME AS QUITE COMPLICATED. QUITE COMPLICATED.
I'M SURE GONZÁLEZ WOULD RATHER BURN THEM THAN HAND THEM OVER TO US.
WOULD YOU SHARE ONE OF YOUR CANARIOS WITH ME, PEÑA? I'M OUT OF TOBACCO.

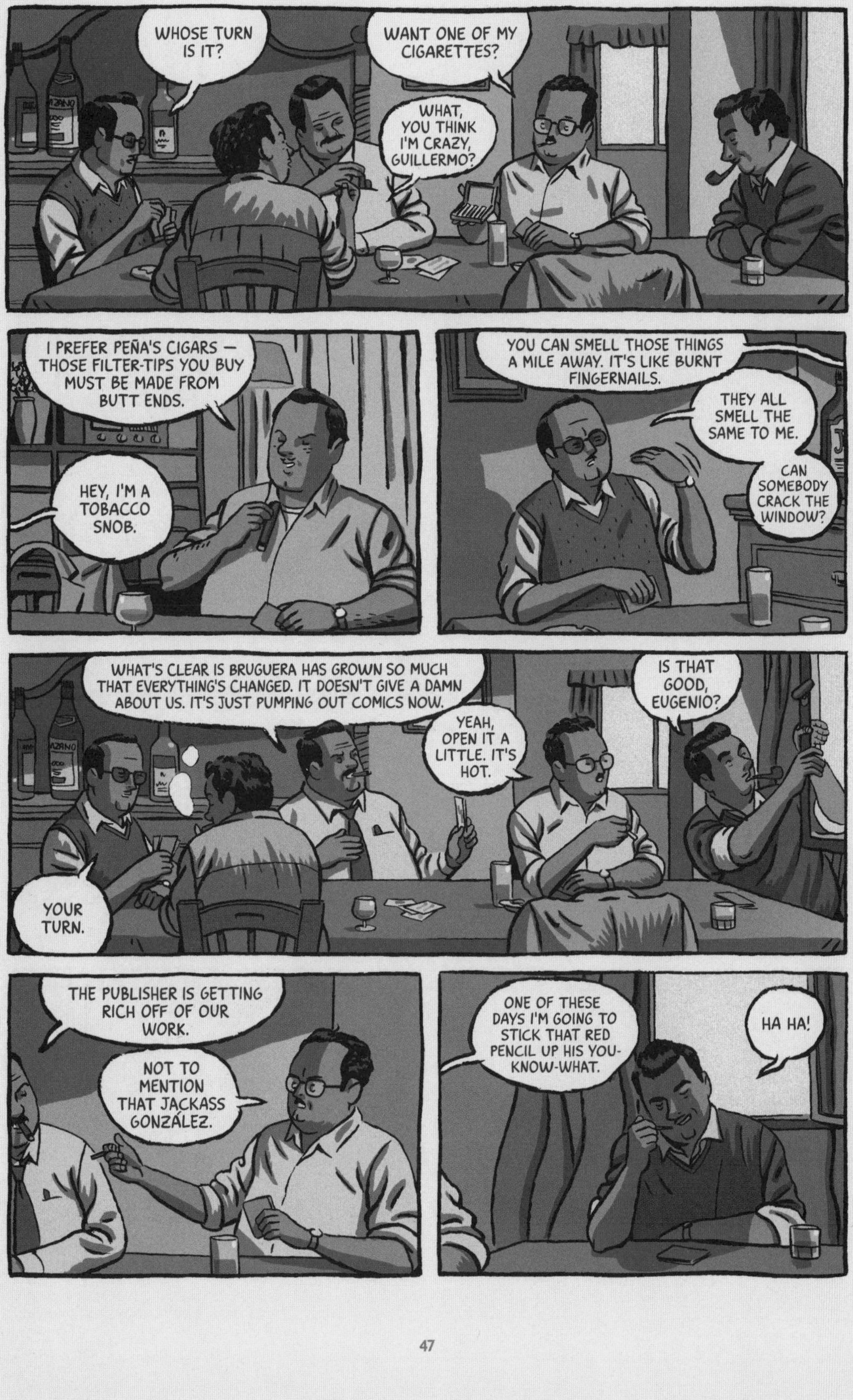
WHOSE TURN IS IT?
WANT ONE OF MY CIGARETTES?
WHAT, YOU THINK I'M CRAZY, GUILLERMO?
I PREFER PEÑA'S CIGARS — THOSE FILTER-TIPS YOU BUY MUST BE MADE FROM BUTT ENDS.
HEY, I'M A TOBACCO SNOB.
YOU CAN SMELL THOSE THINGS A MILE AWAY. IT'S LIKE BURNT FINGERNAILS.
THEY ALL SMELL THE SAME TO ME.
CAN SOMEBODY CRACK THE WINDOW?
WHAT'S CLEAR IS BRUGUERA HAS GROWN SO MUCH THAT EVERYTHING'S CHANGED. IT DOESN'T GIVE A DAMN ABOUT US. IT'S JUST PUMPING OUT COMICS NOW.
YOUR TURN.
YEAH, OPEN IT A LITTLE. IT'S HOT.
IS THAT GOOD, EUGENIO?
THE PUBLISHER IS GETTING RICH OFF OF OUR WORK.
NOT TO MENTION THAT JACKASS GONZÁLEZ.
ONE OF THESE DAYS I'M GOING TO STICK THAT RED PENCIL UP HIS YOU-KNOW-WHAT.
HA HA!

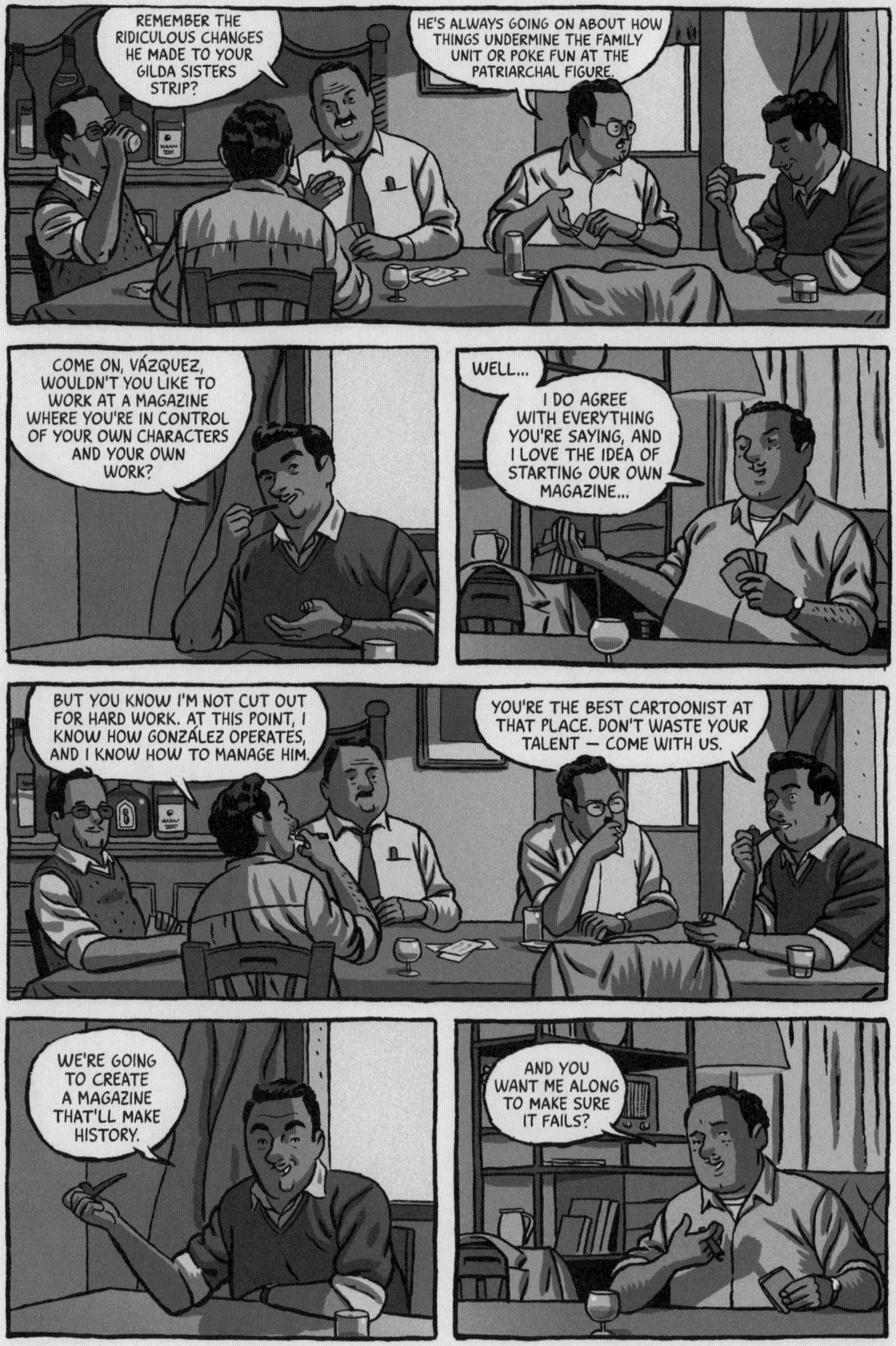
REMEMBER THE RIDICULOUS CHANGES HE MADE TO YOUR GILDA SISTERS STRIP?
HE'S ALWAYS GOING ON ABOUT HOW THINGS UNDERMINE THE FAMILY UNIT OR POKE FUN AT THE PATRIARCHAL FIGURE.
COME ON, VÁZQUEZ, WOULDN'T YOU LIKE TO WORK AT A MAGAZINE WHERE YOU'RE IN CONTROL OF YOUR OWN CHARACTERS AND YOUR OWN WORK?
WELL...
I DO AGREE WITH EVERYTHING YOU'RE SAYING, AND I LOVE THE IDEA OF STARTING OUR OWN MAGAZINE...
BUT YOU KNOW I'M NOT CUT OUT FOR HARD WORK. AT THIS POINT, I KNOW HOW GONZÁLEZ OPERATES, AND I KNOW HOW TO MANAGE HIM.
YOU'RE THE BEST CARTOONIST AT THAT PLACE. DON'T WASTE YOUR TALENT — COME WITH US.
WE'RE GOING TO CREATE A MAGAZINE THAT'LL MAKE HISTORY.
AND YOU WANT ME ALONG TO MAKE SURE IT FAILS?

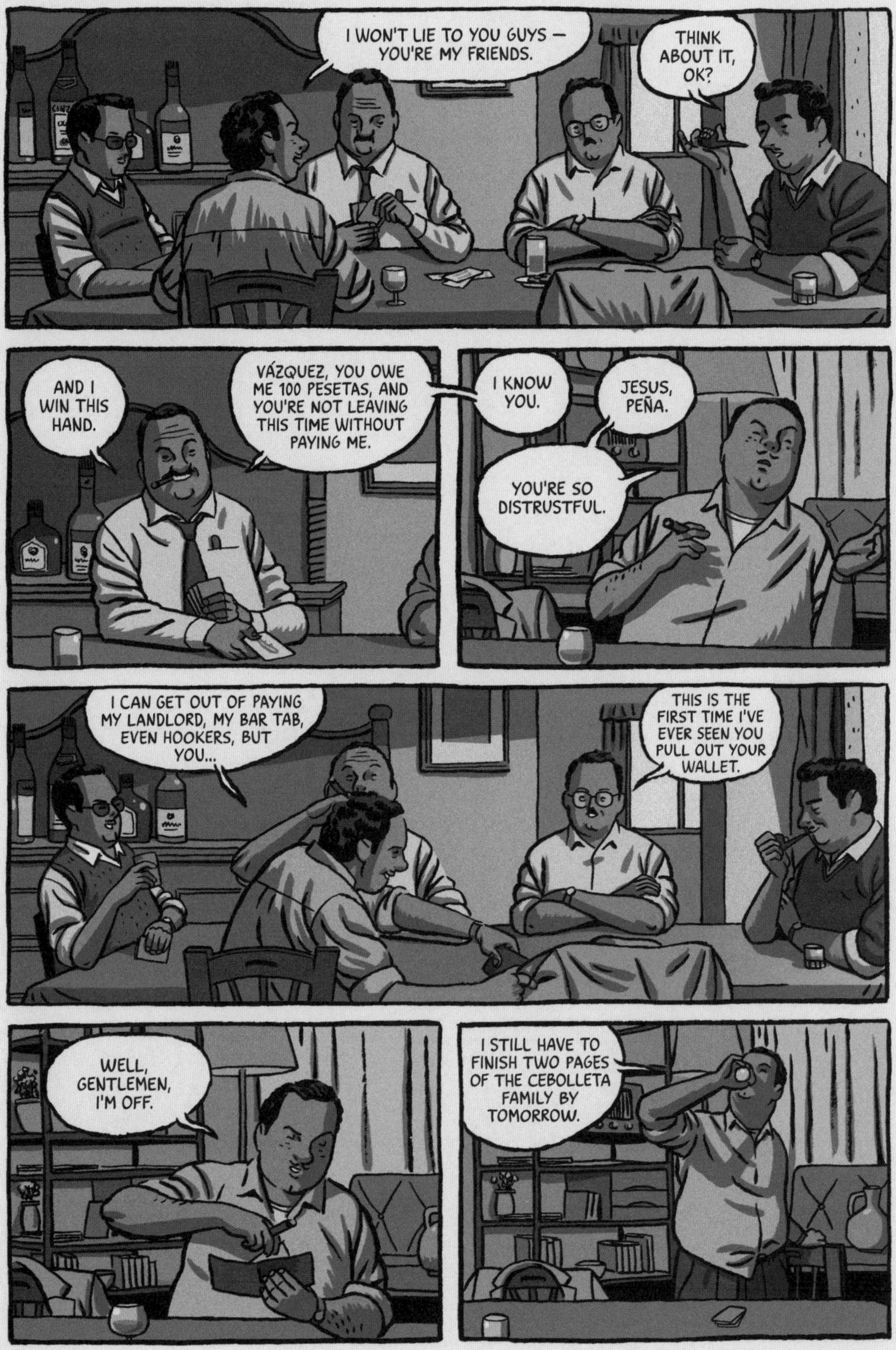
I WON'T LIE TO YOU GUYS — YOU'RE MY FRIENDS.
THINK ABOUT IT, OK?
AND I WIN THIS HAND.
VÁZQUEZ, YOU OWE ME 100 PESETAS, AND YOU'RE NOT LEAVING THIS TIME WITHOUT PAYING ME.
I KNOW YOU.
JESUS, PEÑA.
YOU'RE SO DISTRUSTFUL.
I CAN GET OUT OF PAYING MY LANDLORD, MY BAR TAB, EVEN HOOKERS, BUT YOU...
THIS IS THE FIRST TIME I'VE EVER SEEN YOU PULL OUT YOUR WALLET.
WELL, GENTLEMEN, I'M OFF.
I STILL HAVE TO FINISH TWO PAGES OF THE CEBOLLETA FAMILY BY TOMORROW.

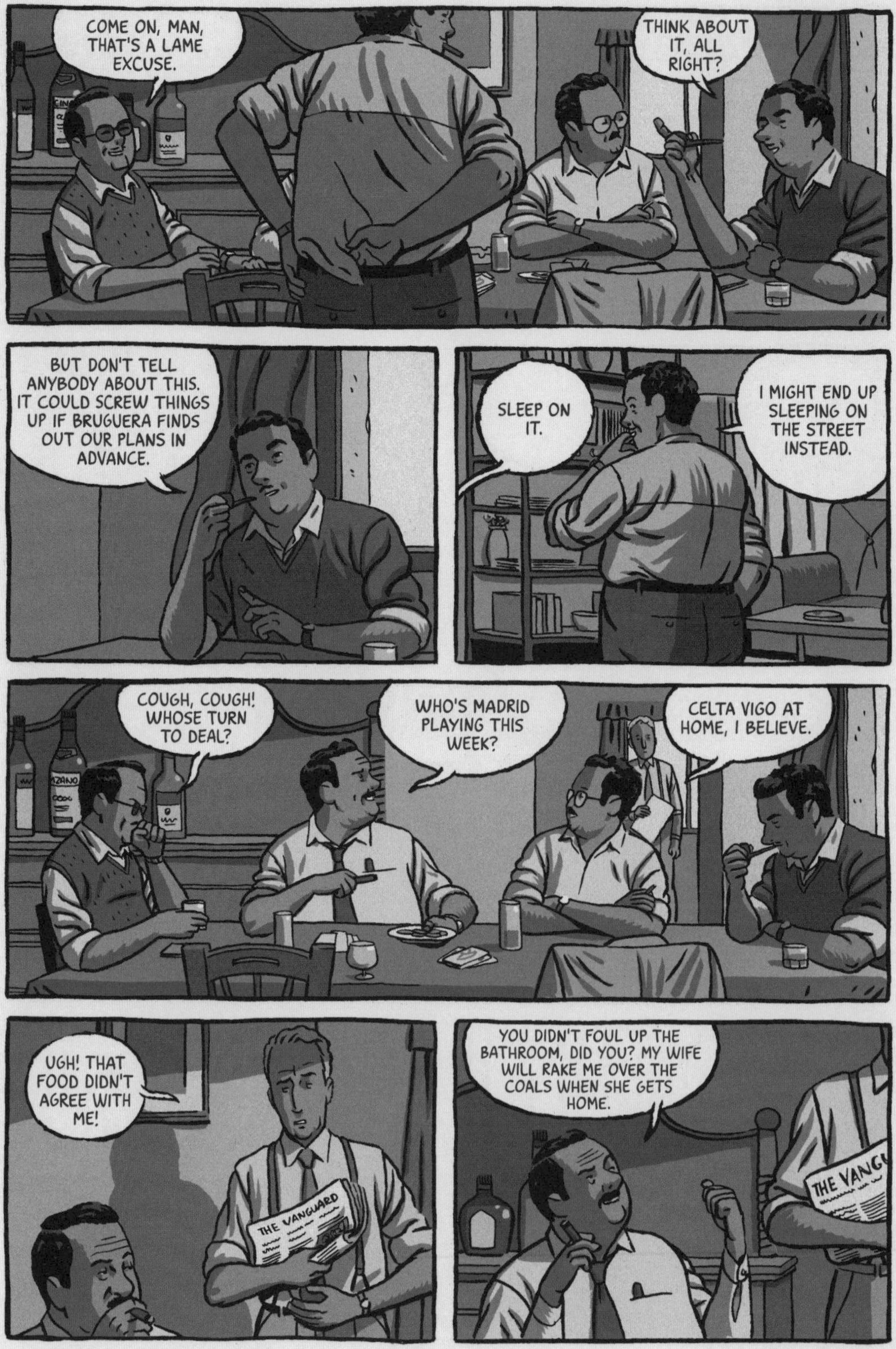
COME ON, MAN, THAT'S A LAME EXCUSE.
THINK ABOUT IT, ALL RIGHT?
BUT DON'T TELL ANYBODY ABOUT THIS. IT COULD SCREW THINGS UP IF BRUGUERA FINDS OUT OUR PLANS IN ADVANCE.
SLEEP ON IT.
I MIGHT END UP SLEEPING ON THE STREET INSTEAD.
COUGH, COUGH! WHOSE TURN TO DEAL?
WHO'S MADRID PLAYING THIS WEEK?
CELTA VIGO AT HOME, I BELIEVE.
UGH! THAT FOOD DIDN'T AGREE WITH ME!
THE VANGUARD
YOU DIDN'T FOUL UP THE BATHROOM, DID YOU? MY WIFE WILL RAKE ME OVER THE COALS WHEN SHE GETS HOME.
THE VANGU

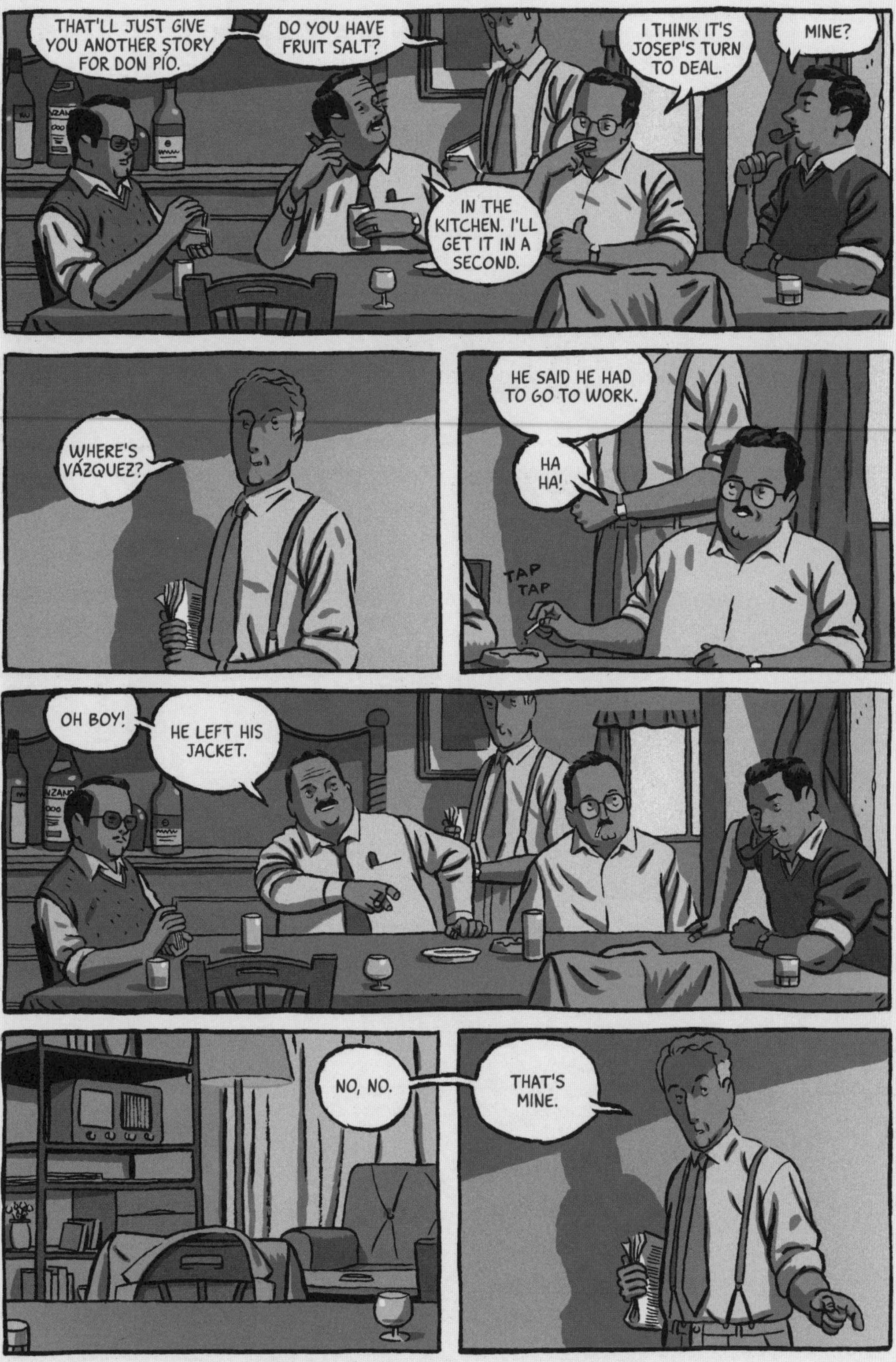
THAT'LL JUST GIVE YOU ANOTHER STORY FOR DON PÍO.
DO YOU HAVE FRUIT SALT?
IN THE KITCHEN. I'LL GET IT IN A SECOND.
I THINK IT'S JOSEP'S TURN TO DEAL.
MINE?
WHERE'S VÁZQUEZ?
HE SAID HE HAD TO GO TO WORK.
HA HA!
TAP TAP
OH BOY!
HE LEFT HIS JACKET.
NO, NO.
THAT'S MINE.

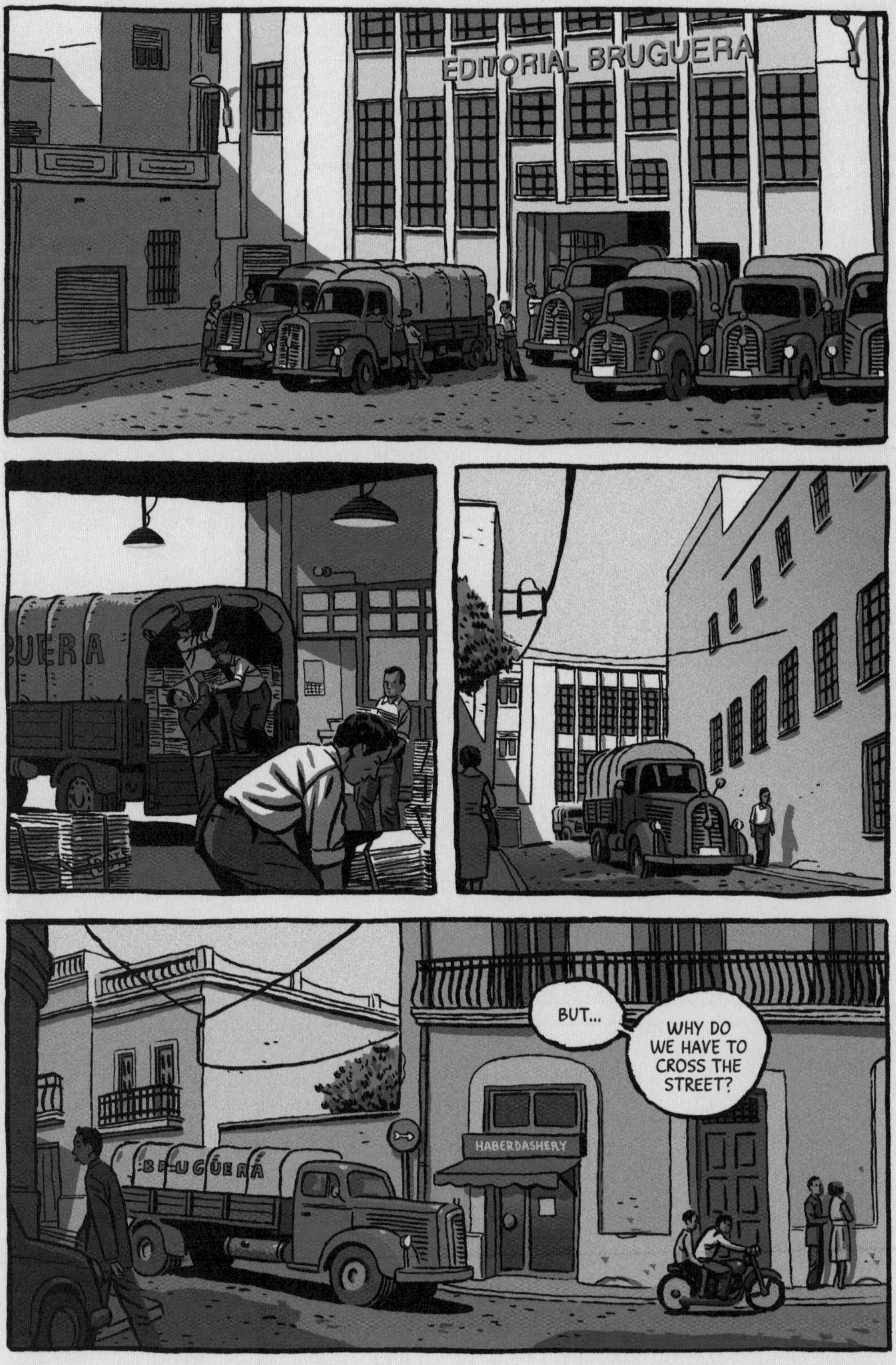
EDITORIAL BRUGUERA
HABERDASHERY
BUT...
WHY DO WE HAVE TO CROSS THE STREET?

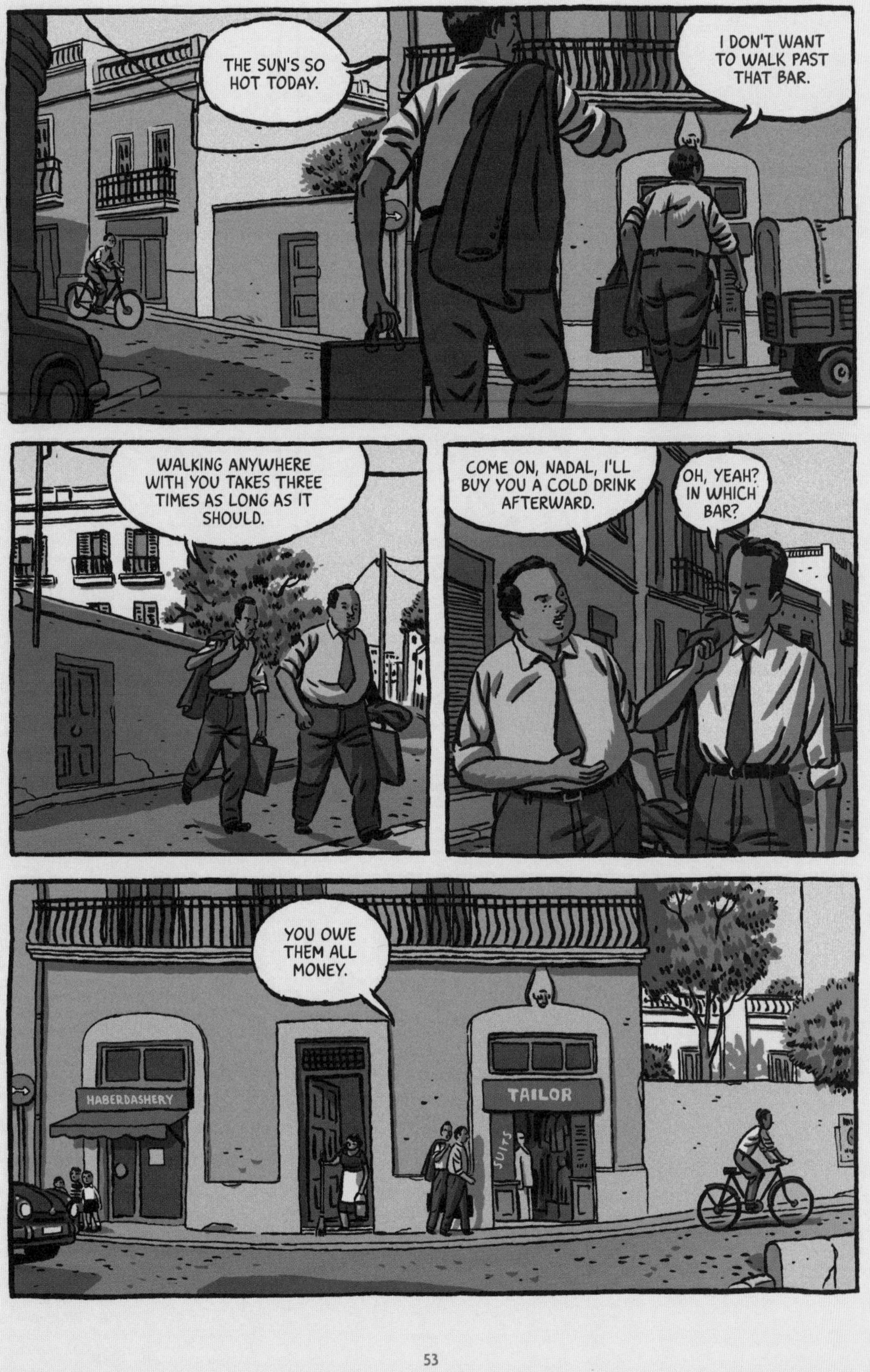
THE SUN'S SO HOT TODAY.
I DON'T WANT TO WALK PAST THAT BAR.
WALKING ANYWHERE WITH YOU TAKES THREE TIMES AS LONG AS IT SHOULD.
COME ON, NADAL, I'LL BUY YOU A COLD DRINK AFTERWARD.
OH, YEAH? IN WHICH BAR?
YOU OWE THEM ALL MONEY.
HABERDASHERY
TAILOR
SUITS

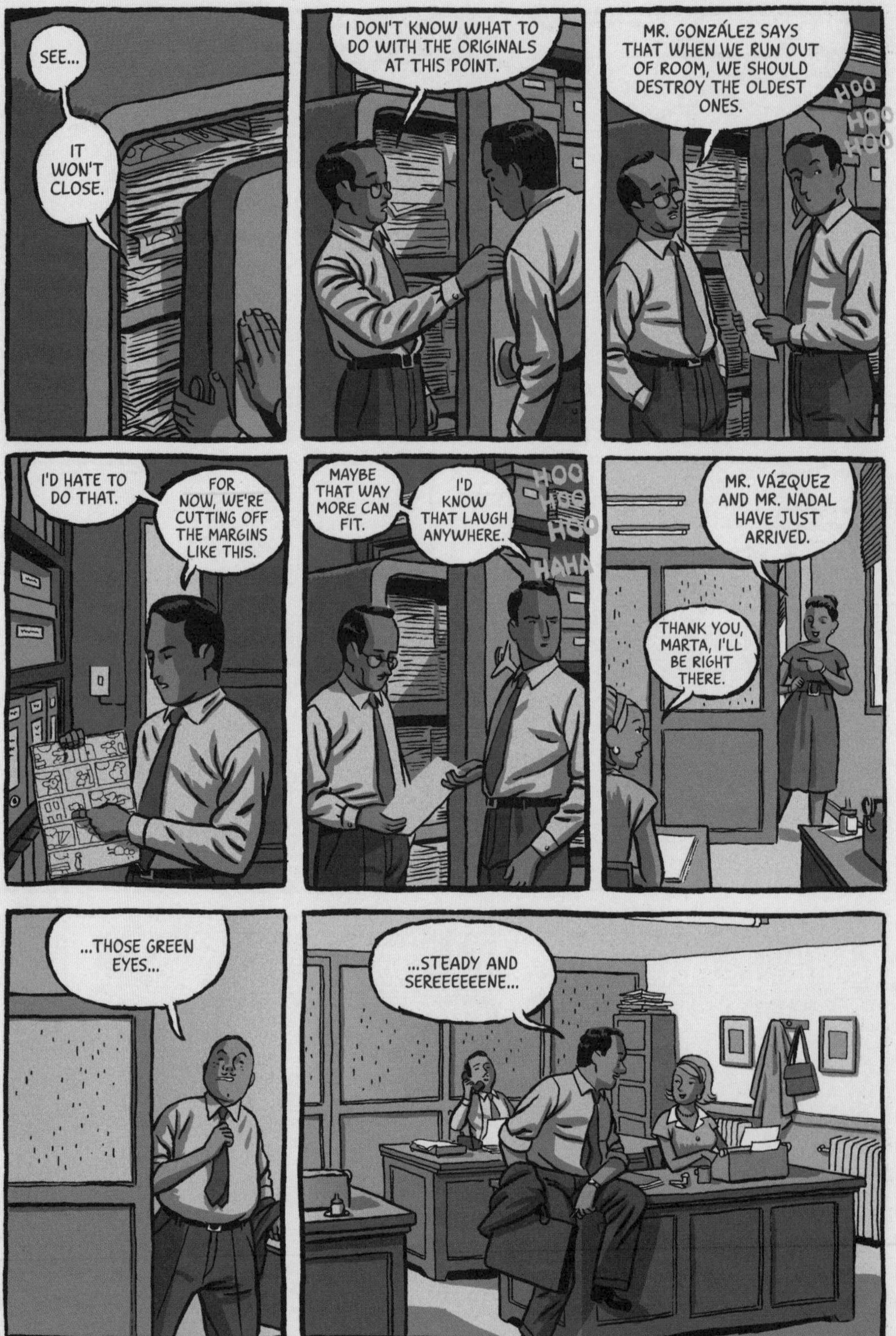
SEE...
IT WON'T CLOSE.
I DON'T KNOW WHAT TO DO WITH THE ORIGINALS AT THIS POINT.
MR. GONZÁLEZ SAYS THAT WHEN WE RUN OUT OF ROOM, WE SHOULD DESTROY THE OLDEST ONES.
HOO HOO HOO
I'D HATE TO DO THAT.
FOR NOW, WE'RE CUTTING OFF THE MARGINS LIKE THIS.
MAYBE THAT WAY MORE CAN FIT.
I'D KNOW THAT LAUGH ANYWHERE.
HOO HOO HOO HAHA
MR. VÁZQUEZ AND MR. NADAL HAVE JUST ARRIVED.
THANK YOU, MARTA, I'LL BE RIGHT THERE.
...THOSE GREEN EYES...
...STEADY AND SEREEEEEENE...

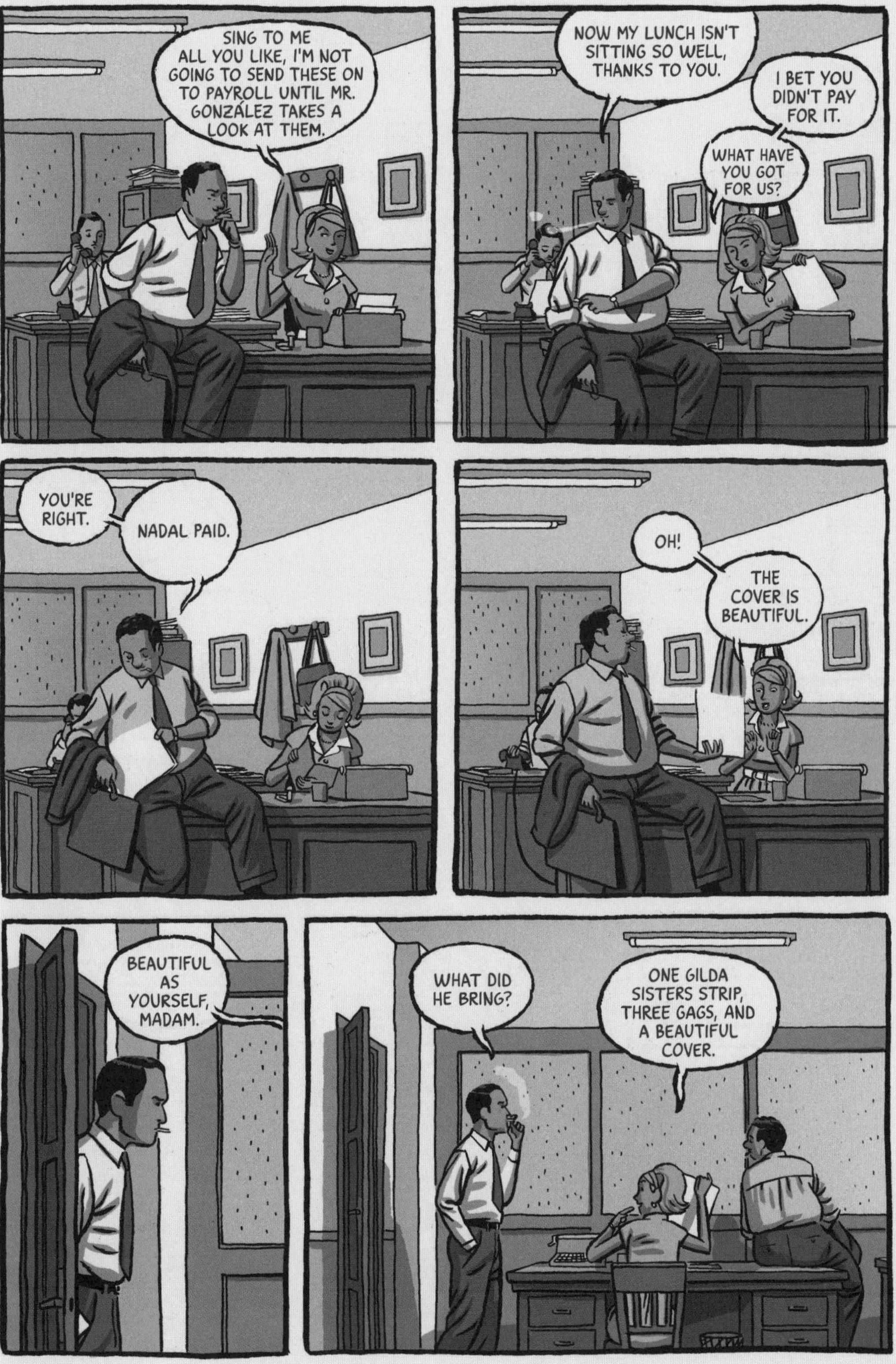
SING TO ME ALL YOU LIKE, I'M NOT GOING TO SEND THESE ON TO PAYROLL UNTIL MR. GONZÁLEZ TAKES A LOOK AT THEM.
NOW MY LUNCH ISN'T SITTING SO WELL, THANKS TO YOU.
I BET YOU DIDN'T PAY FOR IT.
WHAT HAVE YOU GOT FOR US?
YOU'RE RIGHT.
NADAL PAID.
OH!
THE COVER IS BEAUTIFUL.
BEAUTIFUL AS YOURSELF, MADAM.
WHAT DID HE BRING?
ONE GILDA SISTERS STRIP, THREE GAGS, AND A BEAUTIFUL COVER.

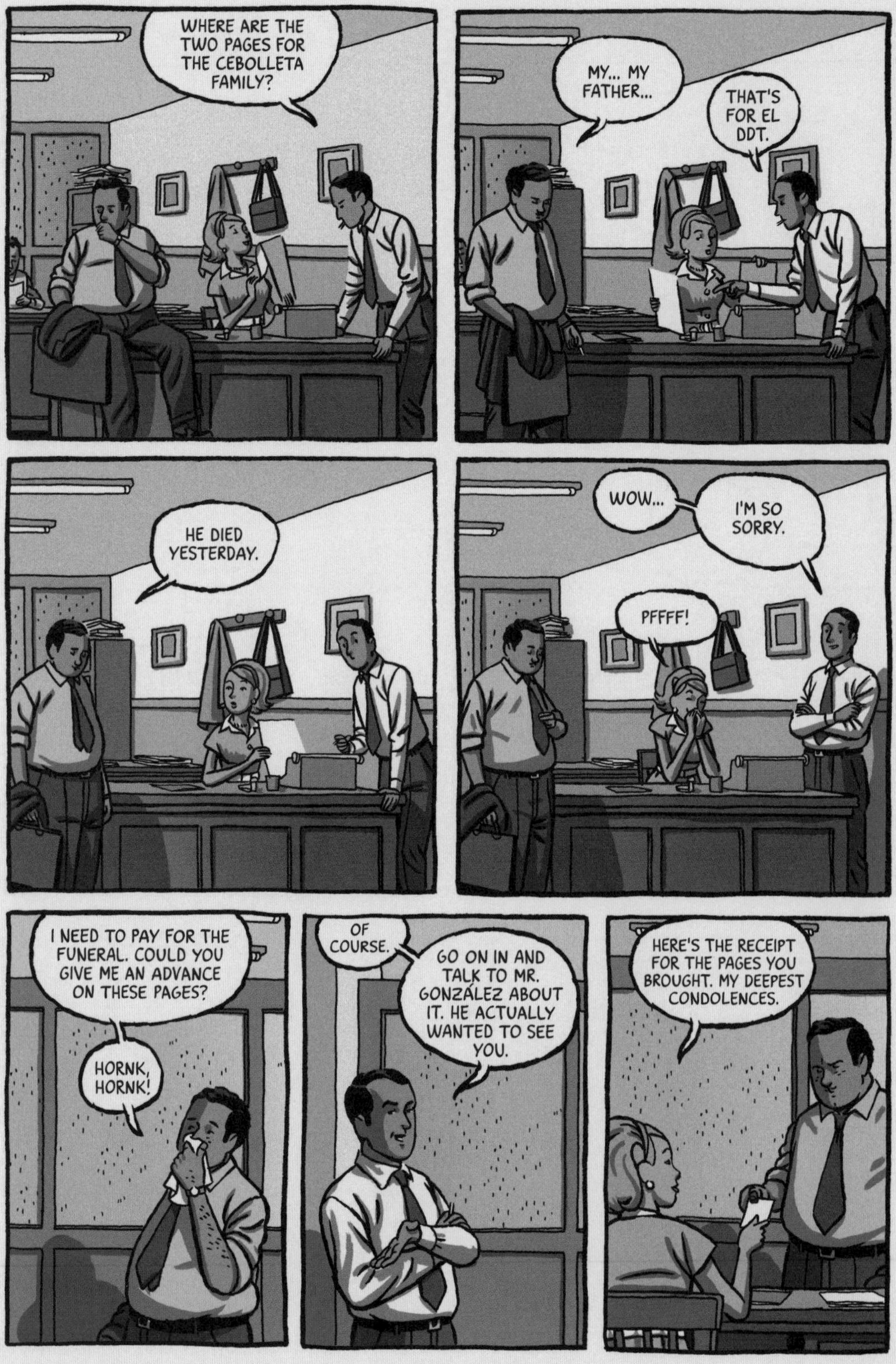
WHERE ARE THE TWO PAGES FOR THE CEBOLLETA FAMILY?
MY... MY FATHER...
THAT'S FOR EL DDT.
HE DIED YESTERDAY.
WOW...
I'M SO SORRY.
PFFFF!
I NEED TO PAY FOR THE FUNERAL. COULD YOU GIVE ME AN ADVANCE ON THESE PAGES?
HORNK, HORNK!
OF COURSE.
GO ON IN AND TALK TO MR. GONZÁLEZ ABOUT IT. HE ACTUALLY WANTED TO SEE YOU.
HERE'S THE RECEIPT FOR THE PAGES YOU BROUGHT. MY DEEPEST CONDOLENCES.

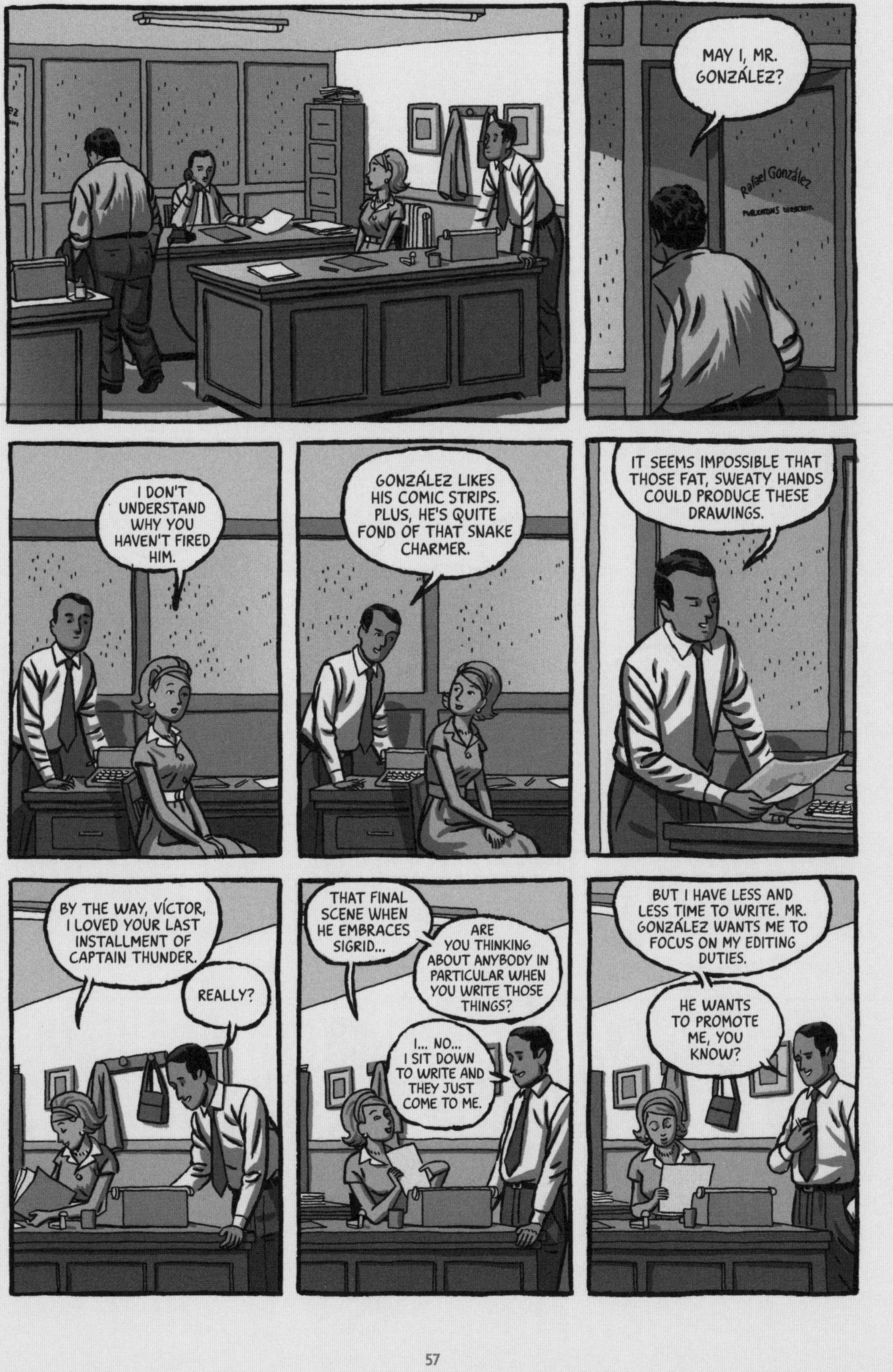
MAY I, MR. GONZÁLEZ?
Rafael González
I DON'T UNDERSTAND WHY YOU HAVEN'T FIRED HIM.
GONZÁLEZ LIKES HIS COMIC STRIPS. PLUS, HE'S QUITE FOND OF THAT SNAKE CHARMER.
IT SEEMS IMPOSSIBLE THAT THOSE FAT, SWEATY HANDS COULD PRODUCE THESE DRAWINGS.
BY THE WAY, VÍCTOR, I LOVED YOUR LAST INSTALLMENT OF CAPTAIN THUNDER.
REALLY?
THAT FINAL SCENE WHEN HE EMBRACES SIGRID...
ARE YOU THINKING ABOUT ANYBODY IN PARTICULAR WHEN YOU WRITE THOSE THINGS?
I... NO... I SIT DOWN TO WRITE AND THEY JUST COME TO ME.
BUT I HAVE LESS AND LESS TIME TO WRITE. MR. GONZÁLEZ WANTS ME TO FOCUS ON MY EDITING DUTIES.
HE WANTS TO PROMOTE ME, YOU KNOW?

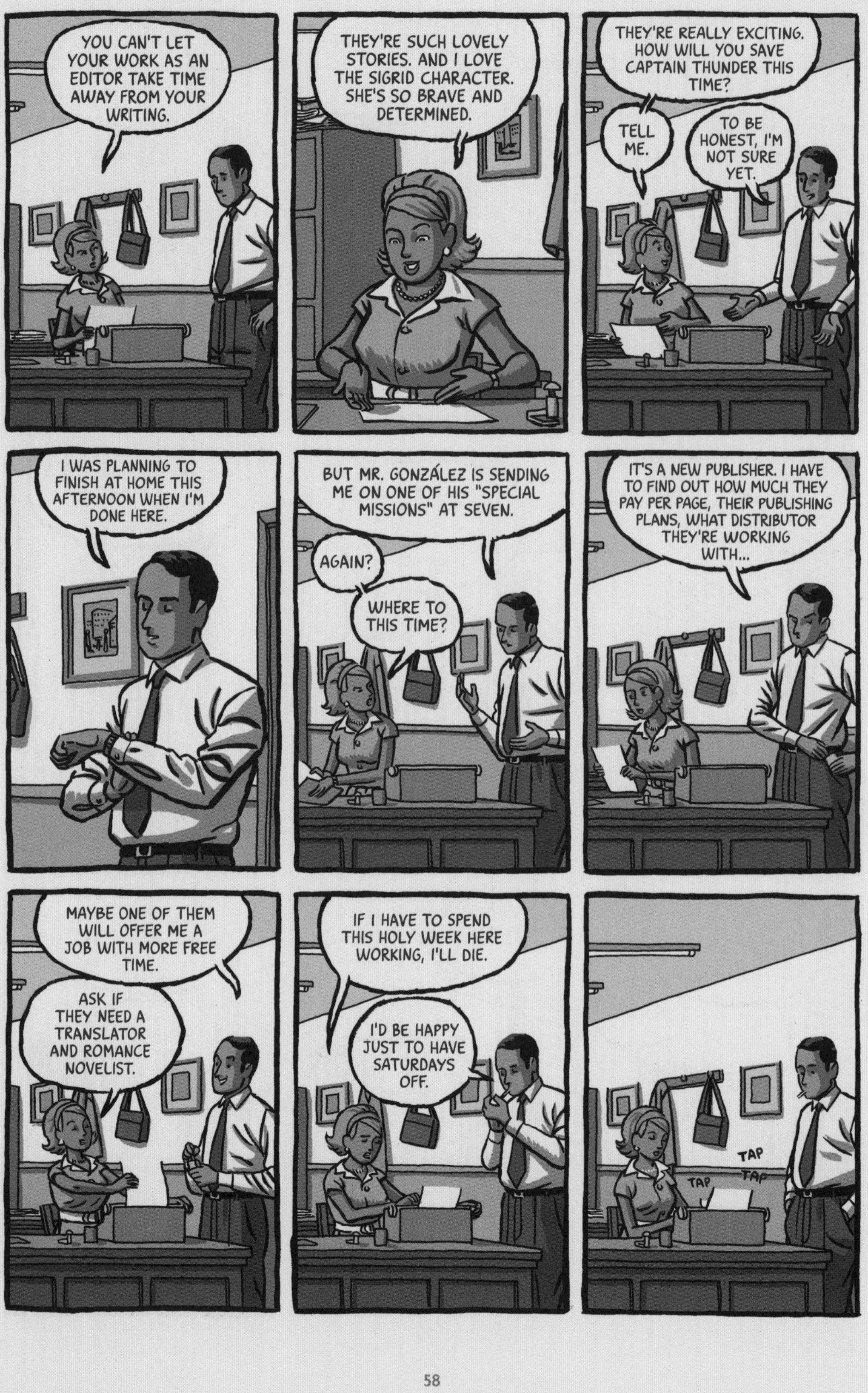
YOU CAN'T LET YOUR WORK AS AN EDITOR TAKE TIME AWAY FROM YOUR WRITING.
THEY'RE SUCH LOVELY STORIES. AND I LOVE THE SIGRID CHARACTER. SHE'S SO BRAVE AND DETERMINED.
THEY'RE REALLY EXCITING. HOW WILL YOU SAVE CAPTAIN THUNDER THIS TIME?
TELL ME.
TO BE HONEST, I'M NOT SURE YET.
I WAS PLANNING TO FINISH AT HOME THIS AFTERNOON WHEN I'M DONE HERE.
BUT MR. GONZÁLEZ IS SENDING ME ON ONE OF HIS "SPECIAL MISSIONS" AT SEVEN.
AGAIN?
WHERE TO THIS TIME?
IT'S A NEW PUBLISHER. I HAVE TO FIND OUT HOW MUCH THEY PAY PER PAGE, THEIR PUBLISHING PLANS, WHAT DISTRIBUTOR THEY'RE WORKING WITH...
MAYBE ONE OF THEM WILL OFFER ME A JOB WITH MORE FREE TIME.
ASK IF THEY NEED A TRANSLATOR AND ROMANCE NOVELIST.
IF I HAVE TO SPEND THIS HOLY WEEK HERE WORKING, I'LL DIE.
I'D BE HAPPY JUST TO HAVE SATURDAYS OFF.
TAP
TAP
TAP

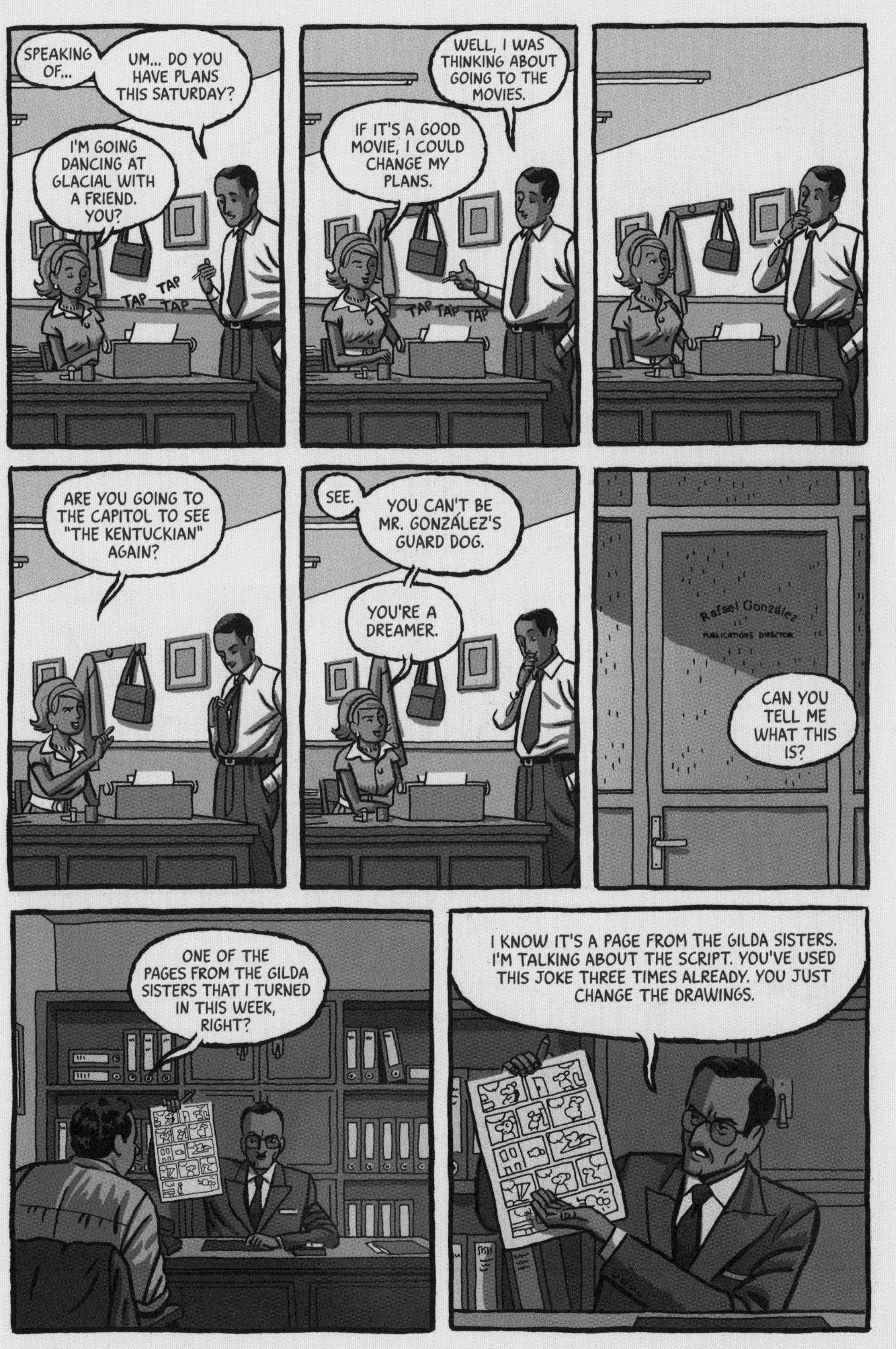
SPEAKING OF...
UM... DO YOU HAVE PLANS THIS SATURDAY?
I'M GOING DANCING AT GLACIAL WITH A FRIEND. YOU?
TAP TAP TAP TAP
WELL, I WAS THINKING ABOUT GOING TO THE MOVIES.
IF IT'S A GOOD MOVIE, I COULD CHANGE MY PLANS.
TAP TAP TAP
ARE YOU GOING TO THE CAPITOL TO SEE "THE KENTUCKIAN" AGAIN?
SEE.
YOU CAN'T BE MR. GONZÁLEZ'S GUARD DOG.
YOU'RE A DREAMER.
Rafael González
PUBLICATIONS DIRECTOR
CAN YOU TELL ME WHAT THIS IS?
ONE OF THE PAGES FROM THE GILDA SISTERS THAT I TURNED IN THIS WEEK, RIGHT?
I KNOW IT'S A PAGE FROM THE GILDA SISTERS. I'M TALKING ABOUT THE SCRIPT. YOU'VE USED THIS JOKE THREE TIMES ALREADY. YOU JUST CHANGE THE DRAWINGS.

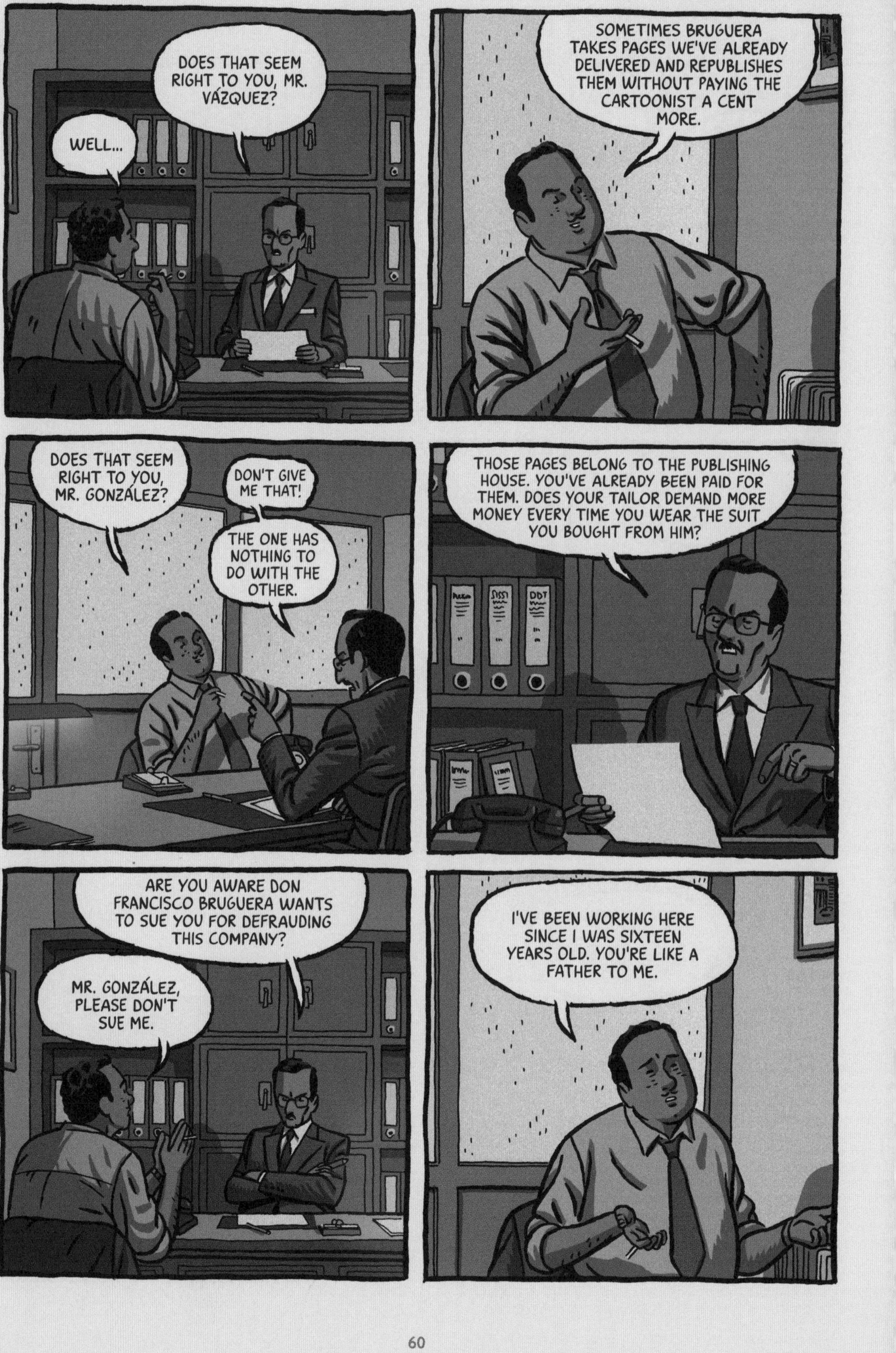
DOES THAT SEEM RIGHT TO YOU, MR. VÁZQUEZ?
WELL...
SOMETIMES BRUGUERA TAKES PAGES WE'VE ALREADY DELIVERED AND REPUBLISHES THEM WITHOUT PAYING THE CARTOONIST A CENT MORE.
DOES THAT SEEM RIGHT TO YOU, MR. GONZÁLEZ?
DON'T GIVE ME THAT!
THE ONE HAS NOTHING TO DO WITH THE OTHER.
THOSE PAGES BELONG TO THE PUBLISHING HOUSE. YOU'VE ALREADY BEEN PAID FOR THEM. DOES YOUR TAILOR DEMAND MORE MONEY EVERY TIME YOU WEAR THE SUIT YOU BOUGHT FROM HIM?
ARE YOU AWARE DON FRANCISCO BRUGUERA WANTS TO SUE YOU FOR DEFRAUDING THIS COMPANY?
MR. GONZÁLEZ, PLEASE DON'T SUE ME.
I'VE BEEN WORKING HERE SINCE I WAS SIXTEEN YEARS OLD. YOU'RE LIKE A FATHER TO ME.

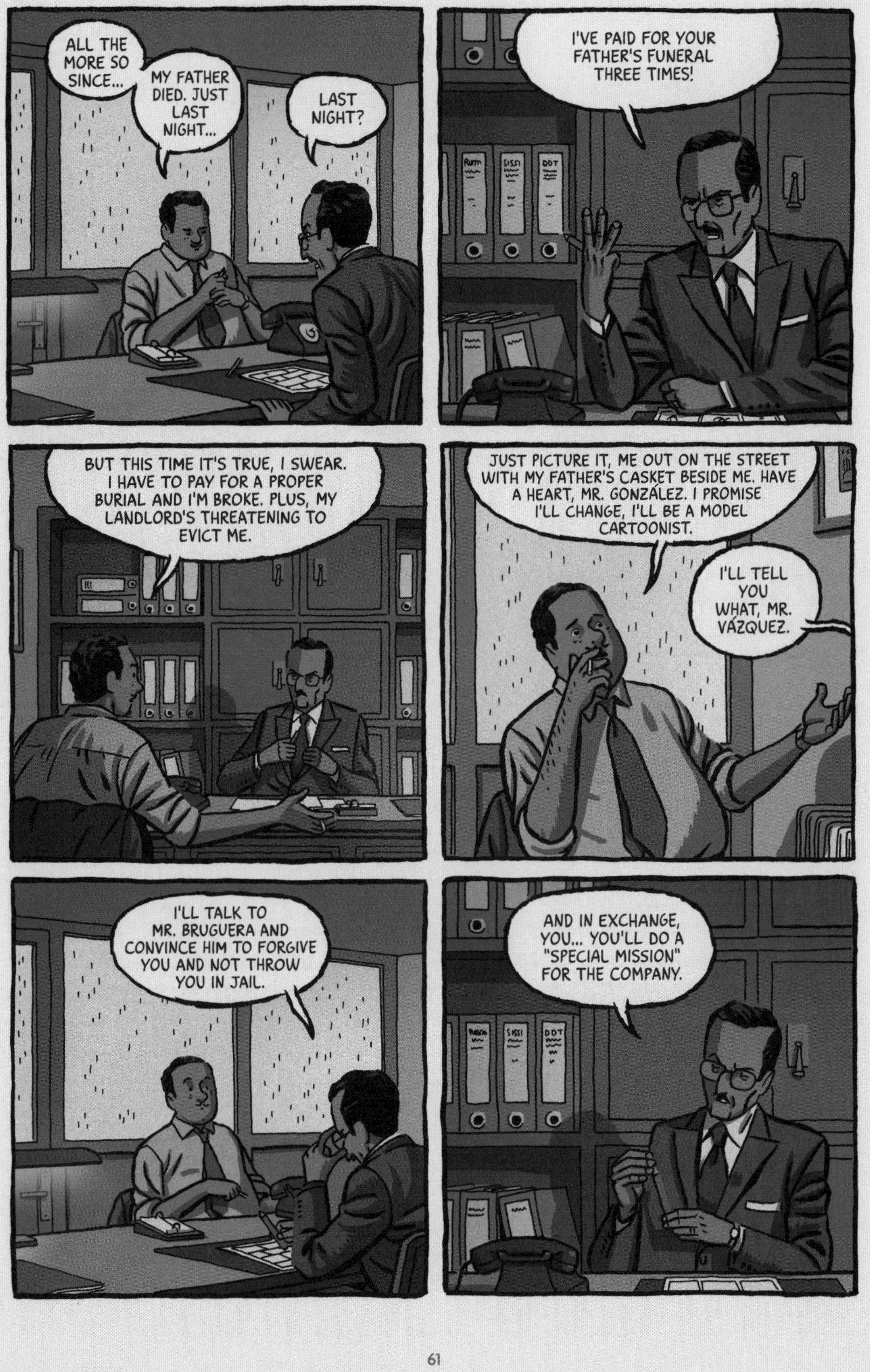
ALL THE MORE SO SINCE...
MY FATHER DIED. JUST LAST NIGHT...
LAST NIGHT?
I'VE PAID FOR YOUR FATHER'S FUNERAL THREE TIMES!
BUT THIS TIME IT'S TRUE, I SWEAR. I HAVE TO PAY FOR A PROPER BURIAL AND I'M BROKE. PLUS, MY LANDLORD'S THREATENING TO EVICT ME.
JUST PICTURE IT, ME OUT ON THE STREET WITH MY FATHER'S CASKET BESIDE ME. HAVE A HEART, MR. GONZÁLEZ. I PROMISE I'LL CHANGE, I'LL BE A MODEL CARTOONIST.
I'LL TELL YOU WHAT, MR. VÁZQUEZ.
I'LL TALK TO MR. BRUGUERA AND CONVINCE HIM TO FORGIVE YOU AND NOT THROW YOU IN JAIL.
AND IN EXCHANGE, YOU... YOU'LL DO A "SPECIAL MISSION" FOR THE COMPANY.

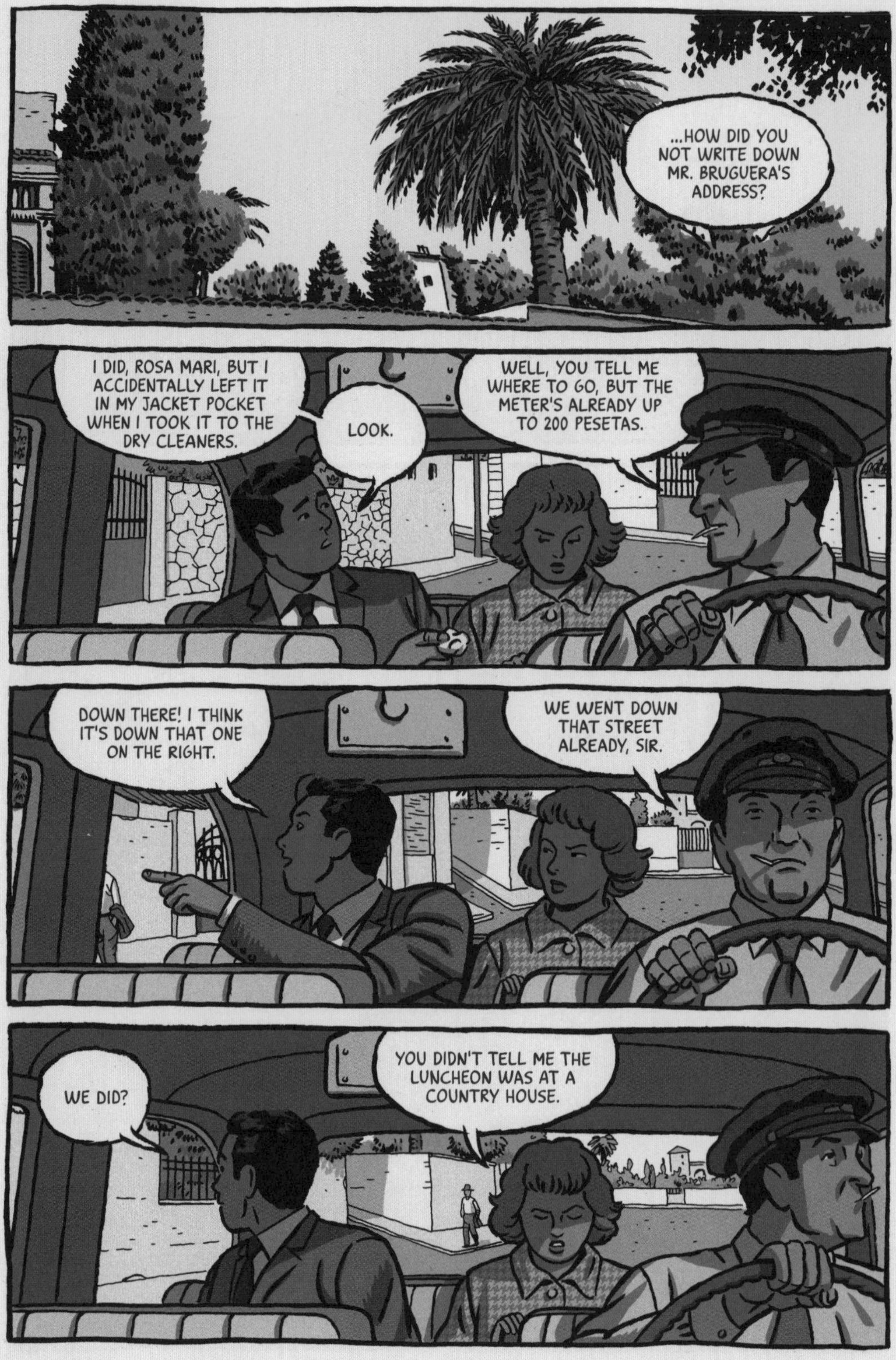
...HOW DID YOU NOT WRITE DOWN MR. BRUGUERA'S ADDRESS?
I DID, ROSA MARI, BUT I ACCIDENTALLY LEFT IT IN MY JACKET POCKET WHEN I TOOK IT TO THE DRY CLEANERS.
LOOK.
WELL, YOU TELL ME WHERE TO GO, BUT THE METER'S ALREADY UP TO 200 PESETAS.
DOWN THERE! I THINK IT'S DOWN THAT ONE ON THE RIGHT.
WE WENT DOWN THAT STREET ALREADY, SIR.
WE DID?
YOU DIDN'T TELL ME THE LUNCHEON WAS AT A COUNTRY HOUSE.

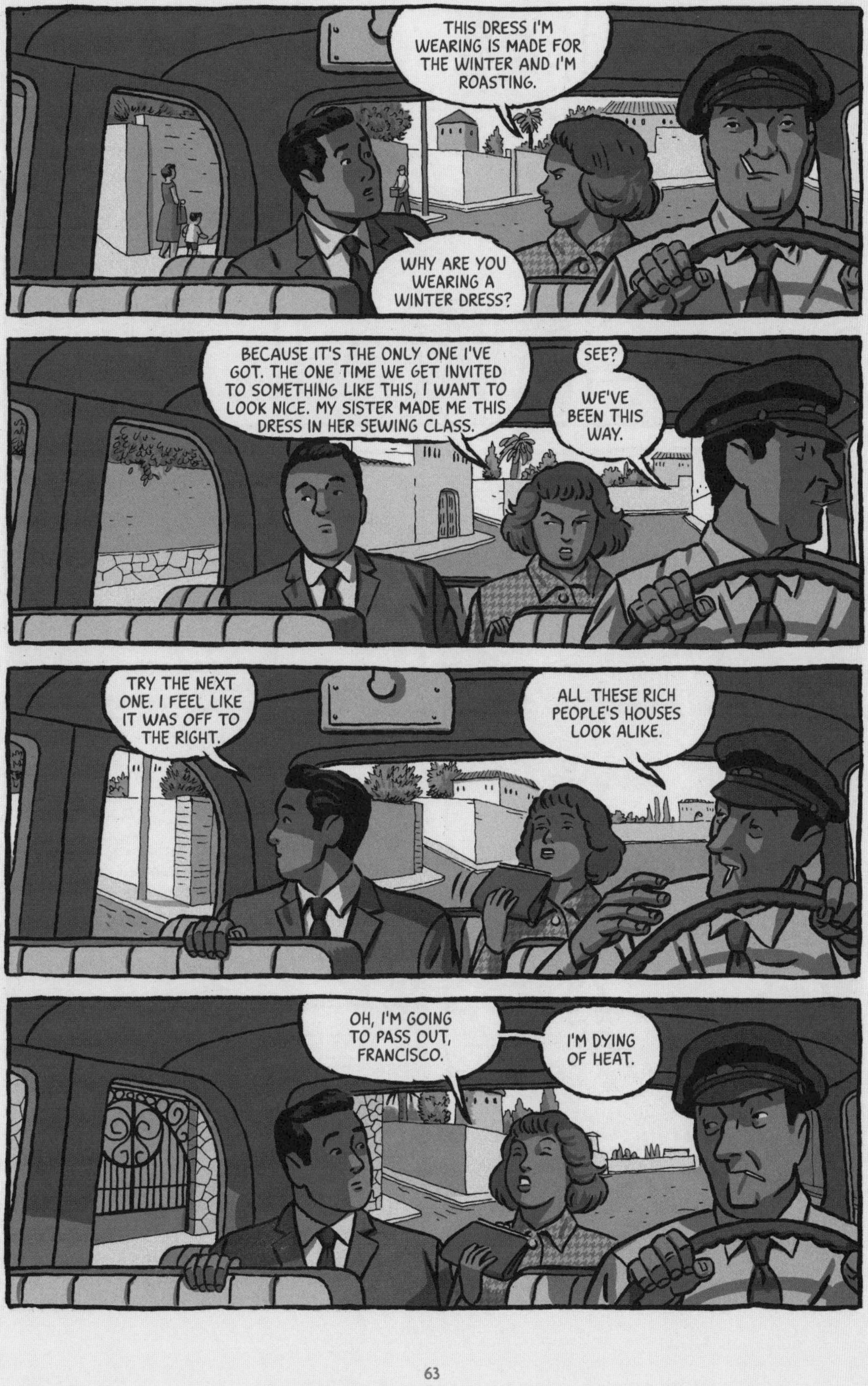
THIS DRESS I'M WEARING IS MADE FOR THE WINTER AND I'M ROASTING.
WHY ARE YOU WEARING A WINTER DRESS?
BECAUSE IT'S THE ONLY ONE I'VE GOT. THE ONE TIME WE GET INVITED TO SOMETHING LIKE THIS, I WANT TO LOOK NICE. MY SISTER MADE ME THIS DRESS IN HER SEWING CLASS.
SEE?
WE'VE BEEN THIS WAY.
TRY THE NEXT ONE. I FEEL LIKE IT WAS OFF TO THE RIGHT.
ALL THESE RICH PEOPLE'S HOUSES LOOK ALIKE.
OH, I'M GOING TO PASS OUT, FRANCISCO.
I'M DYING OF HEAT.

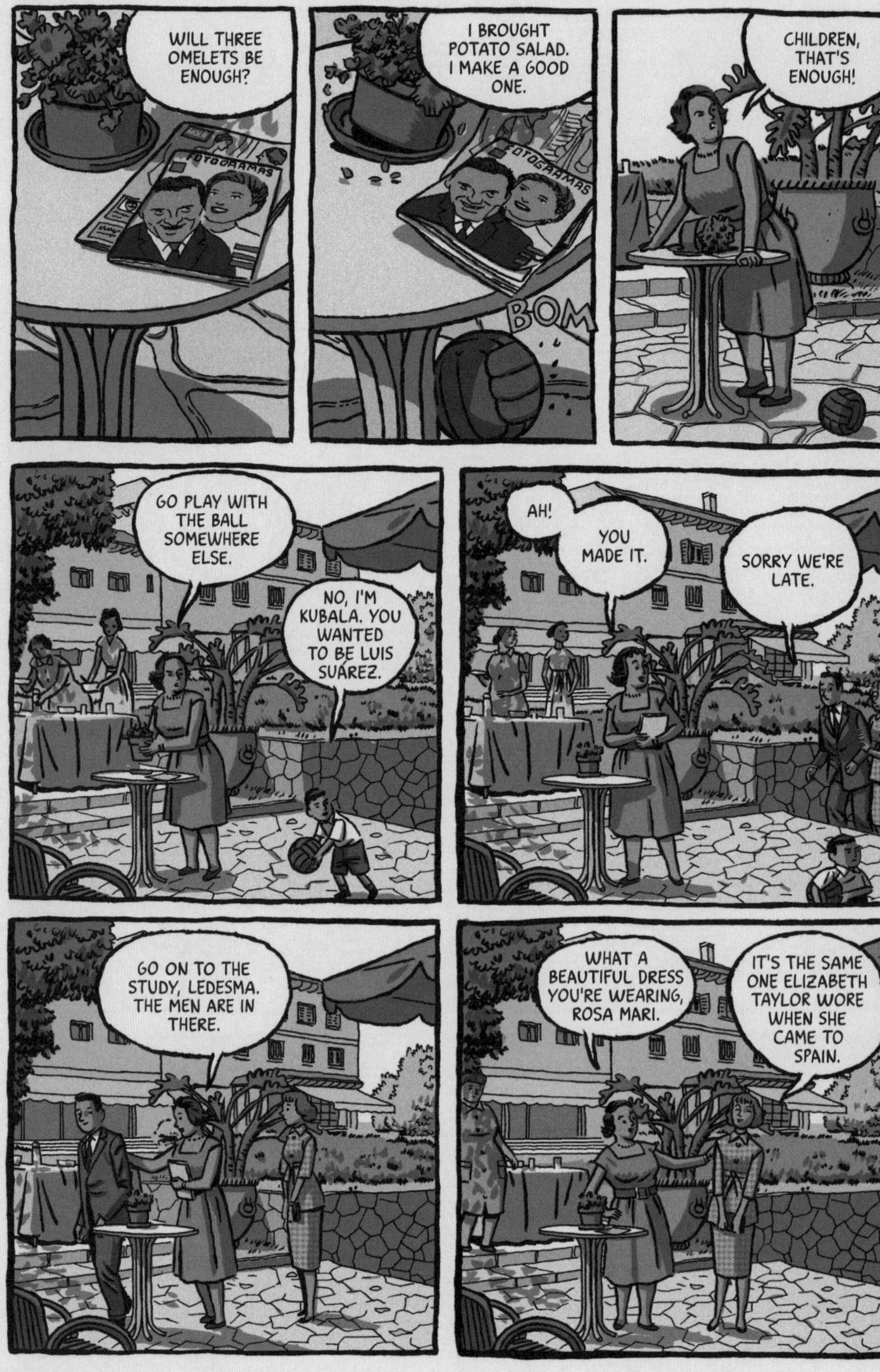
WILL THREE OMELETS BE ENOUGH?
FOTOGRAMAS
I BROUGHT POTATO SALAD. I MAKE A GOOD ONE.
FOTOGRAMAS
BOM
CHILDREN, THAT'S ENOUGH!
GO PLAY WITH THE BALL SOMEWHERE ELSE.
NO, I'M KUBALA. YOU WANTED TO BE LUIS SUÁREZ.
AH!
YOU MADE IT.
SORRY WE'RE LATE.
GO ON TO THE STUDY, LEDESMA. THE MEN ARE IN THERE.
WHAT A BEAUTIFUL DRESS YOU'RE WEARING, ROSA MARI.
IT'S THE SAME ONE ELIZABETH TAYLOR WORE WHEN SHE CAME TO SPAIN.

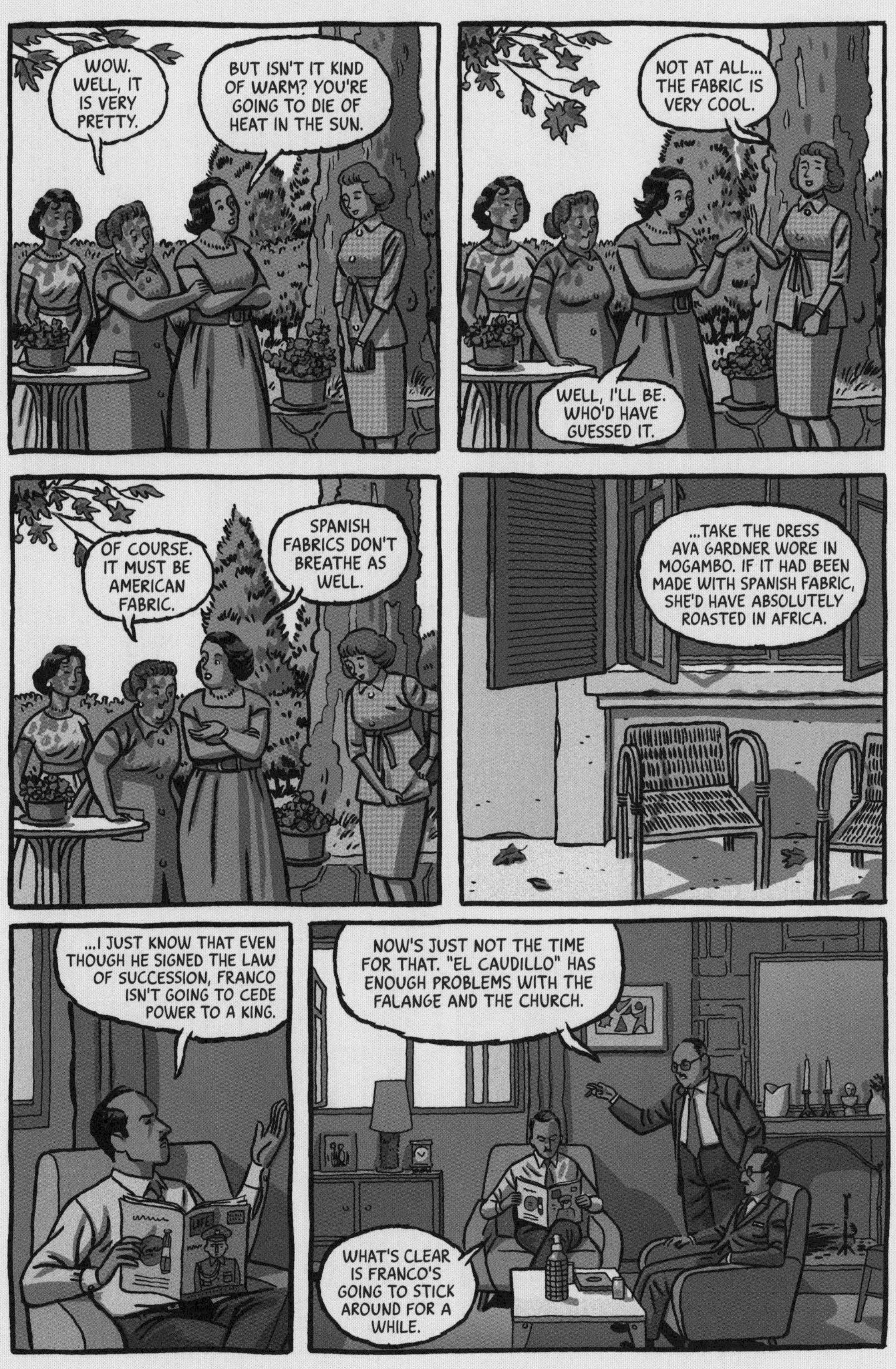
WOW. WELL, IT IS VERY PRETTY.
BUT ISN'T IT KIND OF WARM? YOU'RE GOING TO DIE OF HEAT IN THE SUN.
NOT AT ALL... THE FABRIC IS VERY COOL.
WELL, I'LL BE. WHO'D HAVE GUESSED IT.
OF COURSE. IT MUST BE AMERICAN FABRIC.
SPANISH FABRICS DON'T BREATHE AS WELL.
...TAKE THE DRESS AVA GARDNER WORE IN MOGAMBO. IF IT HAD BEEN MADE WITH SPANISH FABRIC, SHE'D HAVE ABSOLUTELY ROASTED IN AFRICA.
...I JUST KNOW THAT EVEN THOUGH HE SIGNED THE LAW OF SUCCESSION, FRANCO ISN'T GOING TO CEDE POWER TO A KING.
NOW'S JUST NOT THE TIME FOR THAT. "EL CAUDILLO" HAS ENOUGH PROBLEMS WITH THE FALANGE AND THE CHURCH.
WHAT'S CLEAR IS FRANCO'S GOING TO STICK AROUND FOR A WHILE.

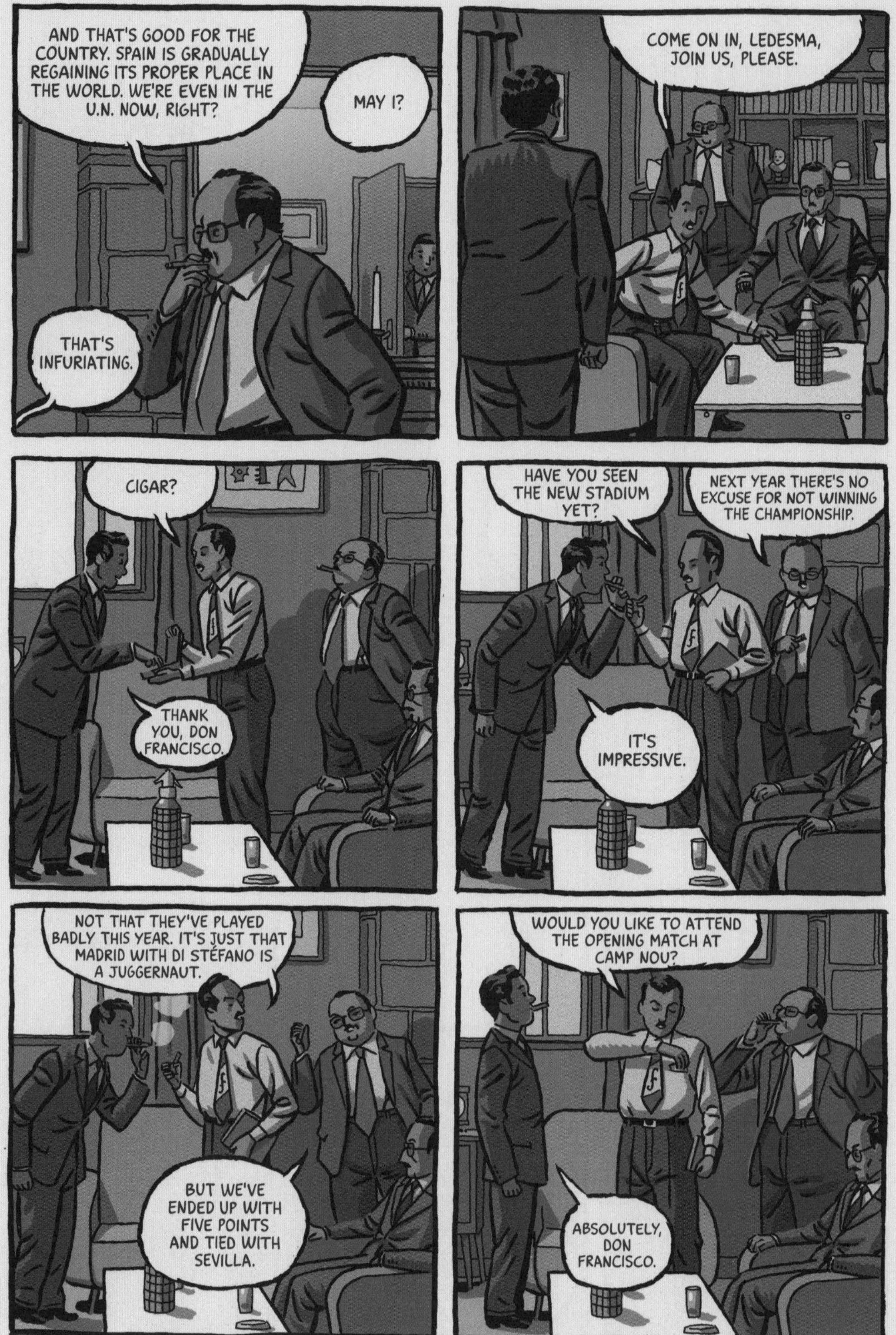
AND THAT'S GOOD FOR THE COUNTRY. SPAIN IS GRADUALLY REGAINING ITS PROPER PLACE IN THE WORLD. WE'RE EVEN IN THE U.N. NOW, RIGHT?
MAY I?
THAT'S INFURIATING.
COME ON IN, LEDESMA, JOIN US, PLEASE.
CIGAR?
THANK YOU, DON FRANCISCO.
HAVE YOU SEEN THE NEW STADIUM YET?
NEXT YEAR THERE'S NO EXCUSE FOR NOT WINNING THE CHAMPIONSHIP.
IT'S IMPRESSIVE.
NOT THAT THEY'VE PLAYED BADLY THIS YEAR. IT'S JUST THAT MADRID WITH DI STÉFANO IS A JUGGERNAUT.
BUT WE'VE ENDED UP WITH FIVE POINTS AND TIED WITH SEVILLA.
WOULD YOU LIKE TO ATTEND THE OPENING MATCH AT CAMP NOU?
ABSOLUTELY, DON FRANCISCO.

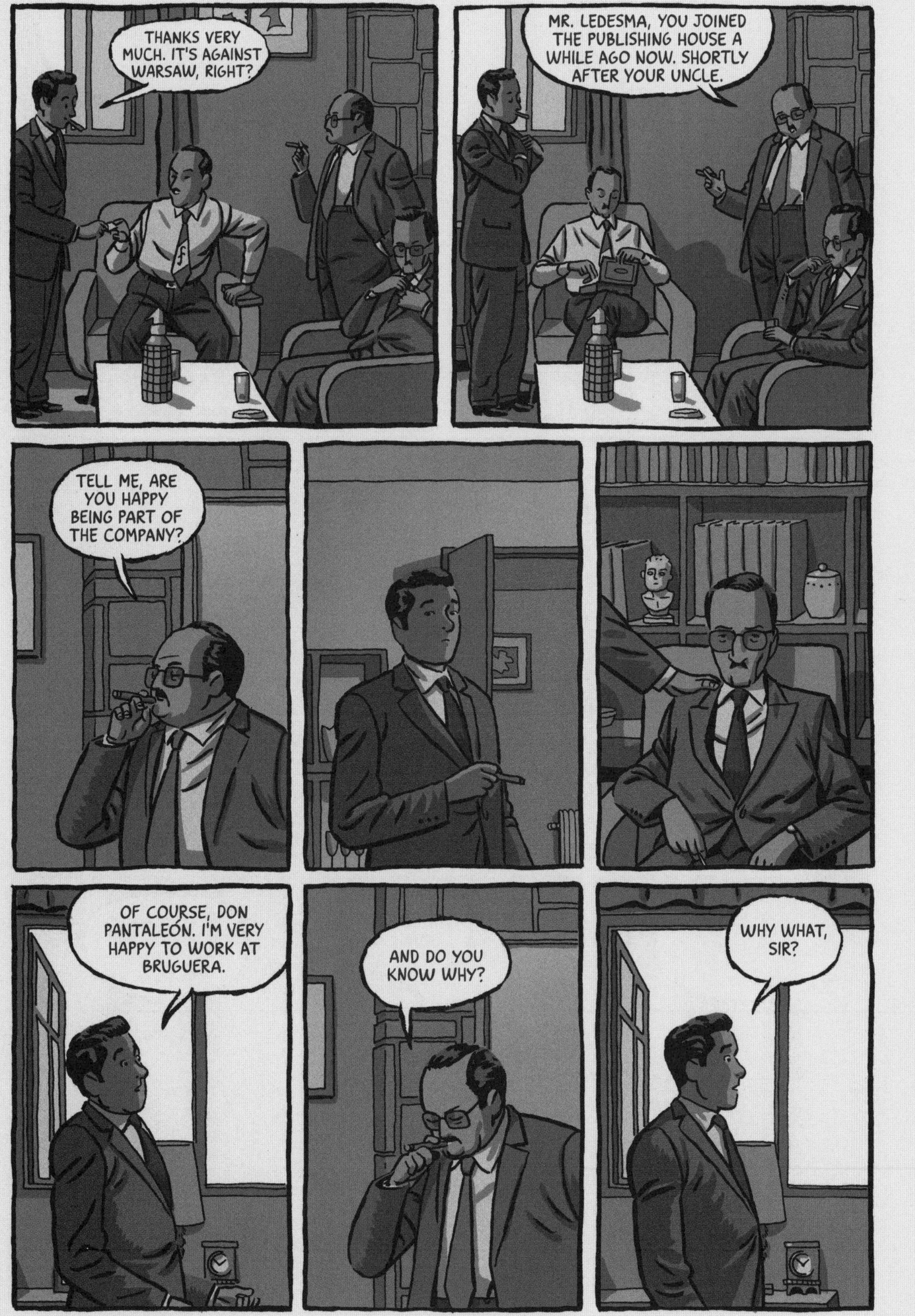
THANKS VERY MUCH. IT'S AGAINST WARSAW, RIGHT?
MR. LEDESMA, YOU JOINED THE PUBLISHING HOUSE A WHILE AGO NOW. SHORTLY AFTER YOUR UNCLE.
TELL ME, ARE YOU HAPPY BEING PART OF THE COMPANY?
OF COURSE, DON PANTALEÓN. I'M VERY HAPPY TO WORK AT BRUGUERA.
AND DO YOU KNOW WHY?
WHY WHAT, SIR?

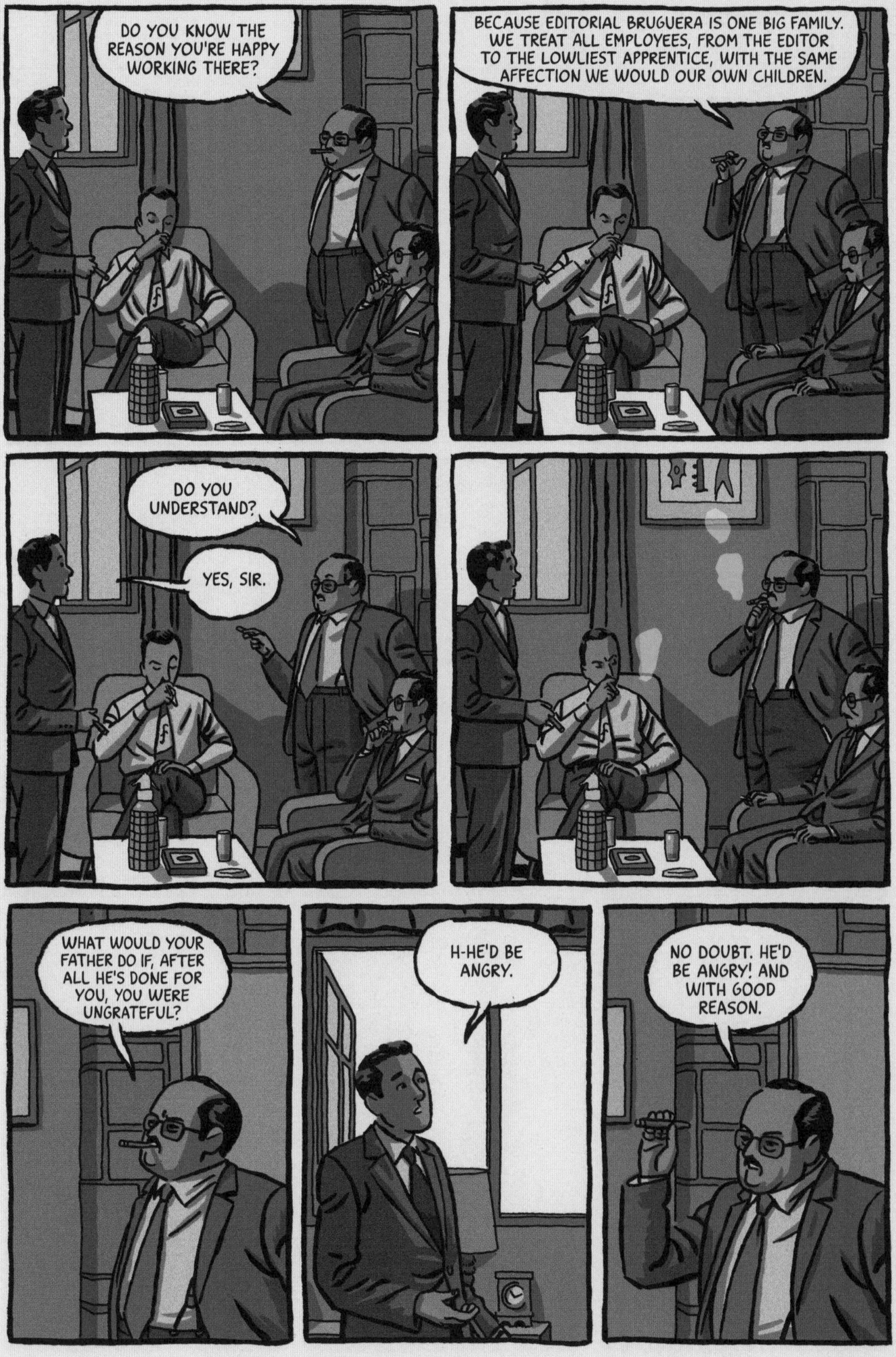
DO YOU KNOW THE REASON YOU'RE HAPPY WORKING THERE?
BECAUSE EDITORIAL BRUGUERA IS ONE BIG FAMILY. WE TREAT ALL EMPLOYEES, FROM THE EDITOR TO THE LOWLIEST APPRENTICE, WITH THE SAME AFFECTION WE WOULD OUR OWN CHILDREN.
DO YOU UNDERSTAND?
YES, SIR.
WHAT WOULD YOUR FATHER DO IF, AFTER ALL HE'S DONE FOR YOU, YOU WERE UNGRATEFUL?
H-HE'D BE ANGRY.
NO DOUBT. HE'D BE ANGRY! AND WITH GOOD REASON.

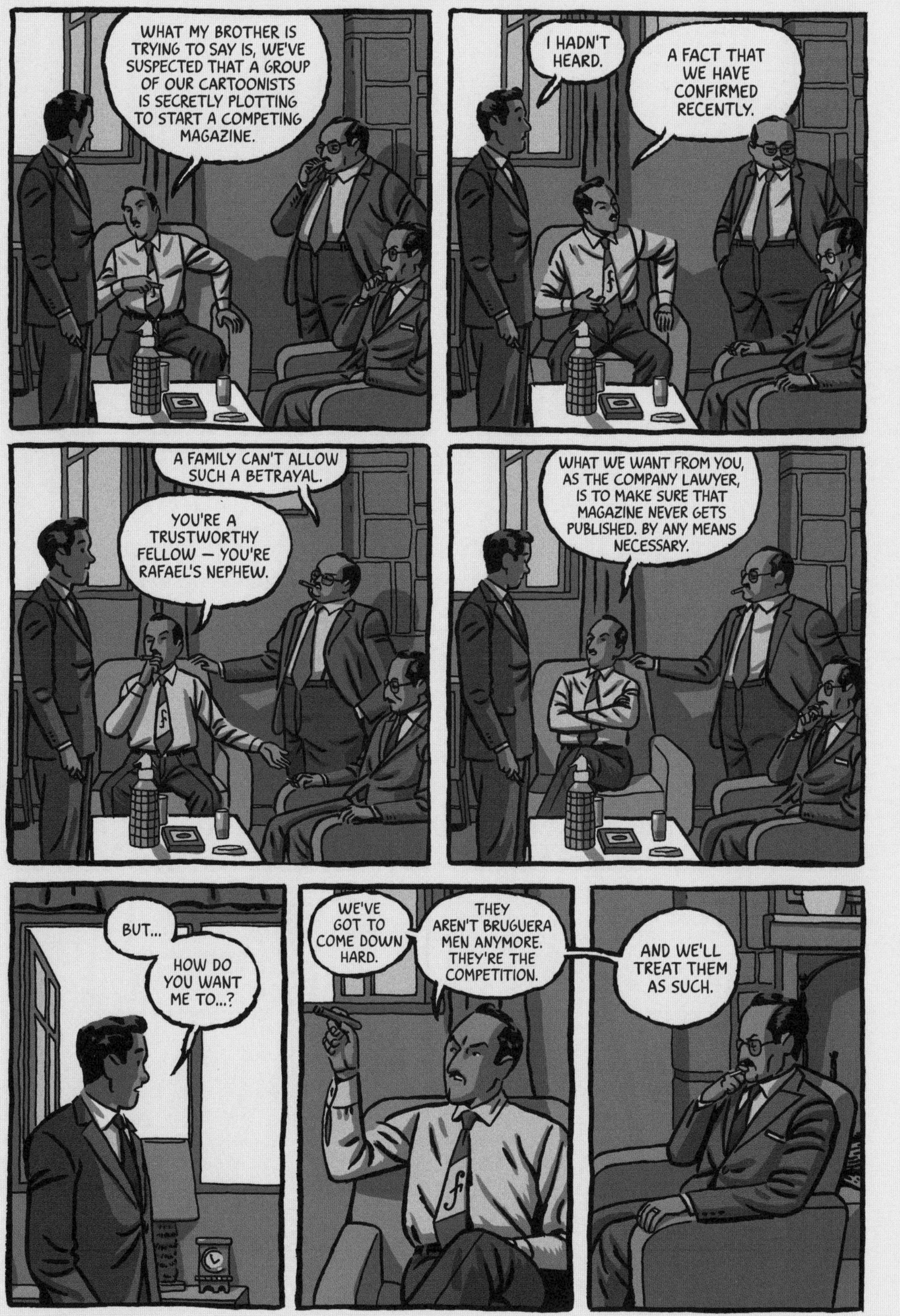
WHAT MY BROTHER IS TRYING TO SAY IS, WE'VE SUSPECTED THAT A GROUP OF OUR CARTOONISTS IS SECRETLY PLOTTING TO START A COMPETING MAGAZINE.
I HADN'T HEARD.
A FACT THAT WE HAVE CONFIRMED RECENTLY.
A FAMILY CAN'T ALLOW SUCH A BETRAYAL.
YOU'RE A TRUSTWORTHY FELLOW — YOU'RE RAFAEL'S NEPHEW.
WHAT WE WANT FROM YOU, AS THE COMPANY LAWYER, IS TO MAKE SURE THAT MAGAZINE NEVER GETS PUBLISHED. BY ANY MEANS NECESSARY.
BUT...
HOW DO YOU WANT ME TO...?
WE'VE GOT TO COME DOWN HARD.
THEY AREN'T BRUGUERA MEN ANYMORE. THEY'RE THE COMPETITION.
AND WE'LL TREAT THEM AS SUCH.

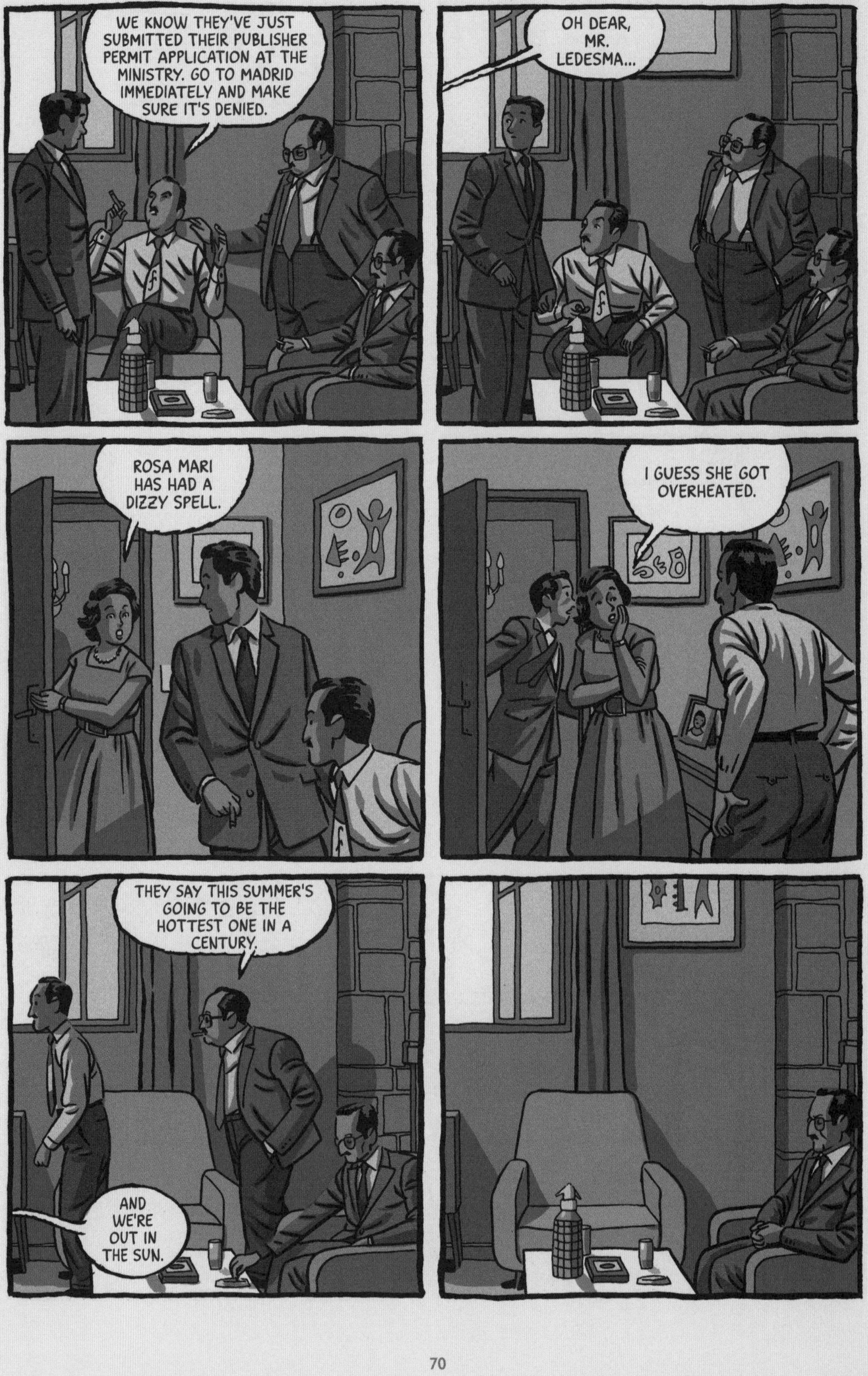
WE KNOW THEY'VE JUST SUBMITTED THEIR PUBLISHER PERMIT APPLICATION AT THE MINISTRY. GO TO MADRID IMMEDIATELY AND MAKE SURE IT'S DENIED.
OH DEAR, MR. LEDESMA...
ROSA MARI HAS HAD A DIZZY SPELL.
I GUESS SHE GOT OVERHEATED.
THEY SAY THIS SUMMER'S GOING TO BE THE HOTTEST ONE IN A CENTURY.
AND WE'RE OUT IN THE SUN.

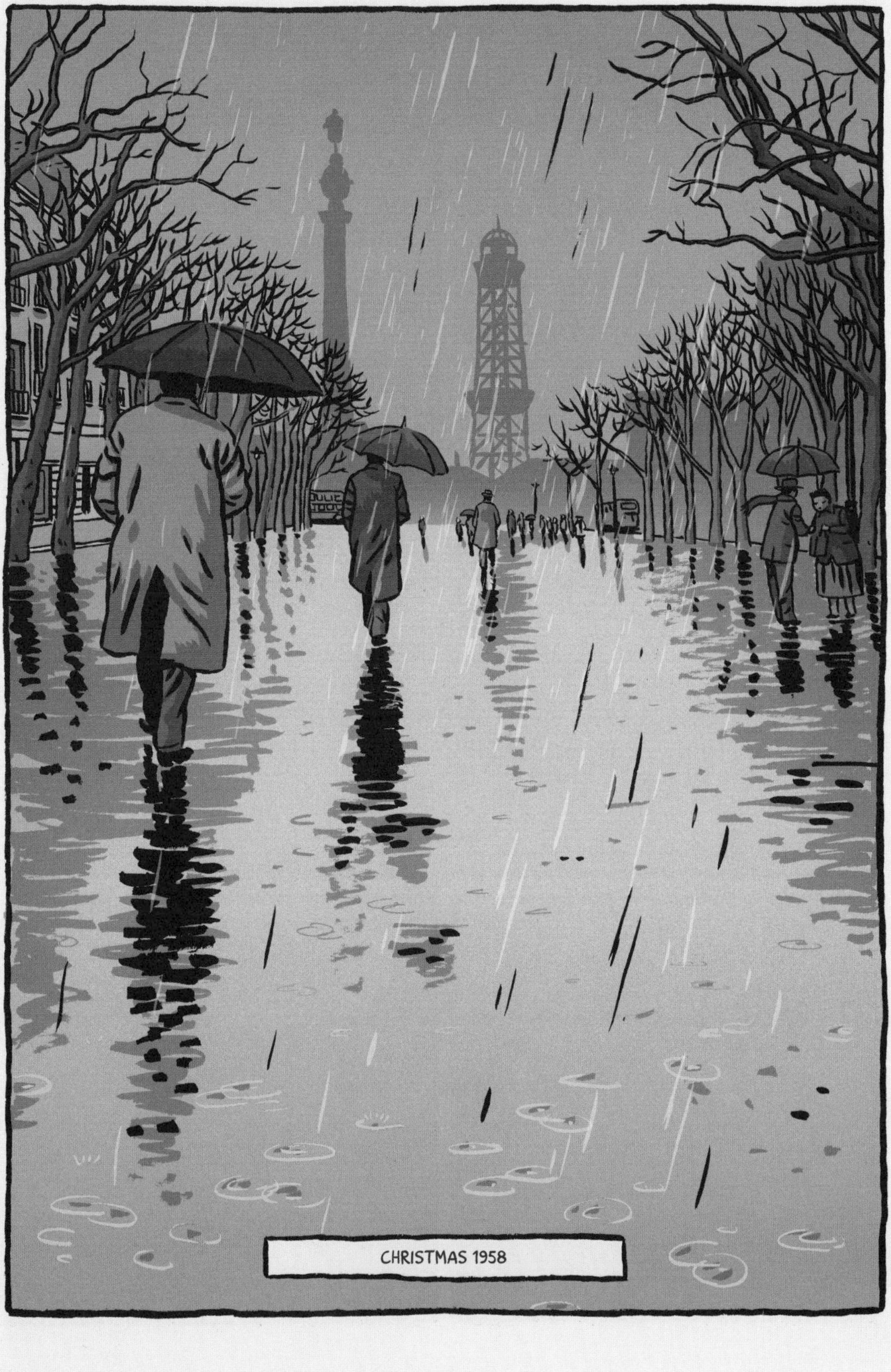
CHRISTMAS 1958

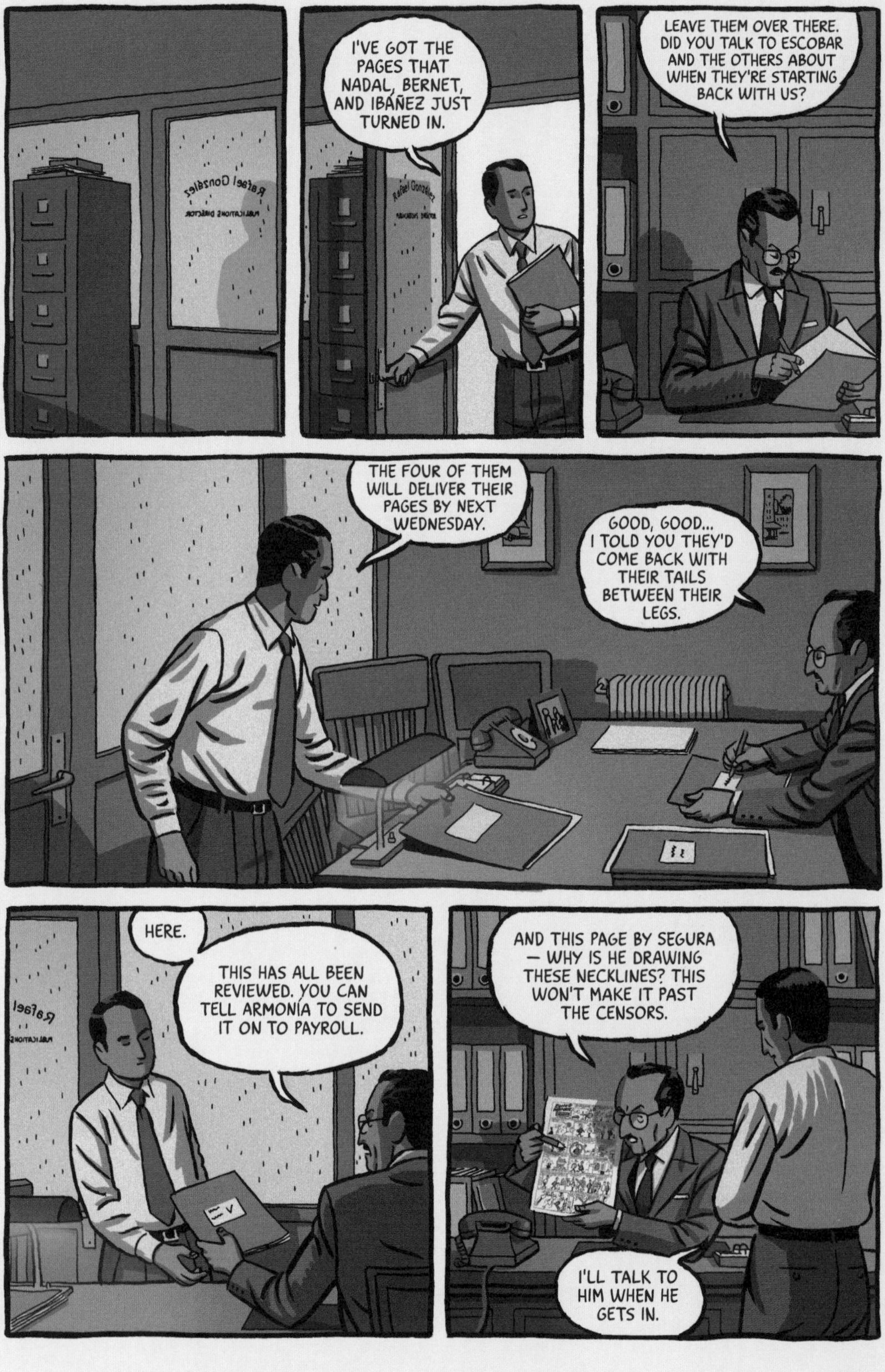
Rafael González
PUBLICATIONS DIRECTOR
I'VE GOT THE PAGES THAT NADAL, BERNET, AND IBÁÑEZ JUST TURNED IN.
LEAVE THEM OVER THERE. DID YOU TALK TO ESCOBAR AND THE OTHERS ABOUT WHEN THEY'RE STARTING BACK WITH US?
THE FOUR OF THEM WILL DELIVER THEIR PAGES BY NEXT WEDNESDAY.
GOOD, GOOD... I TOLD YOU THEY'D COME BACK WITH THEIR TAILS BETWEEN THEIR LEGS.
HERE.
THIS HAS ALL BEEN REVIEWED. YOU CAN TELL ARMONÍA TO SEND IT ON TO PAYROLL.
AND THIS PAGE BY SEGURA — WHY IS HE DRAWING THESE NECKLINES? THIS WON'T MAKE IT PAST THE CENSORS.
I'LL TALK TO HIM WHEN HE GETS IN.

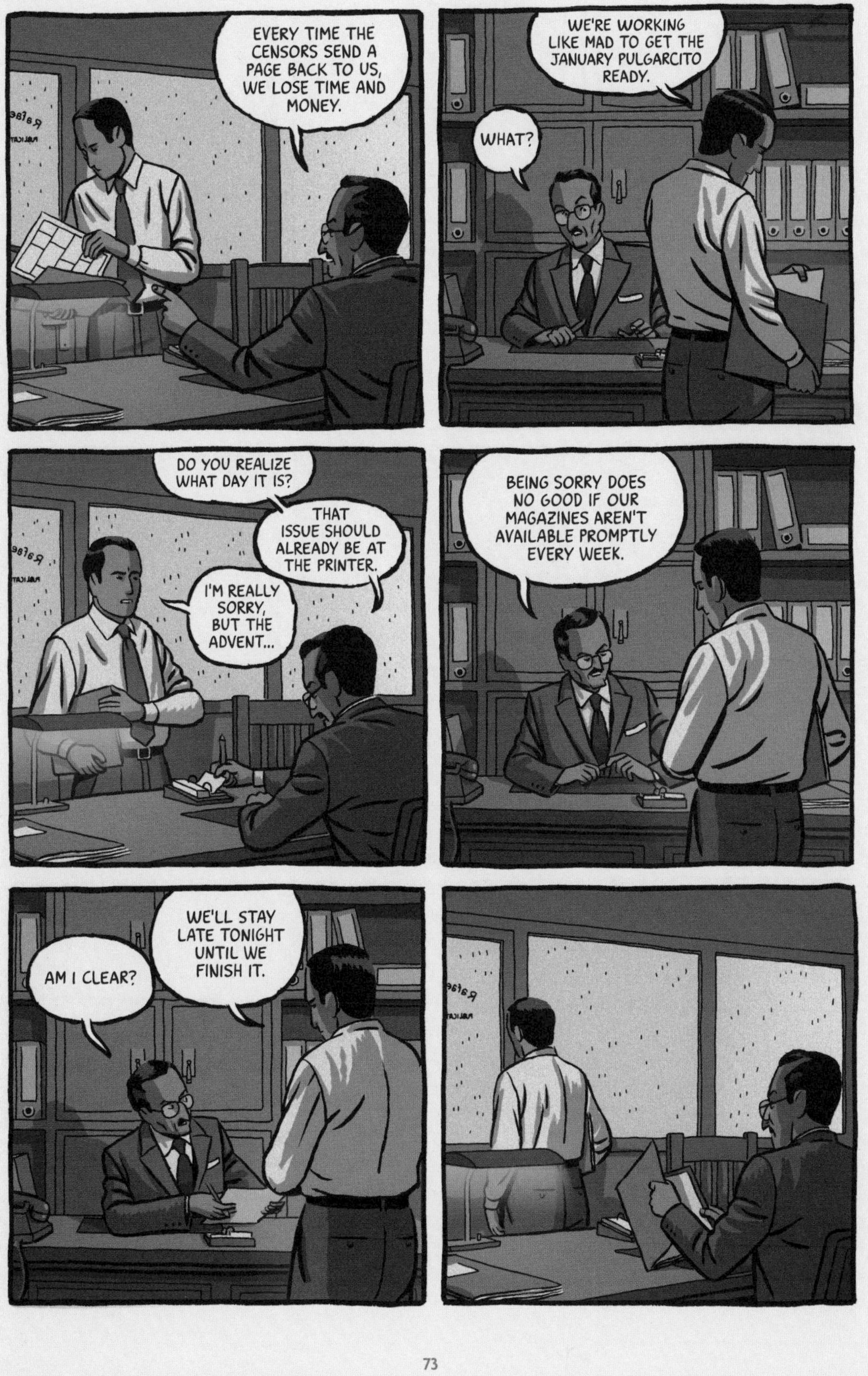
EVERY TIME THE CENSORS SEND A PAGE BACK TO US, WE LOSE TIME AND MONEY.
WE'RE WORKING LIKE MAD TO GET THE JANUARY PULGARCITO READY.
WHAT?
DO YOU REALIZE WHAT DAY IT IS?
THAT ISSUE SHOULD ALREADY BE AT THE PRINTER.
I'M REALLY SORRY, BUT THE ADVENT...
BEING SORRY DOES NO GOOD IF OUR MAGAZINES AREN'T AVAILABLE PROMPTLY EVERY WEEK.
AM I CLEAR?
WE'LL STAY LATE TONIGHT UNTIL WE FINISH IT.

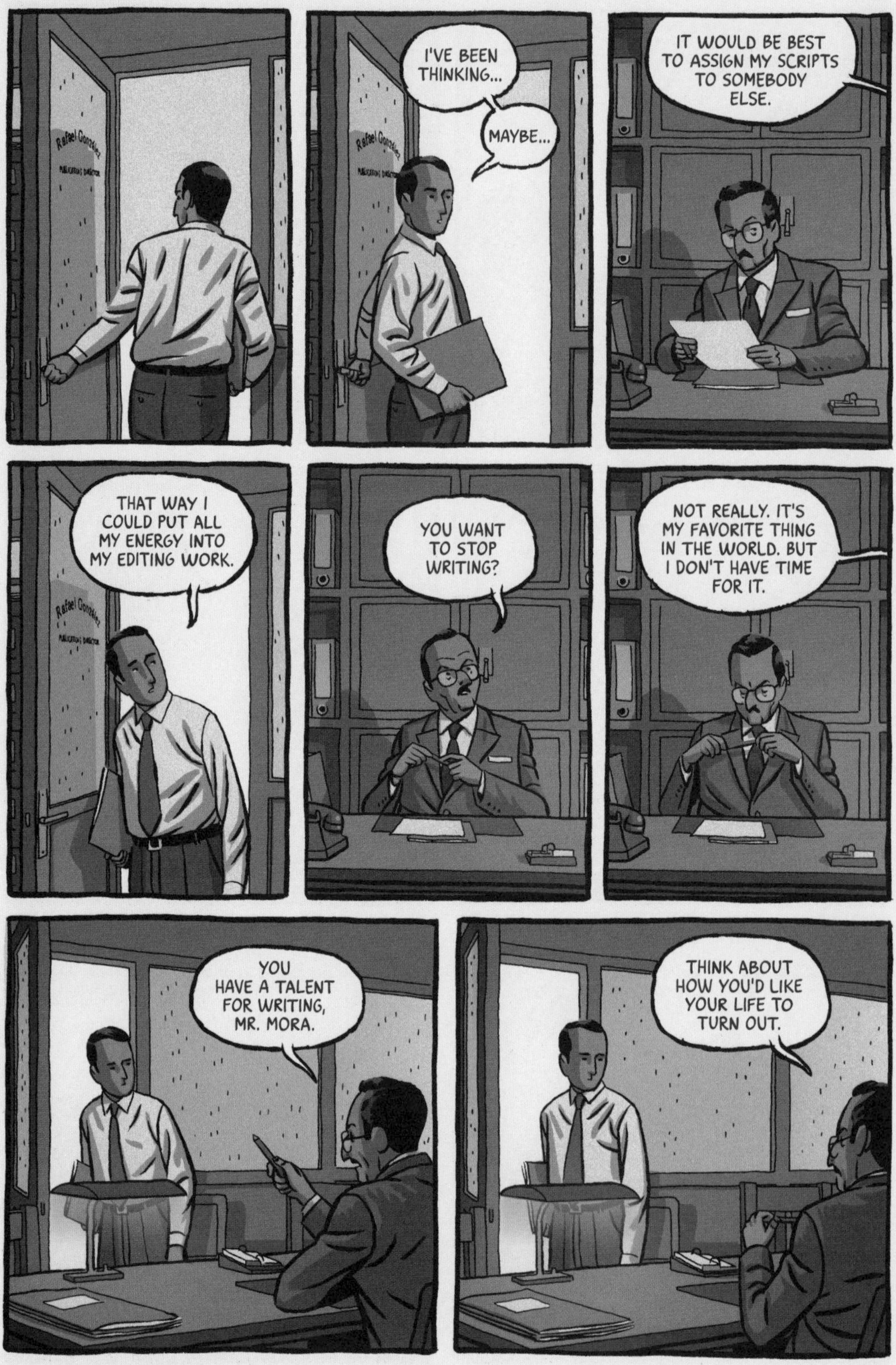
Rafael González
PUBLICATIONS DIRECTOR
I'VE BEEN THINKING...
MAYBE...
IT WOULD BE BEST TO ASSIGN MY SCRIPTS TO SOMEBODY ELSE.
THAT WAY I COULD PUT ALL MY ENERGY INTO MY EDITING WORK.
Rafael González
YOU WANT TO STOP WRITING?
NOT REALLY. IT'S MY FAVORITE THING IN THE WORLD. BUT I DON'T HAVE TIME FOR IT.
YOU HAVE A TALENT FOR WRITING, MR. MORA.
THINK ABOUT HOW YOU'D LIKE YOUR LIFE TO TURN OUT.

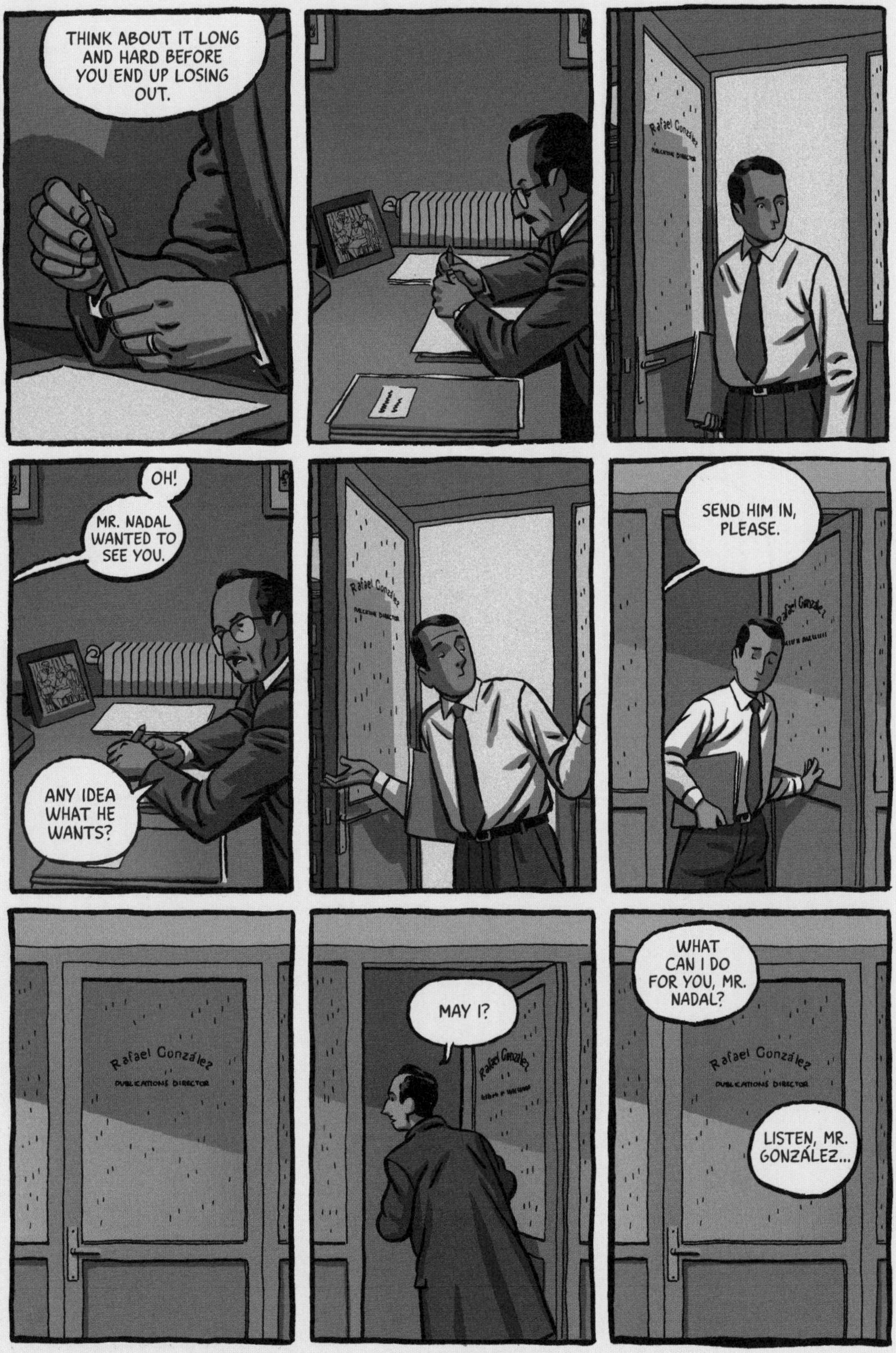

THINK ABOUT IT LONG AND HARD BEFORE YOU END UP LOSING OUT.
OH!
MR. NADAL WANTED TO SEE YOU.
ANY IDEA WHAT HE WANTS?
SEND HIM IN, PLEASE.
Rafael González
PUBLICATIONS DIRECTOR
MAY I?
WHAT CAN I DO FOR YOU, MR. NADAL?
Rafael González
PUBLICATIONS DIRECTOR
LISTEN, MR. GONZÁLEZ...

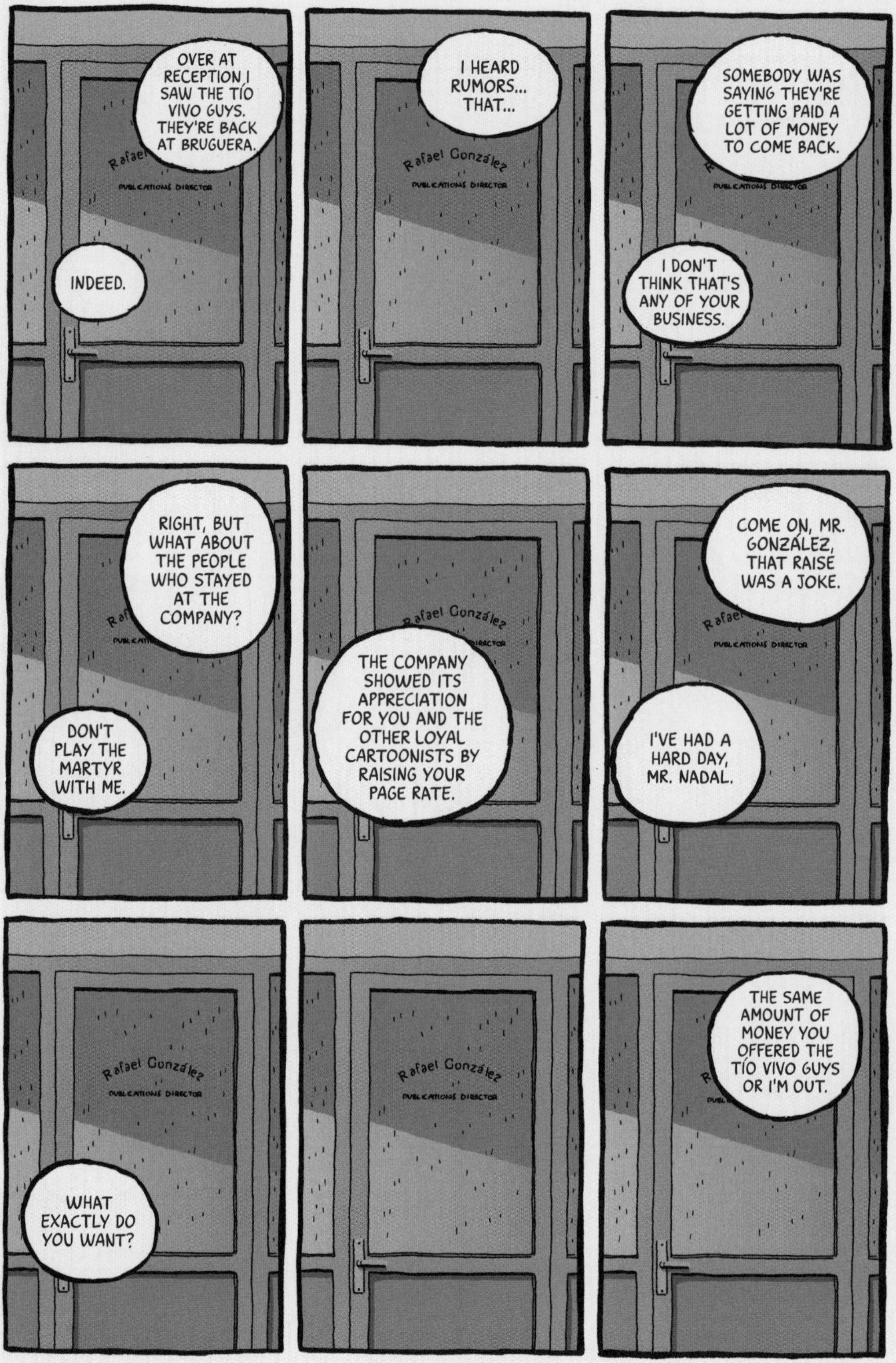
OVER AT RECEPTION I SAW THE TÍO VIVO GUYS. THEY'RE BACK AT BRUGUERA.
Rafael
PUBLICATIONS DIRECTOR
INDEED.
I HEARD RUMORS... THAT...
Rafael González
PUBLICATIONS DIRECTOR
SOMEBODY WAS SAYING THEY'RE GETTING PAID A LOT OF MONEY TO COME BACK.
I DON'T THINK THAT'S ANY OF YOUR BUSINESS.
RIGHT, BUT WHAT ABOUT THE PEOPLE WHO STAYED AT THE COMPANY?
DON'T PLAY THE MARTYR WITH ME.
THE COMPANY SHOWED ITS APPRECIATION FOR YOU AND THE OTHER LOYAL CARTOONISTS BY RAISING YOUR PAGE RATE.
COME ON, MR. GONZÁLEZ, THAT RAISE WAS A JOKE.
I'VE HAD A HARD DAY, MR. NADAL.
Rafael González
PUBLICATIONS DIRECTOR
WHAT EXACTLY DO YOU WANT?
Rafael González
PUBLICATIONS DIRECTOR
THE SAME AMOUNT OF MONEY YOU OFFERED THE TÍO VIVO GUYS OR I'M OUT.

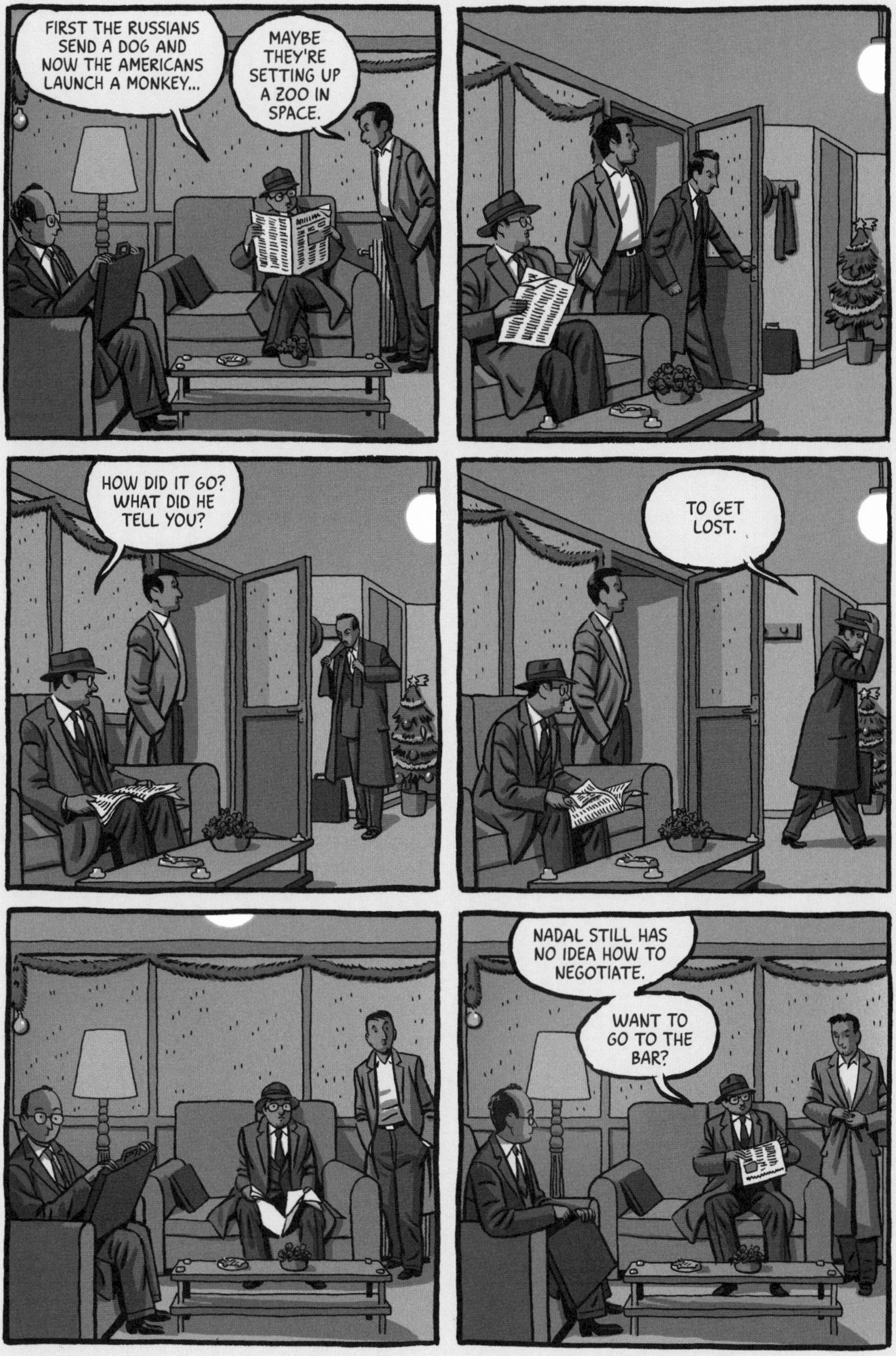
FIRST THE RUSSIANS SEND A DOG AND NOW THE AMERICANS LAUNCH A MONKEY...
MAYBE THEY'RE SETTING UP A ZOO IN SPACE.
HOW DID IT GO? WHAT DID HE TELL YOU?
TO GET LOST.
NADAL STILL HAS NO IDEA HOW TO NEGOTIATE.
WANT TO GO TO THE BAR?

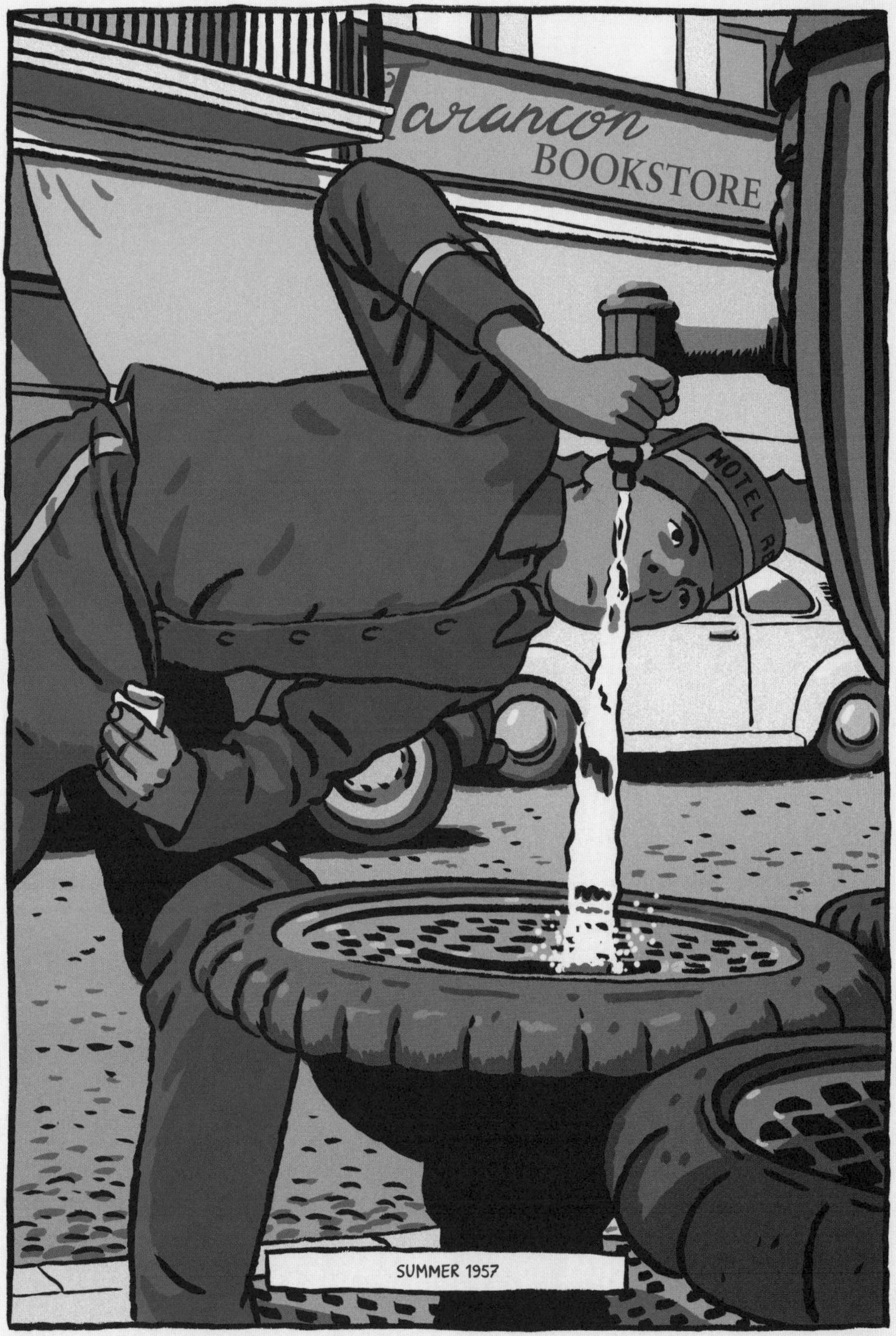
BOOKSTORE
HOTEL
SUMMER 1957

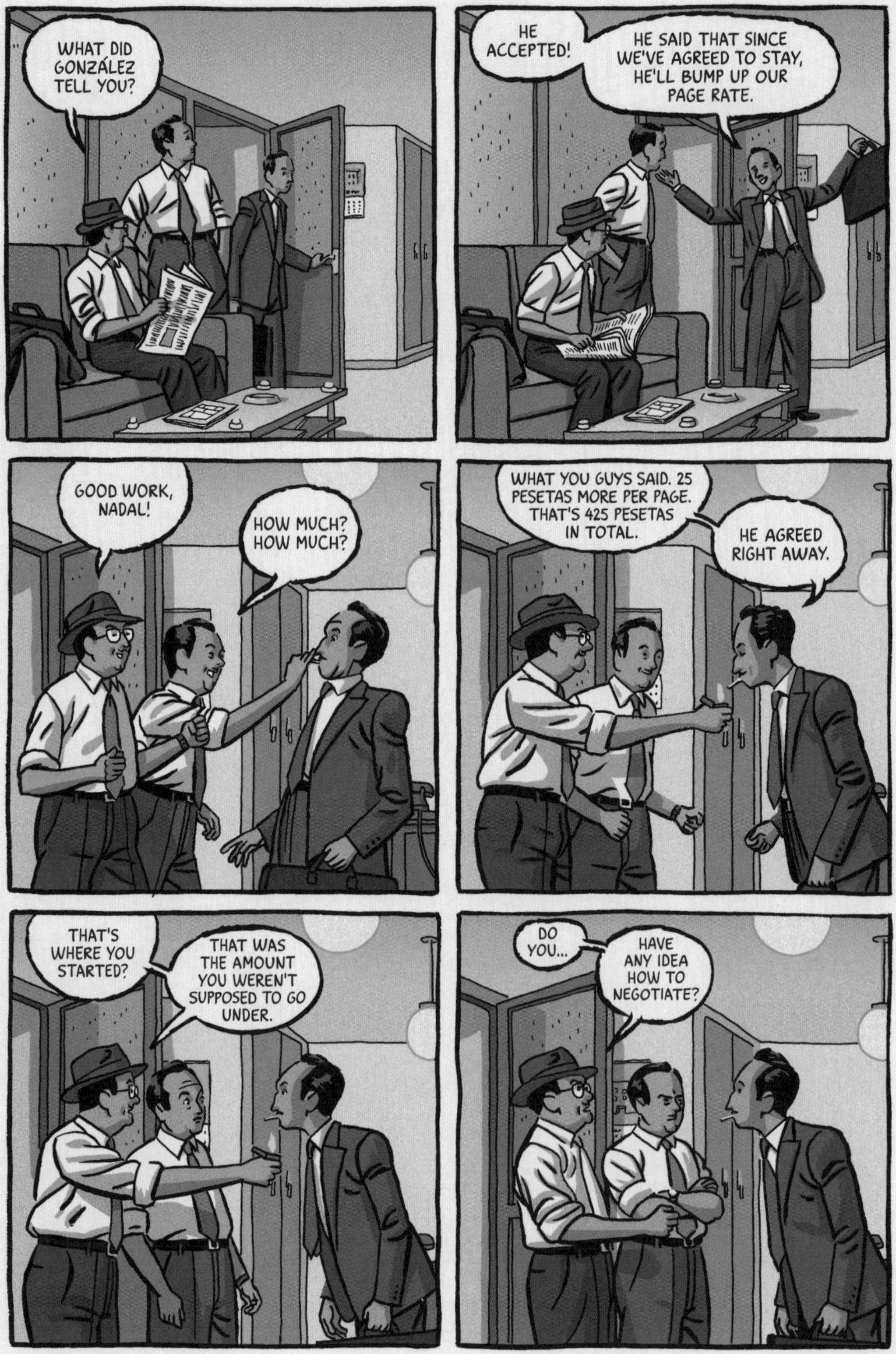
WHAT DID GONZÁLEZ TELL YOU?
HE ACCEPTED!
HE SAID THAT SINCE WE'VE AGREED TO STAY, HE'LL BUMP UP OUR PAGE RATE.
GOOD WORK, NADAL!
HOW MUCH? HOW MUCH?
WHAT YOU GUYS SAID. 25 PESETAS MORE PER PAGE. THAT'S 425 PESETAS IN TOTAL.
HE AGREED RIGHT AWAY.
THAT'S WHERE YOU STARTED?
THAT WAS THE AMOUNT YOU WEREN'T SUPPOSED TO GO UNDER.
DO YOU...
HAVE ANY IDEA HOW TO NEGOTIATE?

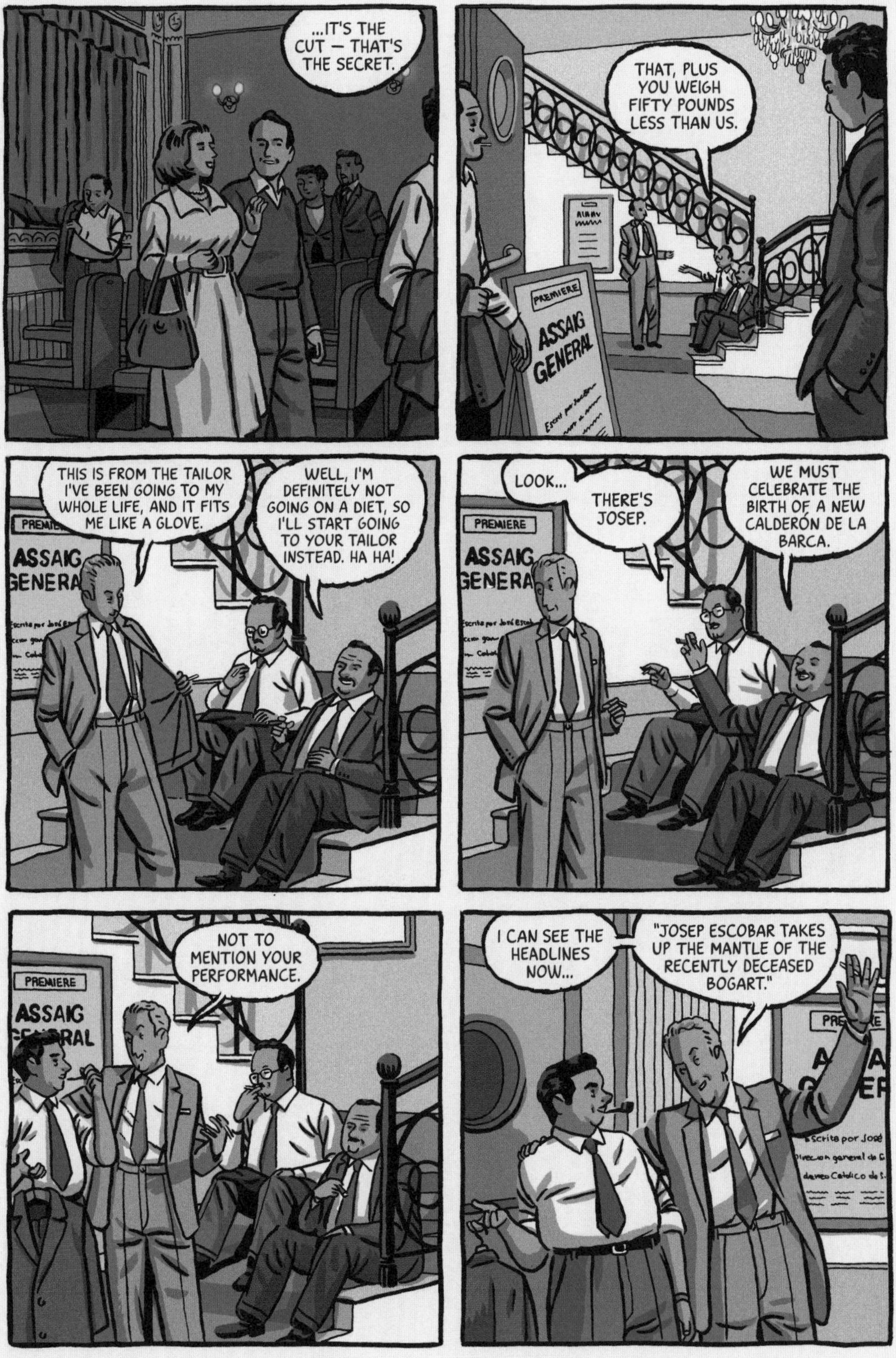
...IT'S THE CUT — THAT'S THE SECRET.
THAT, PLUS YOU WEIGH FIFTY POUNDS LESS THAN US.
PREMIERE
ASSAIG GENERAL
THIS IS FROM THE TAILOR I'VE BEEN GOING TO MY WHOLE LIFE, AND IT FITS ME LIKE A GLOVE.
WELL, I'M DEFINITELY NOT GOING ON A DIET, SO I'LL START GOING TO YOUR TAILOR INSTEAD. HA HA!
LOOK...
THERE'S JOSEP.
WE MUST CELEBRATE THE BIRTH OF A NEW CALDERÓN DE LA BARCA.
NOT TO MENTION YOUR PERFORMANCE.
I CAN SEE THE HEADLINES NOW...
"JOSEP ESCOBAR TAKES UP THE MANTLE OF THE RECENTLY DECEASED BOGART."

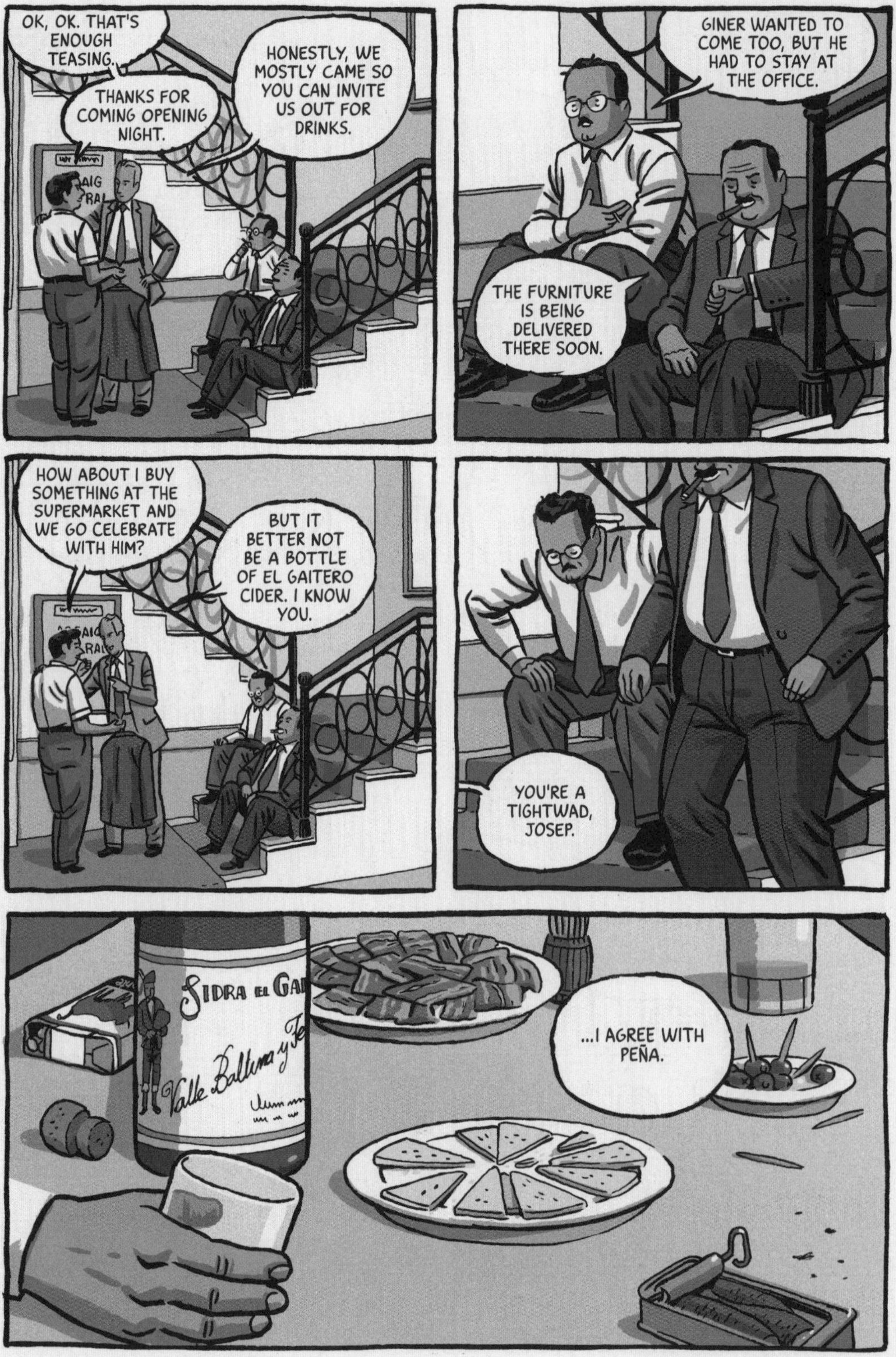
OK, OK. THAT'S ENOUGH TEASING.
THANKS FOR COMING OPENING NIGHT.
HONESTLY, WE MOSTLY CAME SO YOU CAN INVITE US OUT FOR DRINKS.
GINER WANTED TO COME TOO, BUT HE HAD TO STAY AT THE OFFICE.
THE FURNITURE IS BEING DELIVERED THERE SOON.
HOW ABOUT I BUY SOMETHING AT THE SUPERMARKET AND WE GO CELEBRATE WITH HIM?
BUT IT BETTER NOT BE A BOTTLE OF EL GAITERO CIDER. I KNOW YOU.
YOU'RE A TIGHTWAD, JOSEP.
...I AGREE WITH PEÑA.

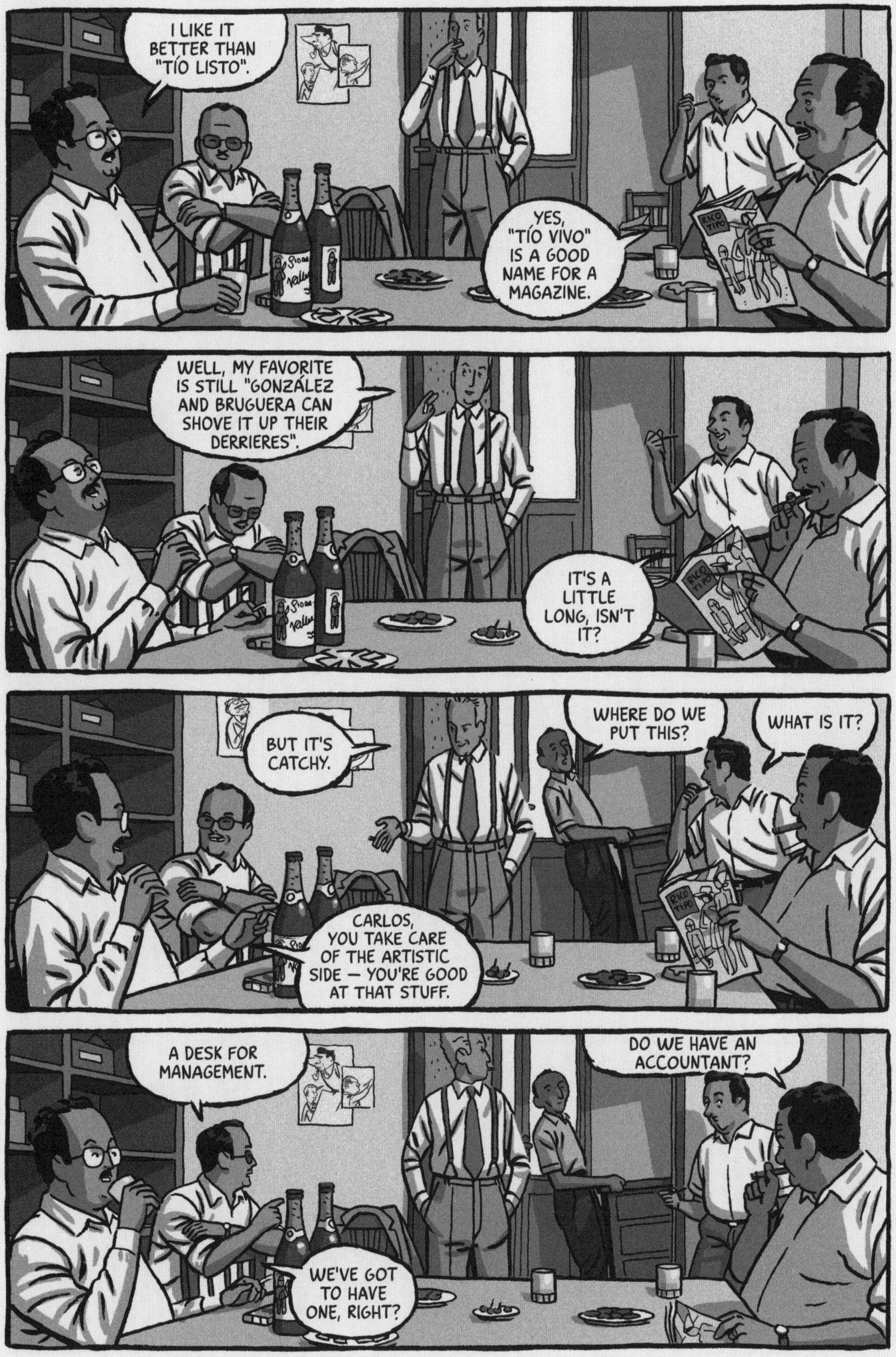
I LIKE IT BETTER THAN "TÍO LISTO".
YES, "TÍO VIVO" IS A GOOD NAME FOR A MAGAZINE.
WELL, MY FAVORITE IS STILL "GONZÁLEZ AND BRUGUERA CAN SHOVE IT UP THEIR DERRIERES".
IT'S A LITTLE LONG, ISN'T IT?
BUT IT'S CATCHY.
WHERE DO WE PUT THIS?
WHAT IS IT?
CARLOS, YOU TAKE CARE OF THE ARTISTIC SIDE — YOU'RE GOOD AT THAT STUFF.
A DESK FOR MANAGEMENT.
DO WE HAVE AN ACCOUNTANT?
WE'VE GOT TO HAVE ONE, RIGHT?

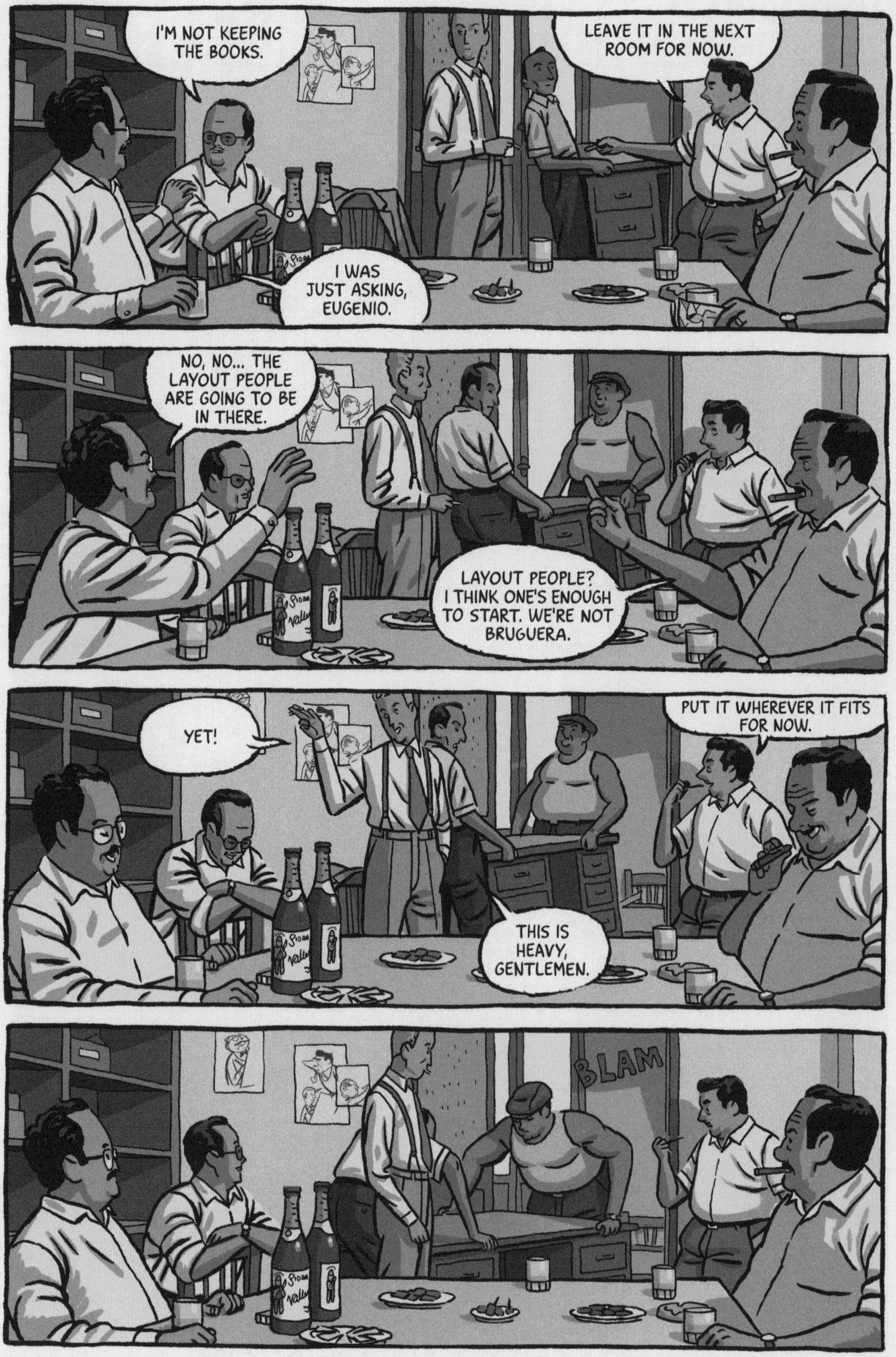
I'M NOT KEEPING THE BOOKS.
LEAVE IT IN THE NEXT ROOM FOR NOW.
I WAS JUST ASKING, EUGENIO.
NO, NO... THE LAYOUT PEOPLE ARE GOING TO BE IN THERE.
LAYOUT PEOPLE? I THINK ONE'S ENOUGH TO START. WE'RE NOT BRUGUERA.
YET!
PUT IT WHEREVER IT FITS FOR NOW.
THIS IS HEAVY, GENTLEMEN.
BLAM

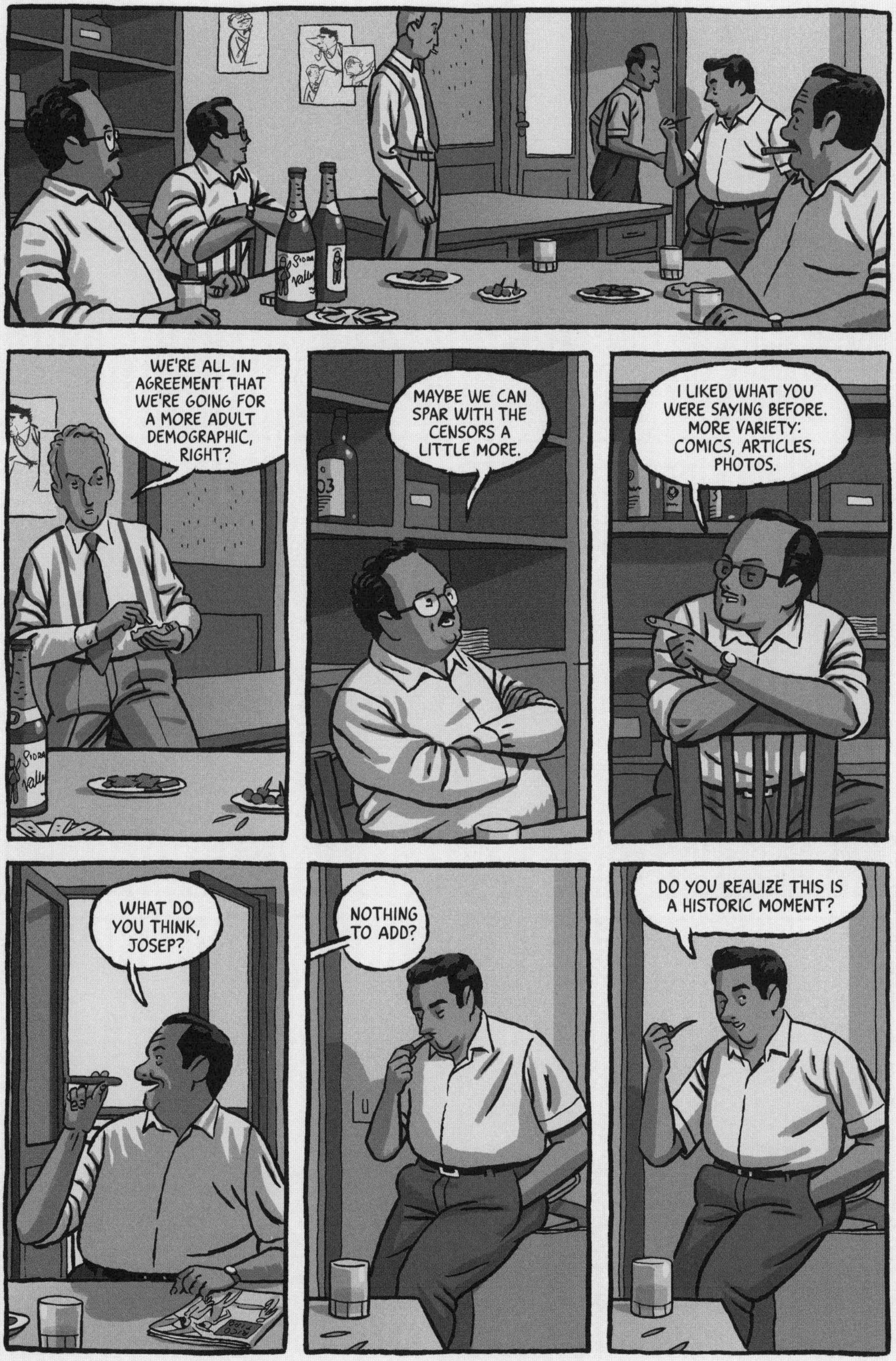
WE'RE ALL IN AGREEMENT THAT WE'RE GOING FOR A MORE ADULT DEMOGRAPHIC, RIGHT?
MAYBE WE CAN SPAR WITH THE CENSORS A LITTLE MORE.
I LIKED WHAT YOU WERE SAYING BEFORE. MORE VARIETY: COMICS, ARTICLES, PHOTOS.
WHAT DO YOU THINK, JOSEP?
NOTHING TO ADD?
DO YOU REALIZE THIS IS A HISTORIC MOMENT?

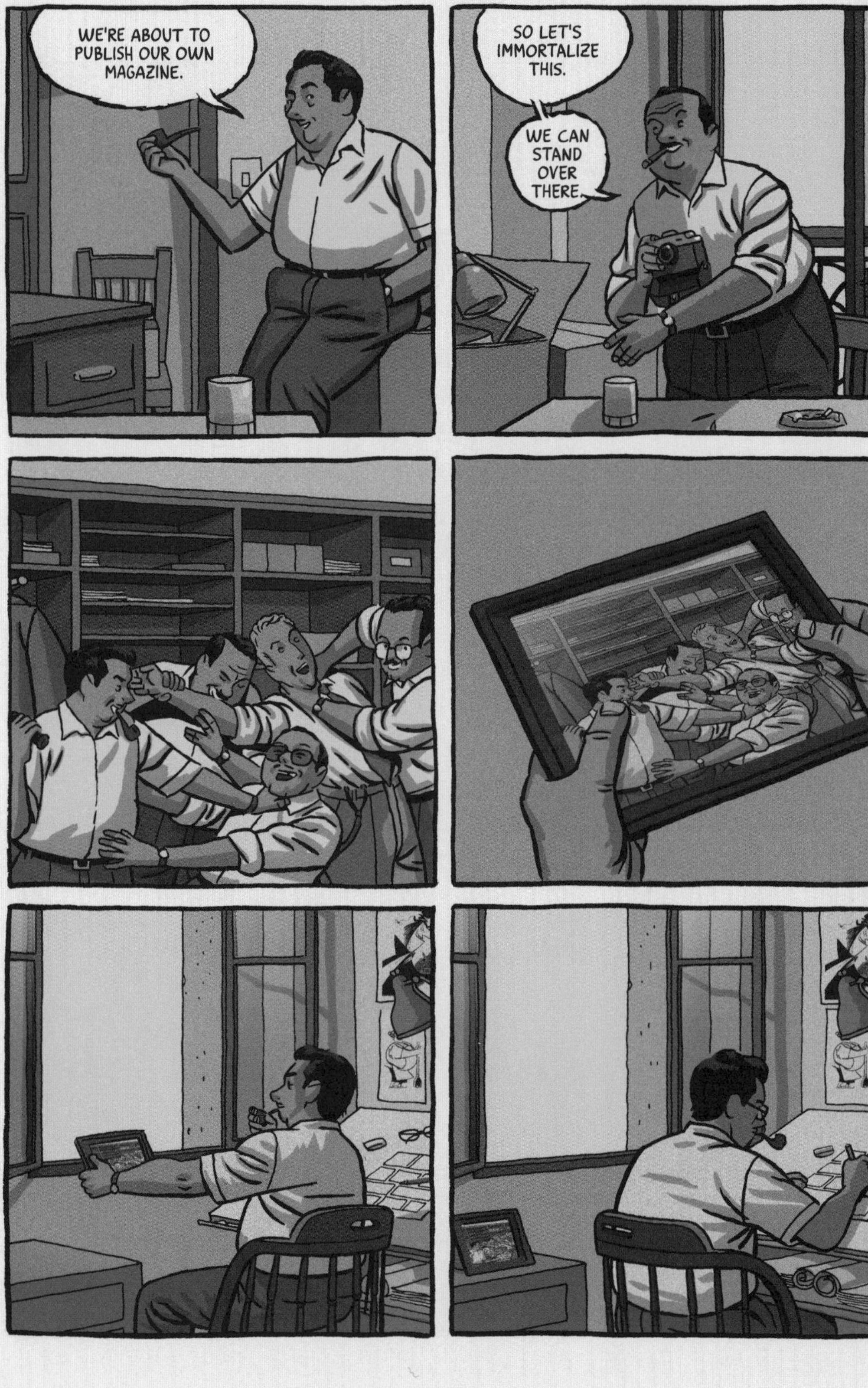
WE'RE ABOUT TO PUBLISH OUR OWN MAGAZINE.
SO LET'S IMMORTALIZE THIS.
WE CAN STAND OVER THERE.

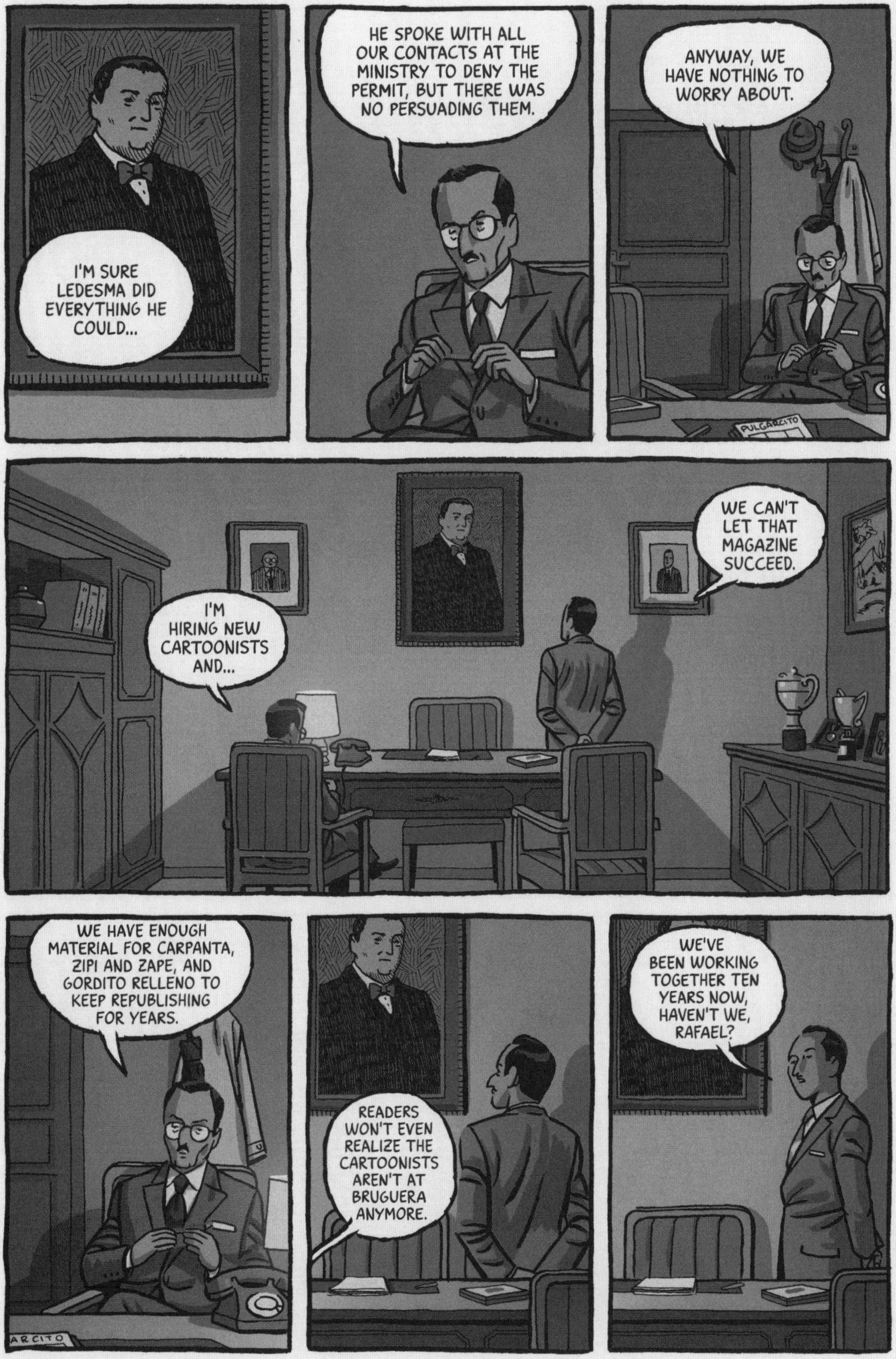

I'M SURE LEDESMA DID EVERYTHING HE COULD...
HE SPOKE WITH ALL OUR CONTACTS AT THE MINISTRY TO DENY THE PERMIT, BUT THERE WAS NO PERSUADING THEM.
ANYWAY, WE HAVE NOTHING TO WORRY ABOUT.
PULGARCITO
I'M HIRING NEW CARTOONISTS AND...
WE CAN'T LET THAT MAGAZINE SUCCEED.
WE HAVE ENOUGH MATERIAL FOR CARPANTA, ZIPI AND ZAPE, AND GORDITO RELLENO TO KEEP REPUBLISHING FOR YEARS.
ARCITO
READERS WON'T EVEN REALIZE THE CARTOONISTS AREN'T AT BRUGUERA ANYMORE.
WE'VE BEEN WORKING TOGETHER TEN YEARS NOW, HAVEN'T WE, RAFAEL?

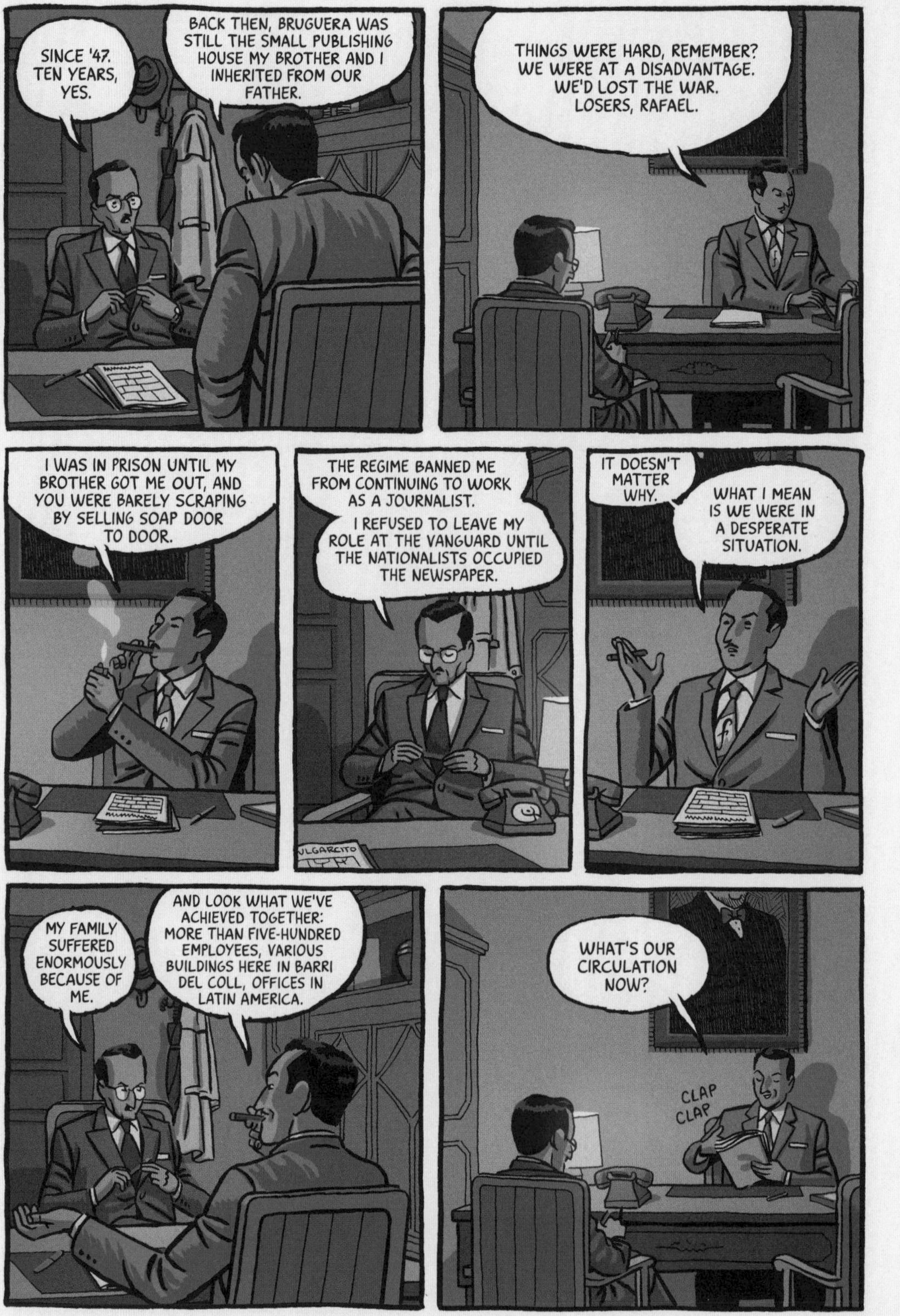

SINCE '47. TEN YEARS, YES.
BACK THEN, BRUGUERA WAS STILL THE SMALL PUBLISHING HOUSE MY BROTHER AND I INHERITED FROM OUR FATHER.
THINGS WERE HARD, REMEMBER? WE WERE AT A DISADVANTAGE. WE'D LOST THE WAR. LOSERS, RAFAEL.
I WAS IN PRISON UNTIL MY BROTHER GOT ME OUT, AND YOU WERE BARELY SCRAPING BY SELLING SOAP DOOR TO DOOR.
THE REGIME BANNED ME FROM CONTINUING TO WORK AS A JOURNALIST.
I REFUSED TO LEAVE MY ROLE AT THE VANGUARD UNTIL THE NATIONALISTS OCCUPIED THE NEWSPAPER.
IT DOESN'T MATTER WHY.
WHAT I MEAN IS WE WERE IN A DESPERATE SITUATION.
MY FAMILY SUFFERED ENORMOUSLY BECAUSE OF ME.
AND LOOK WHAT WE'VE ACHIEVED TOGETHER: MORE THAN FIVE-HUNDRED EMPLOYEES, VARIOUS BUILDINGS HERE IN BARRI DEL COLL, OFFICES IN LATIN AMERICA.
WHAT'S OUR CIRCULATION NOW?
CLAP CLAP

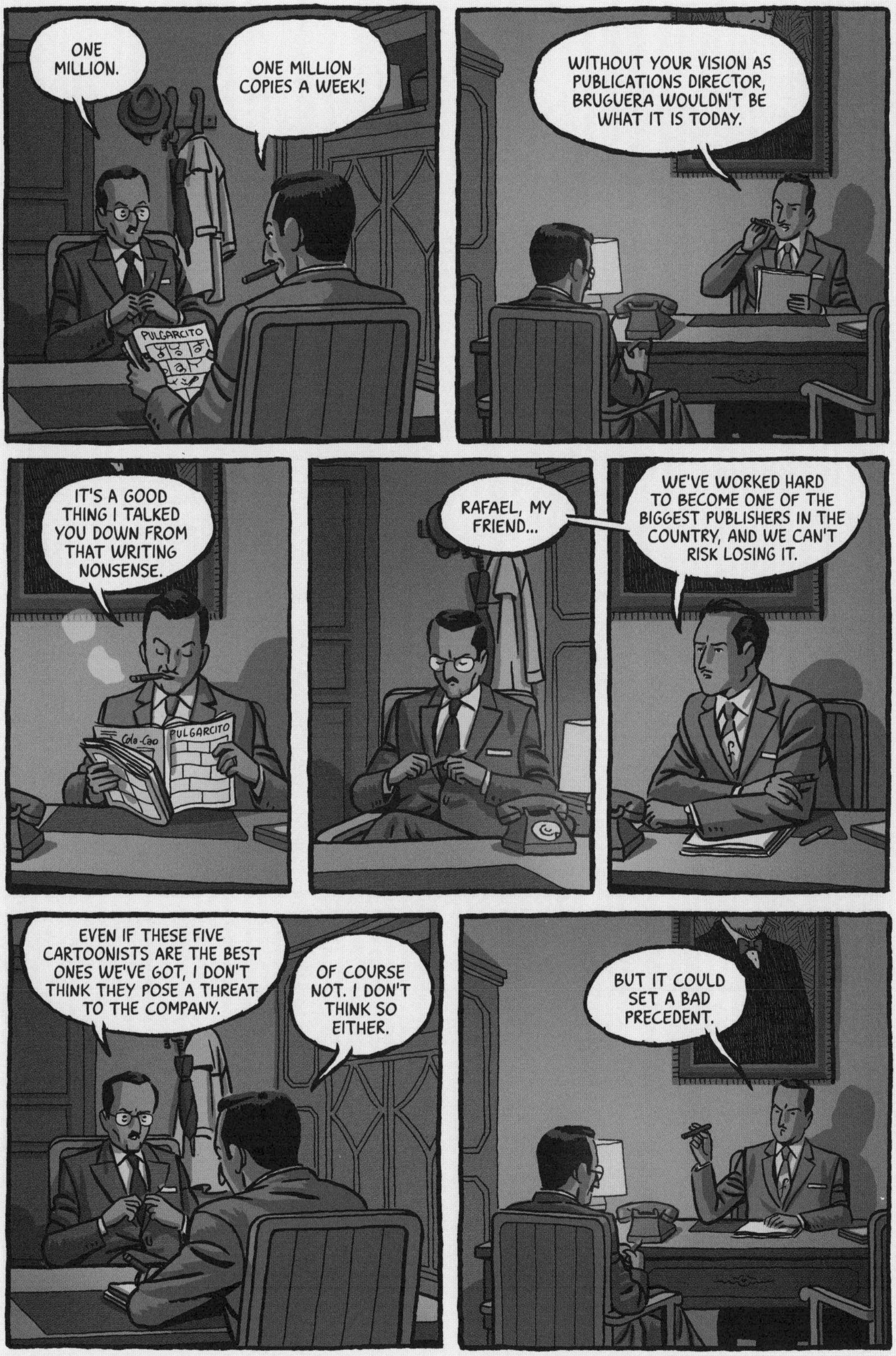

ONE MILLION.
ONE MILLION COPIES A WEEK!
PULGARCITO
WITHOUT YOUR VISION AS PUBLICATIONS DIRECTOR, BRUGUERA WOULDN'T BE WHAT IT IS TODAY.
IT'S A GOOD THING I TALKED YOU DOWN FROM THAT WRITING NONSENSE.
Cola-Cao
PULGARCITO
RAFAEL, MY FRIEND...
WE'VE WORKED HARD TO BECOME ONE OF THE BIGGEST PUBLISHERS IN THE COUNTRY, AND WE CAN'T RISK LOSING IT.
EVEN IF THESE FIVE CARTOONISTS ARE THE BEST ONES WE'VE GOT, I DON'T THINK THEY POSE A THREAT TO THE COMPANY.
OF COURSE NOT. I DON'T THINK SO EITHER.
BUT IT COULD SET A BAD PRECEDENT.

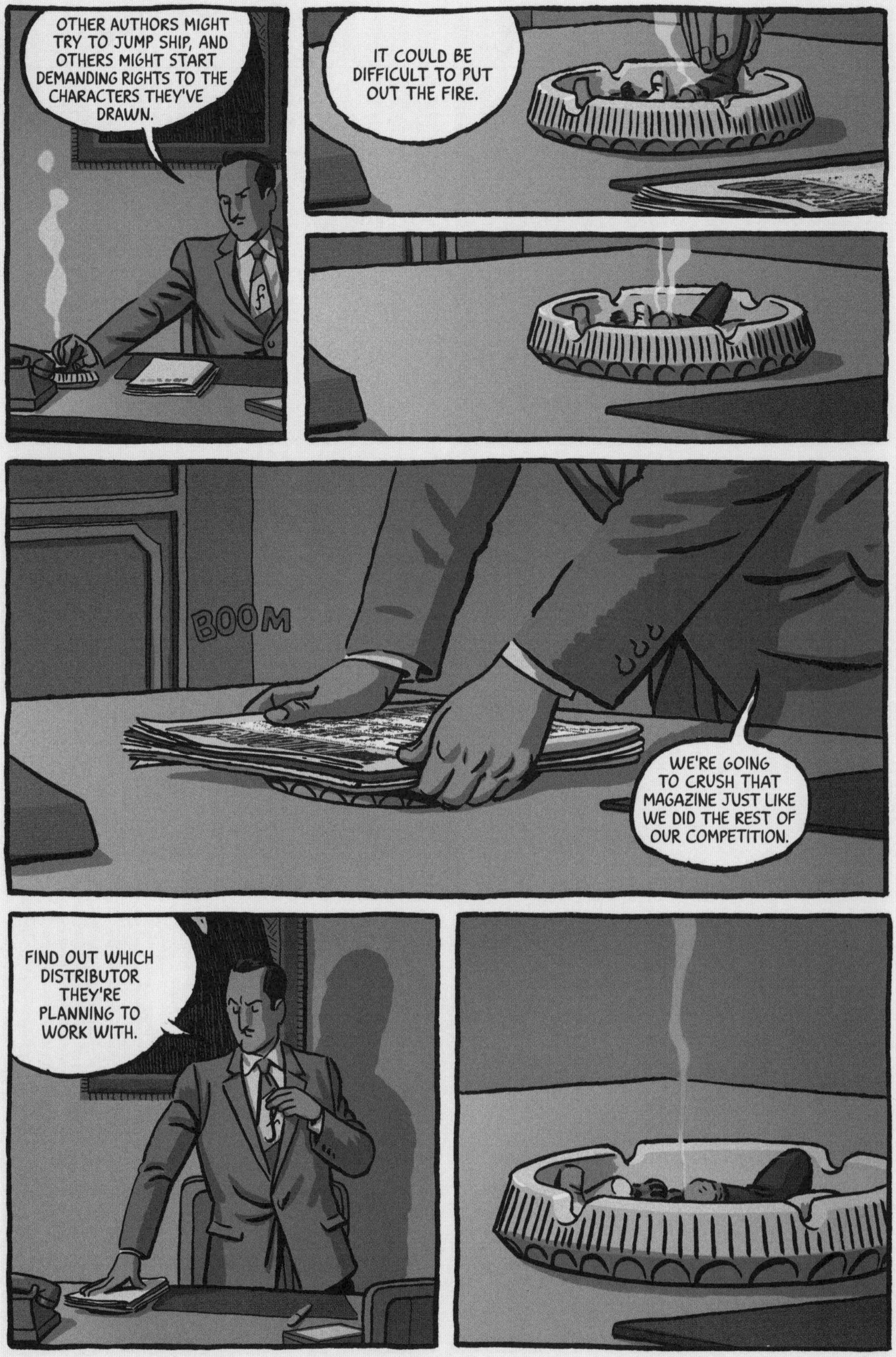
OTHER AUTHORS MIGHT TRY TO JUMP SHIP, AND OTHERS MIGHT START DEMANDING RIGHTS TO THE CHARACTERS THEY'VE DRAWN.
IT COULD BE DIFFICULT TO PUT OUT THE FIRE.
BOOM
WE'RE GOING TO CRUSH THAT MAGAZINE JUST LIKE WE DID THE REST OF OUR COMPETITION.
FIND OUT WHICH DISTRIBUTOR THEY'RE PLANNING TO WORK WITH.

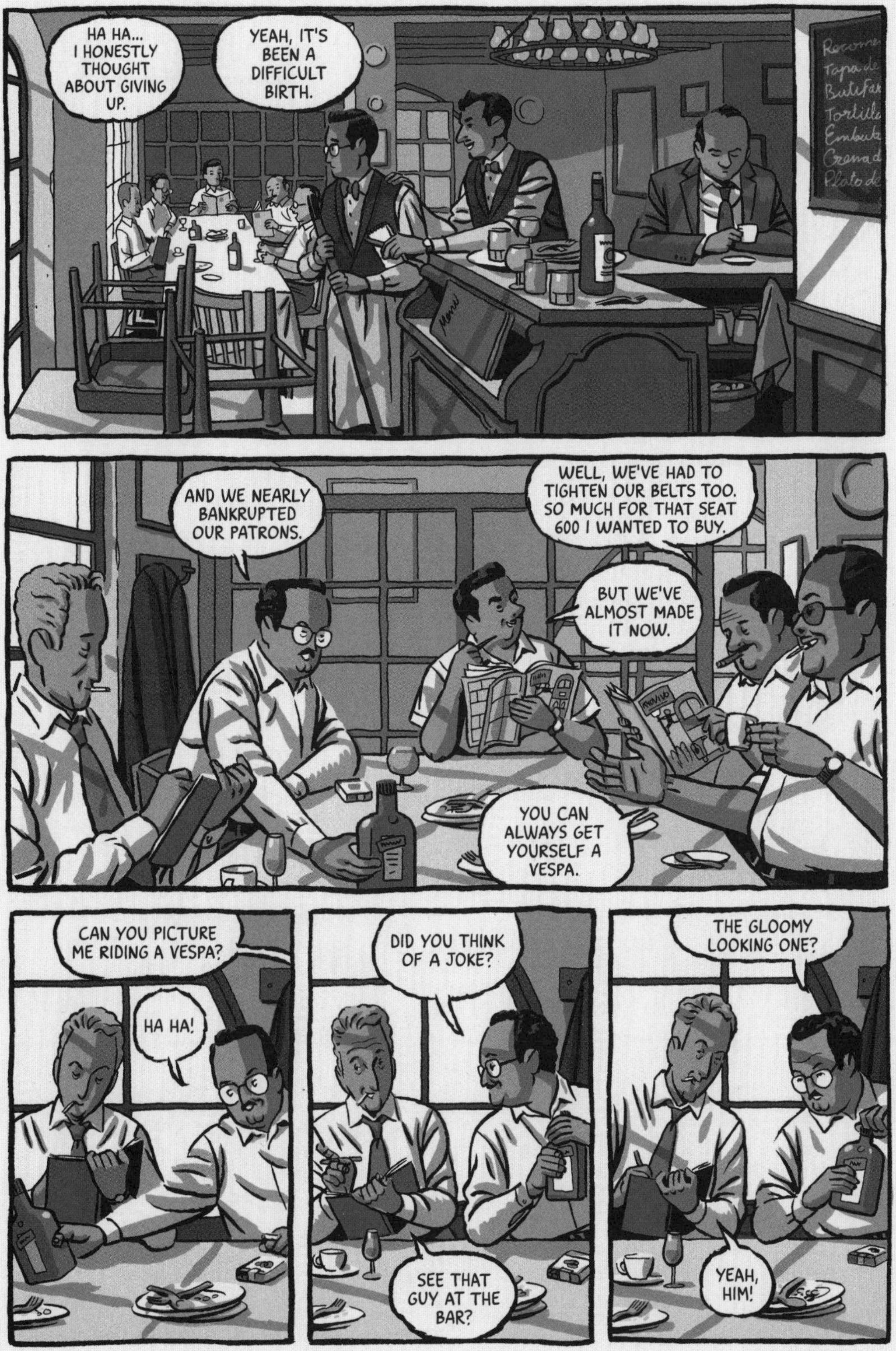

HA HA... I HONESTLY THOUGHT ABOUT GIVING UP.
YEAH, IT'S BEEN A DIFFICULT BIRTH.
AND WE NEARLY BANKRUPTED OUR PATRONS.
WELL, WE'VE HAD TO TIGHTEN OUR BELTS TOO. SO MUCH FOR THAT SEAT 600 I WANTED TO BUY.
BUT WE'VE ALMOST MADE IT NOW.
YOU CAN ALWAYS GET YOURSELF A VESPA.
CAN YOU PICTURE ME RIDING A VESPA?
HA HA!
DID YOU THINK OF A JOKE?
SEE THAT GUY AT THE BAR?
THE GLOOMY LOOKING ONE?
YEAH, HIM!

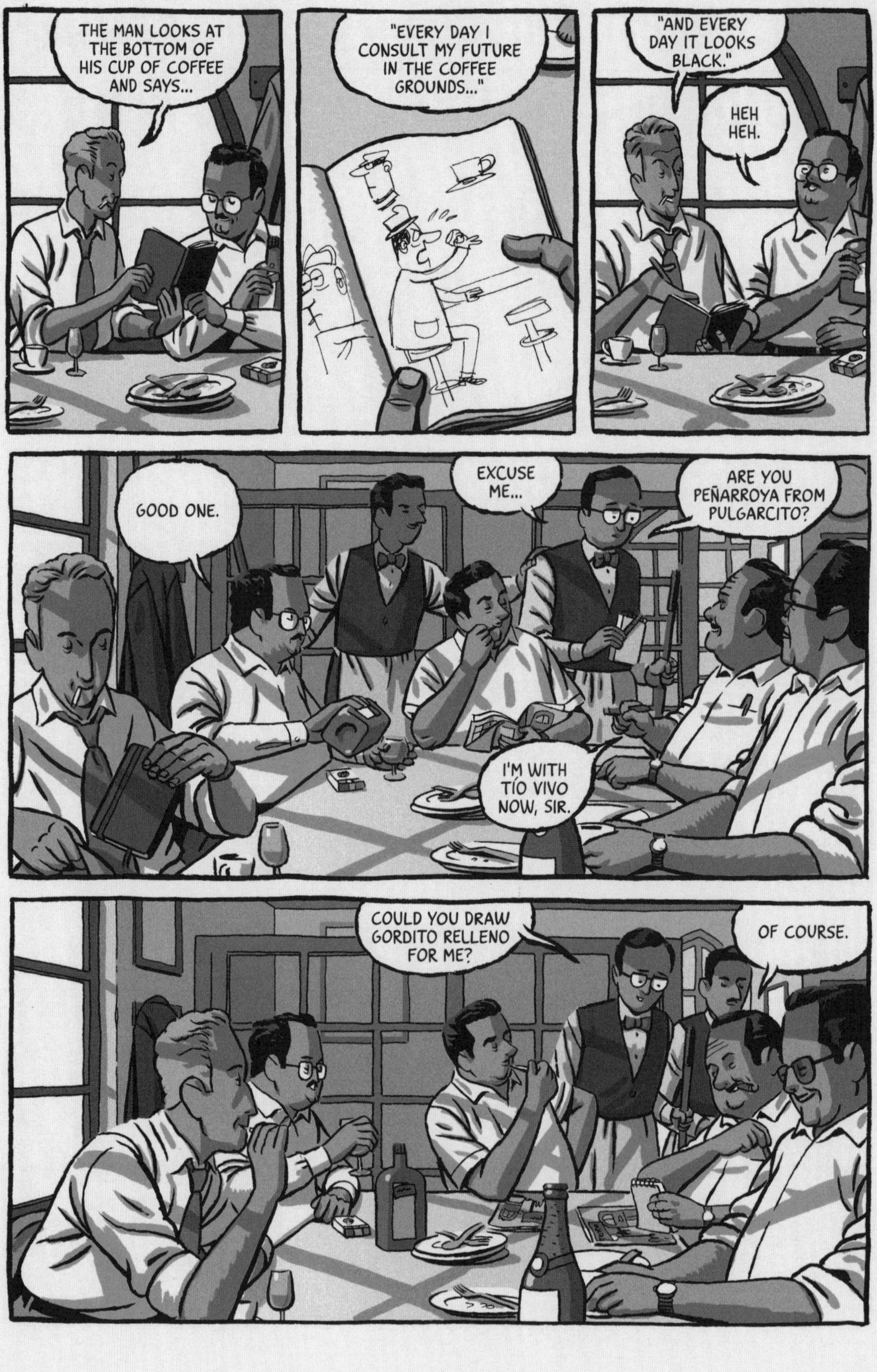
THE MAN LOOKS AT THE BOTTOM OF HIS CUP OF COFFEE AND SAYS...
"EVERY DAY I CONSULT MY FUTURE IN THE COFFEE GROUNDS..."
"AND EVERY DAY IT LOOKS BLACK."
HEH HEH.
GOOD ONE.
EXCUSE ME...
ARE YOU PEÑARROYA FROM PULGARCITO?
I'M WITH TÍO VIVO NOW, SIR.
COULD YOU DRAW GORDITO RELLENO FOR ME?
OF COURSE.

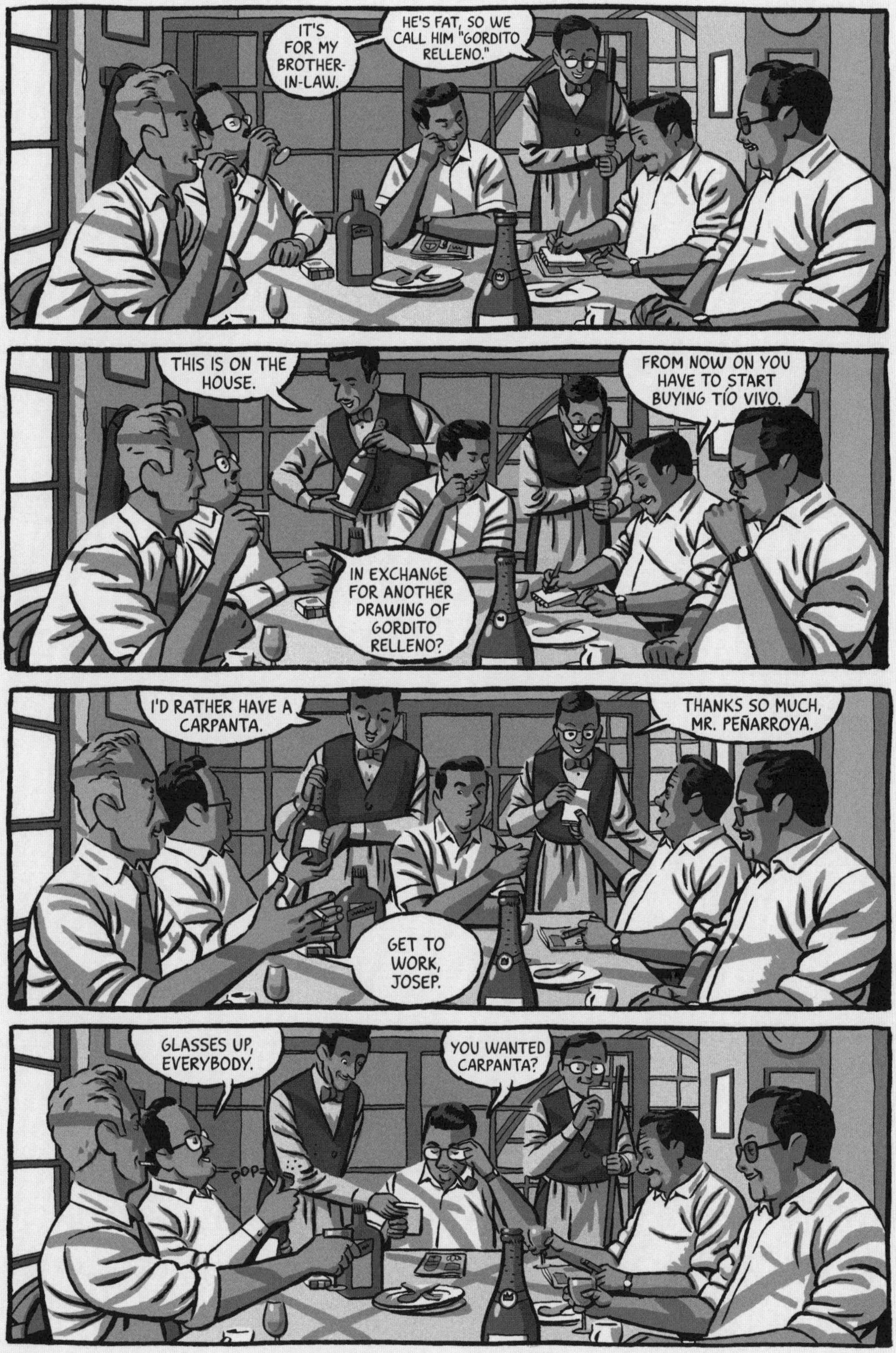
IT'S FOR MY BROTHER-IN-LAW.
HE'S FAT, SO WE CALL HIM "GORDITO RELLENO."
THIS IS ON THE HOUSE.
FROM NOW ON YOU HAVE TO START BUYING TÍO VIVO.
IN EXCHANGE FOR ANOTHER DRAWING OF GORDITO RELLENO?
I'D RATHER HAVE A CARPANTA.
THANKS SO MUCH, MR. PEÑARROYA.
GET TO WORK, JOSEP.
GLASSES UP, EVERYBODY.
POP
YOU WANTED CARPANTA?

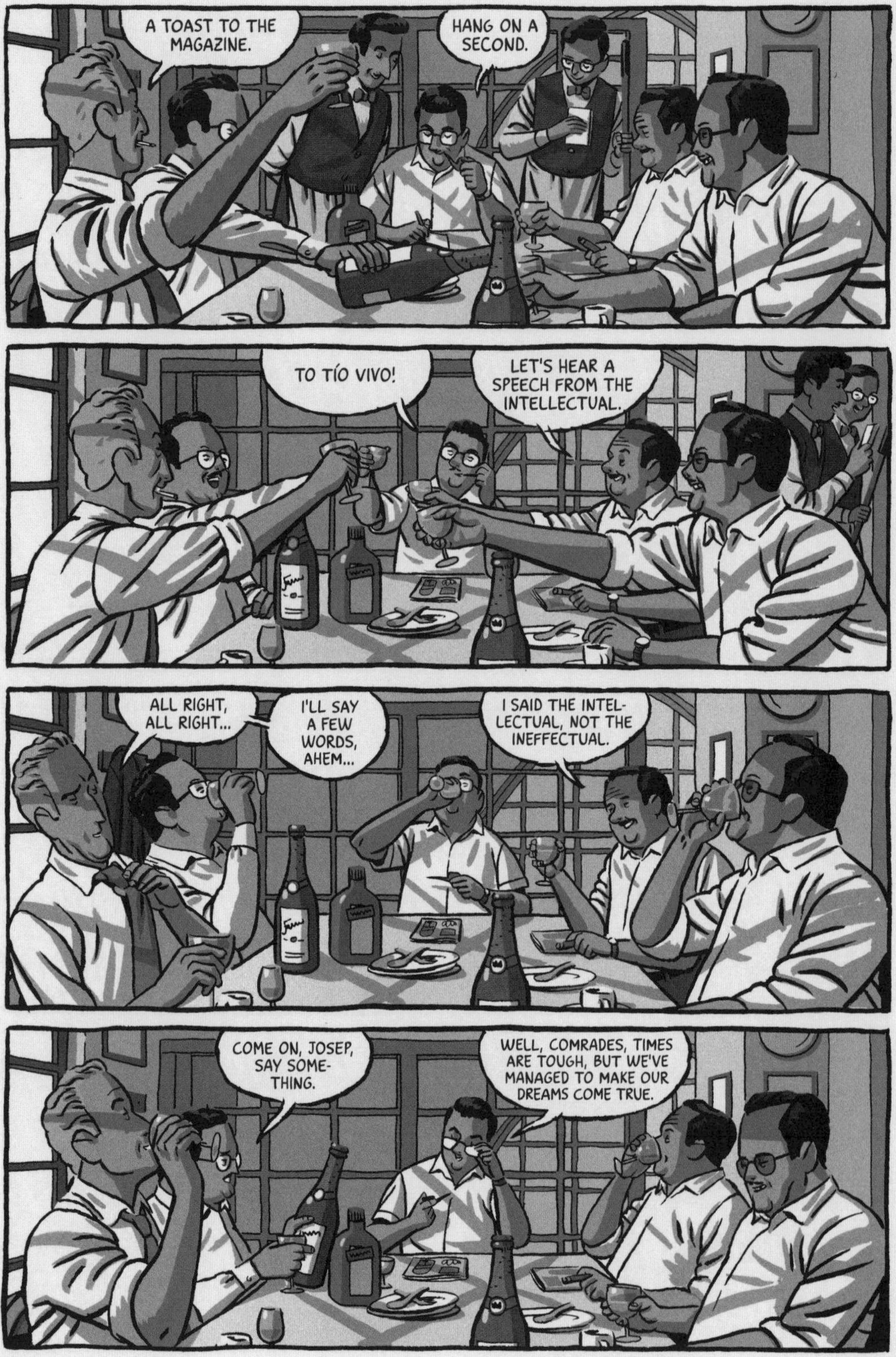
A TOAST TO THE MAGAZINE.
HANG ON A SECOND.
TO TÍO VIVO!
LET'S HEAR A SPEECH FROM THE INTELLECTUAL.
ALL RIGHT, ALL RIGHT...
I'LL SAY A FEW WORDS, AHEM...
I SAID THE INTEL-LECTUAL, NOT THE INEFFECTUAL.
COME ON, JOSEP, SAY SOME-THING.
WELL, COMRADES, TIMES ARE TOUGH, BUT WE'VE MANAGED TO MAKE OUR DREAMS COME TRUE.

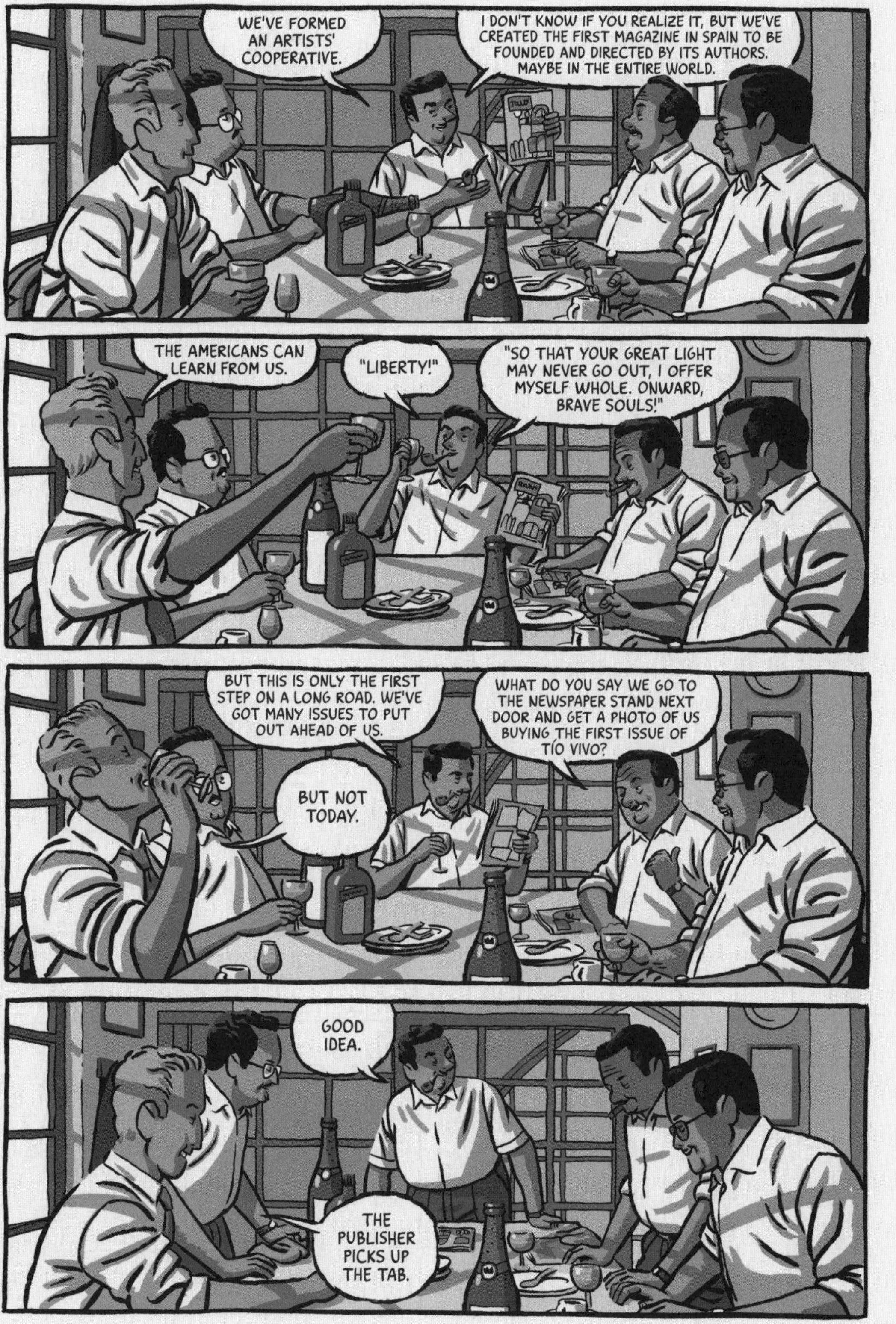
WE'VE FORMED AN ARTISTS' COOPERATIVE.
I DON'T KNOW IF YOU REALIZE IT, BUT WE'VE CREATED THE FIRST MAGAZINE IN SPAIN TO BE FOUNDED AND DIRECTED BY ITS AUTHORS. MAYBE IN THE ENTIRE WORLD.
THE AMERICANS CAN LEARN FROM US.
"LIBERTY!"
"SO THAT YOUR GREAT LIGHT MAY NEVER GO OUT, I OFFER MYSELF WHOLE. ONWARD, BRAVE SOULS!"
BUT THIS IS ONLY THE FIRST STEP ON A LONG ROAD. WE'VE GOT MANY ISSUES TO PUT OUT AHEAD OF US.
WHAT DO YOU SAY WE GO TO THE NEWSPAPER STAND NEXT DOOR AND GET A PHOTO OF US BUYING THE FIRST ISSUE OF TÍO VIVO?
BUT NOT TODAY.
GOOD IDEA.
THE PUBLISHER PICKS UP THE TAB.

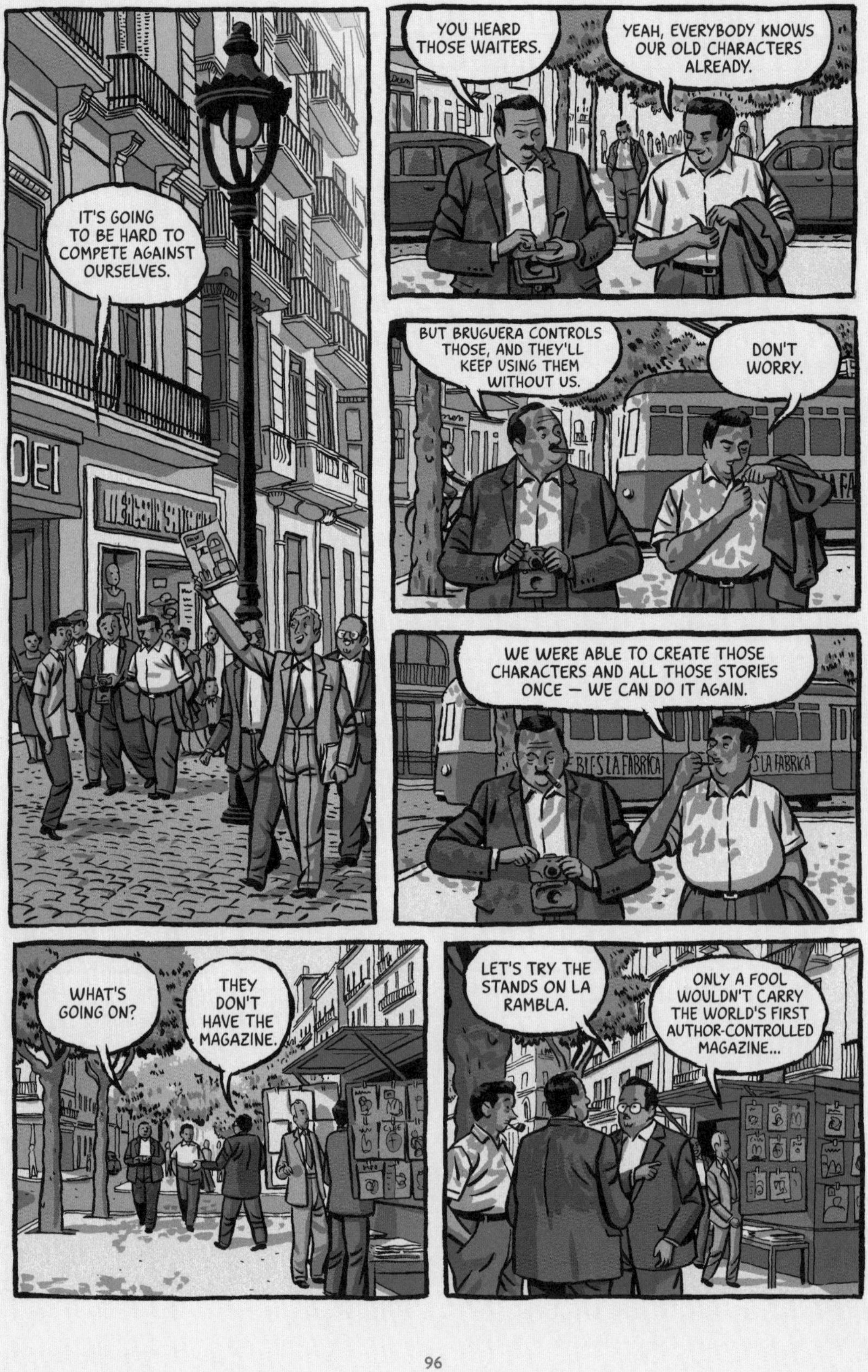
IT'S GOING TO BE HARD TO COMPETE AGAINST OURSELVES.
YOU HEARD THOSE WAITERS.
YEAH, EVERYBODY KNOWS OUR OLD CHARACTERS ALREADY.
BUT BRUGUERA CONTROLS THOSE, AND THEY'LL KEEP USING THEM WITHOUT US.
DON'T WORRY.
WE WERE ABLE TO CREATE THOSE CHARACTERS AND ALL THOSE STORIES ONCE — WE CAN DO IT AGAIN.
LA FABRICA
WHAT'S GOING ON?
THEY DON'T HAVE THE MAGAZINE.
LET'S TRY THE STANDS ON LA RAMBLA.
ONLY A FOOL WOULDN'T CARRY THE WORLD'S FIRST AUTHOR-CONTROLLED MAGAZINE...

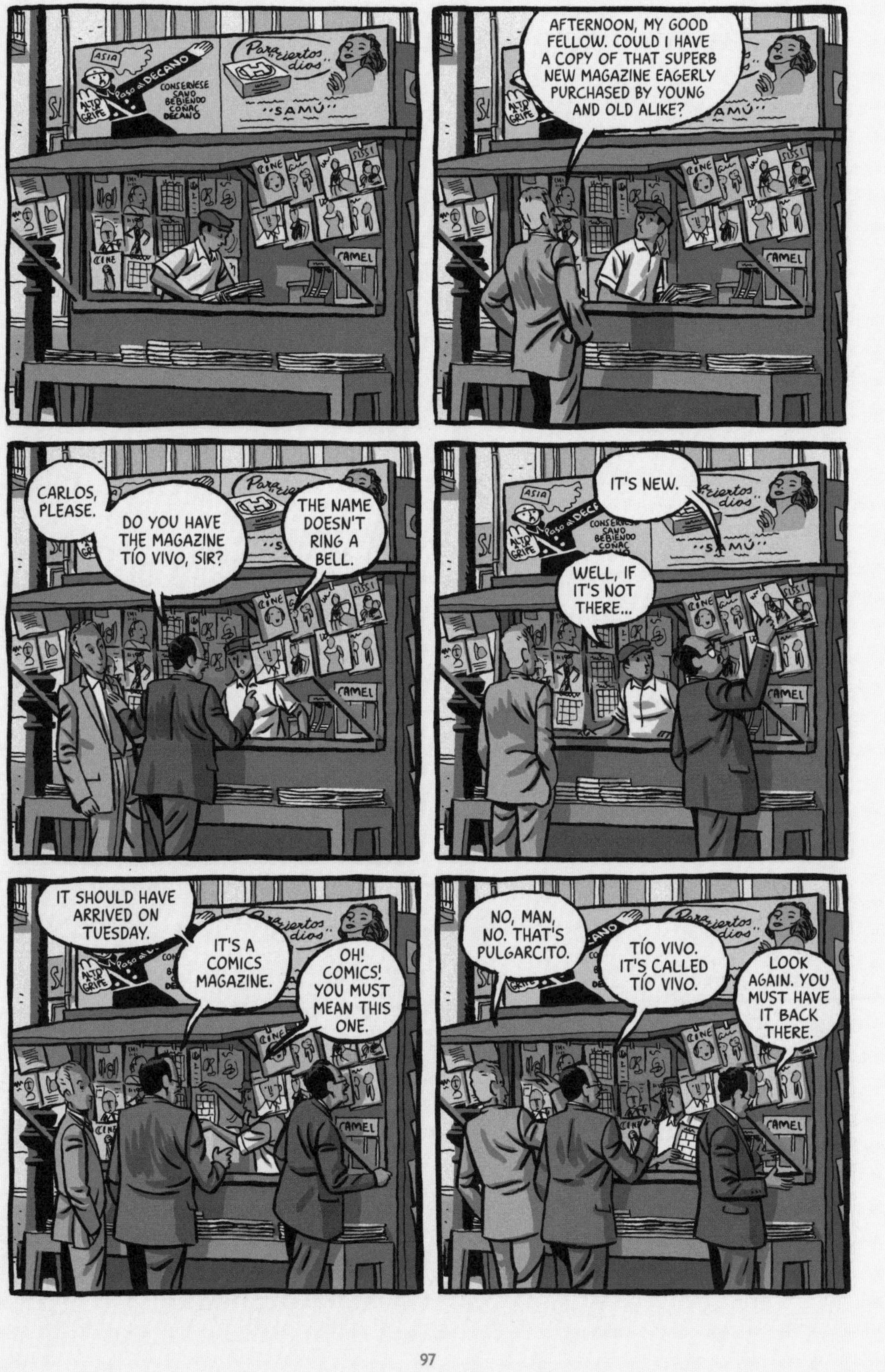
ASIA
Paso al DECANO
CONSERVESE SANO BEBIENDO CONAC DECANO
ALTO GRIPE
Para ciertos dios
SAMÚ
CINE
CAMEL
AFTERNOON, MY GOOD FELLOW. COULD I HAVE A COPY OF THAT SUPERB NEW MAGAZINE EAGERLY PURCHASED BY YOUNG AND OLD ALIKE?
CARLOS, PLEASE.
DO YOU HAVE THE MAGAZINE TÍO VIVO, SIR?
THE NAME DOESN'T RING A BELL.
IT'S NEW.
WELL, IF IT'S NOT THERE...
IT SHOULD HAVE ARRIVED ON TUESDAY.
IT'S A COMICS MAGAZINE.
OH! COMICS! YOU MUST MEAN THIS ONE.
NO, MAN, NO. THAT'S PULGARCITO.
TÍO VIVO. IT'S CALLED TÍO VIVO.
LOOK AGAIN. YOU MUST HAVE IT BACK THERE.

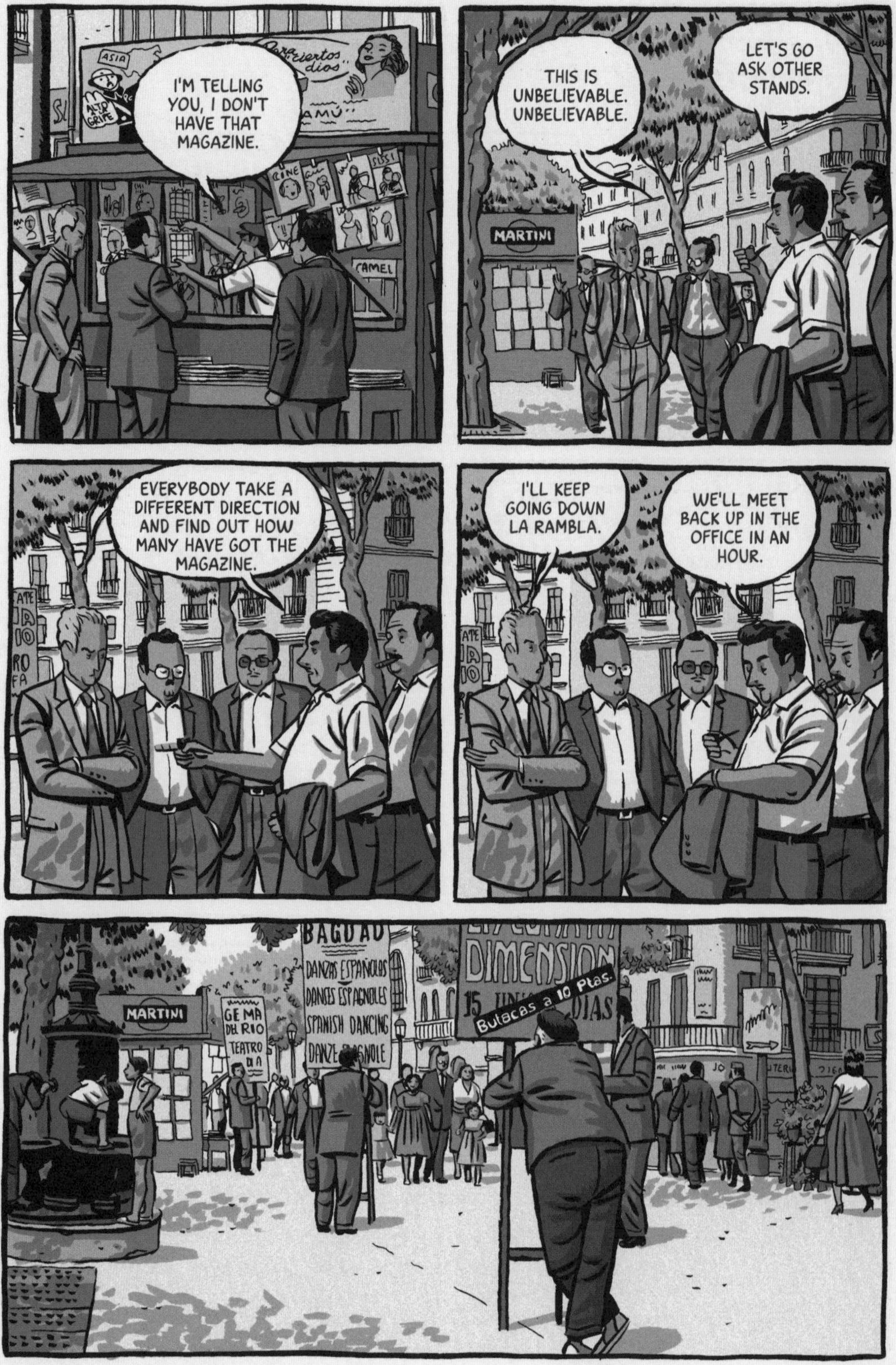
ASIA
ALTO A LA GRIPE
CINE
CAMEL
I'M TELLING YOU, I DON'T HAVE THAT MAGAZINE.
MARTINI
THIS IS UNBELIEVABLE. UNBELIEVABLE.
LET'S GO ASK OTHER STANDS.
EVERYBODY TAKE A DIFFERENT DIRECTION AND FIND OUT HOW MANY HAVE GOT THE MAGAZINE.
I'LL KEEP GOING DOWN LA RAMBLA.
WE'LL MEET BACK UP IN THE OFFICE IN AN HOUR.
MARTINI
GEMA DEL RIO
TEATRO
BAGDAD
DANZAS ESPAÑOLAS
DANCES ESPAGNOLES
SPANISH DANCING
DIMENSION
Butacas a 10 Ptas.

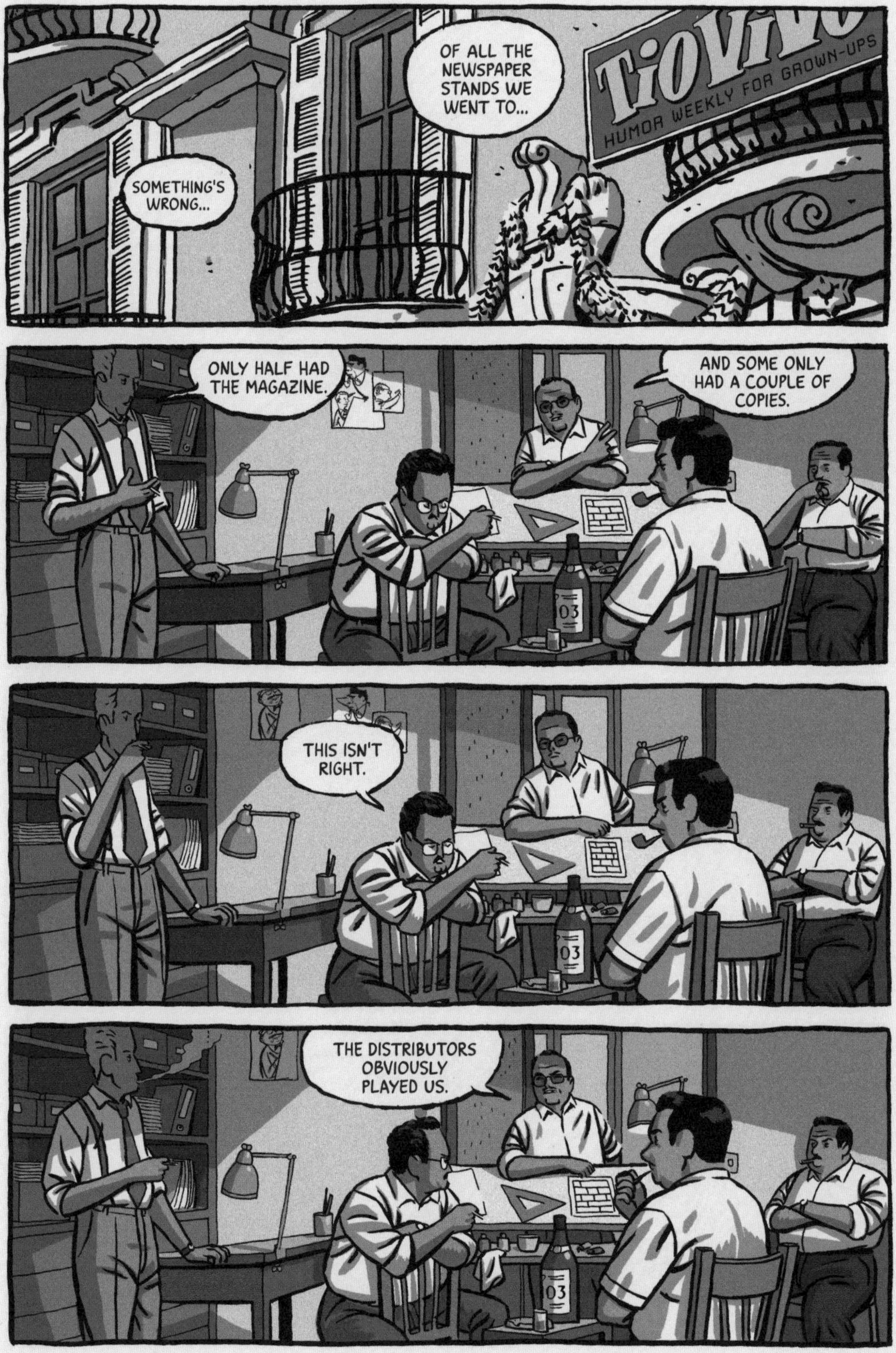
SOMETHING'S WRONG...
OF ALL THE NEWSPAPER STANDS WE WENT TO...
TIOVIVO
HUMOR WEEKLY FOR GROWN-UPS
ONLY HALF HAD THE MAGAZINE.
AND SOME ONLY HAD A COUPLE OF COPIES.
THIS ISN'T RIGHT.
THE DISTRIBUTORS OBVIOUSLY PLAYED US.

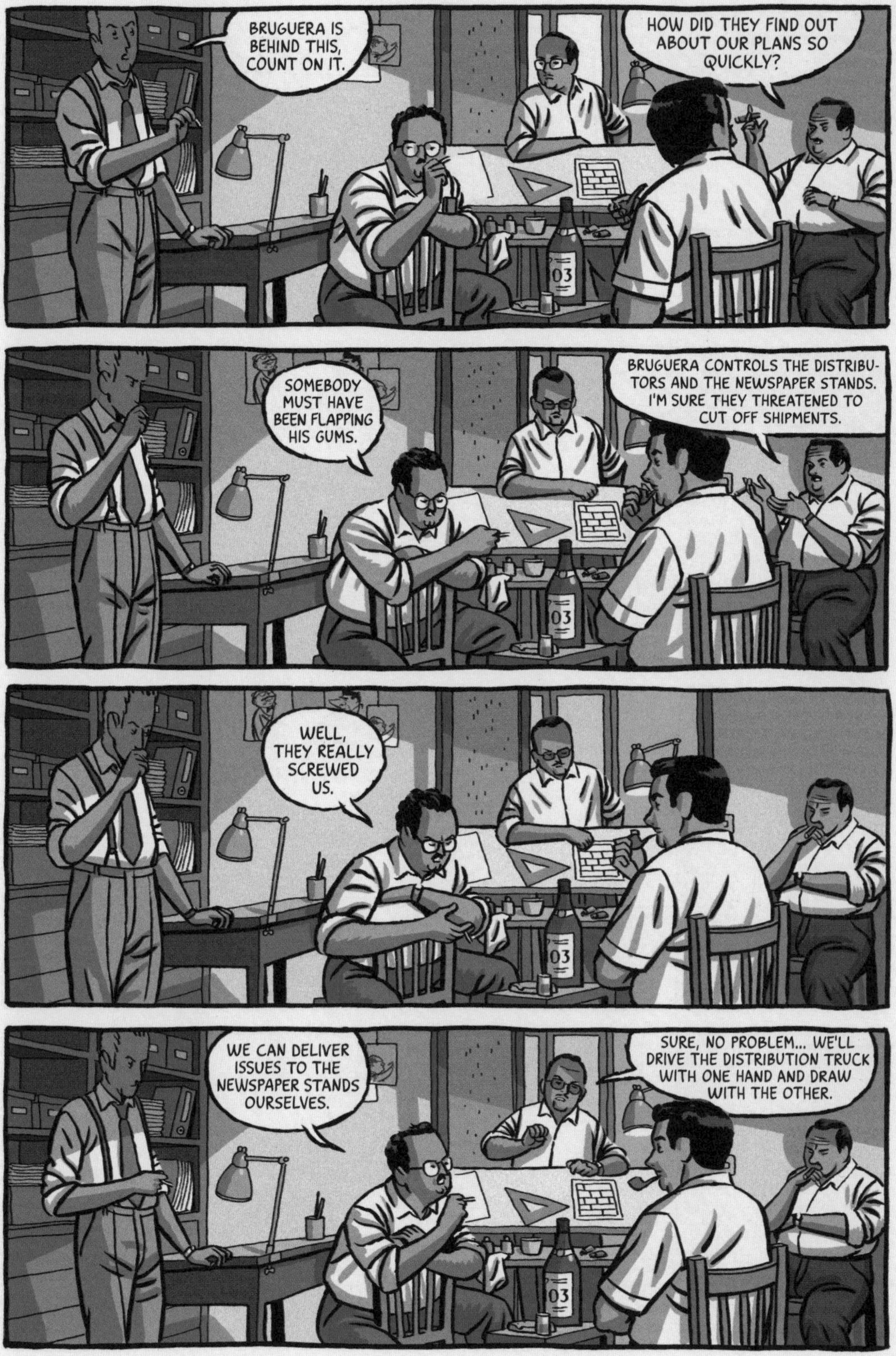
BRUGUERA IS BEHIND THIS, COUNT ON IT.
HOW DID THEY FIND OUT ABOUT OUR PLANS SO QUICKLY?
SOMEBODY MUST HAVE BEEN FLAPPING HIS GUMS.
BRUGUERA CONTROLS THE DISTRIBUTORS AND THE NEWSPAPER STANDS. I'M SURE THEY THREATENED TO CUT OFF SHIPMENTS.
WELL, THEY REALLY SCREWED US.
WE CAN DELIVER ISSUES TO THE NEWSPAPER STANDS OURSELVES.
SURE, NO PROBLEM... WE'LL DRIVE THE DISTRIBUTION TRUCK WITH ONE HAND AND DRAW WITH THE OTHER.

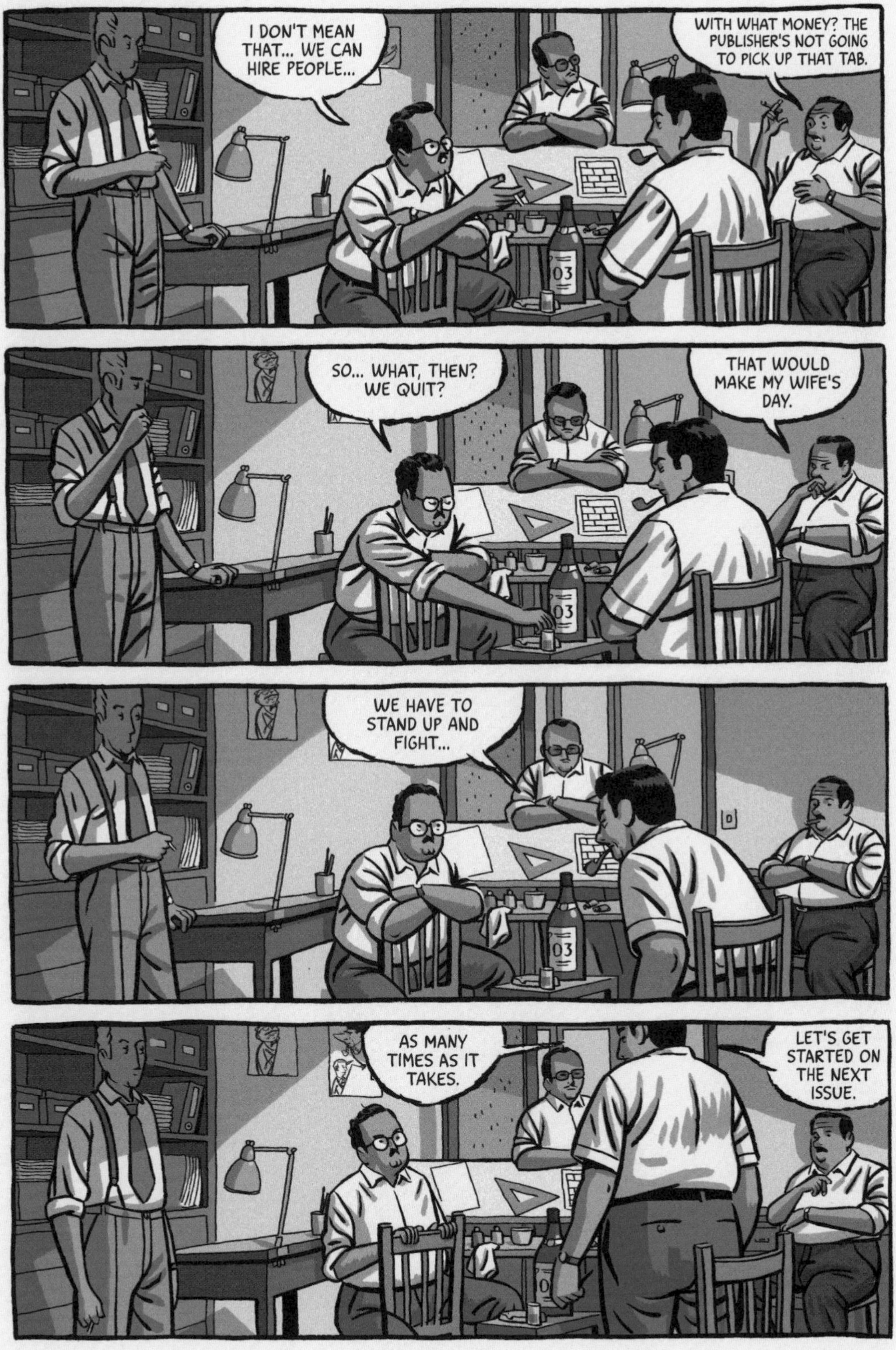
I DON'T MEAN THAT... WE CAN HIRE PEOPLE...
WITH WHAT MONEY? THE PUBLISHER'S NOT GOING TO PICK UP THAT TAB.
SO... WHAT, THEN? WE QUIT?
THAT WOULD MAKE MY WIFE'S DAY.
WE HAVE TO STAND UP AND FIGHT...
AS MANY TIMES AS IT TAKES.
LET'S GET STARTED ON THE NEXT ISSUE.

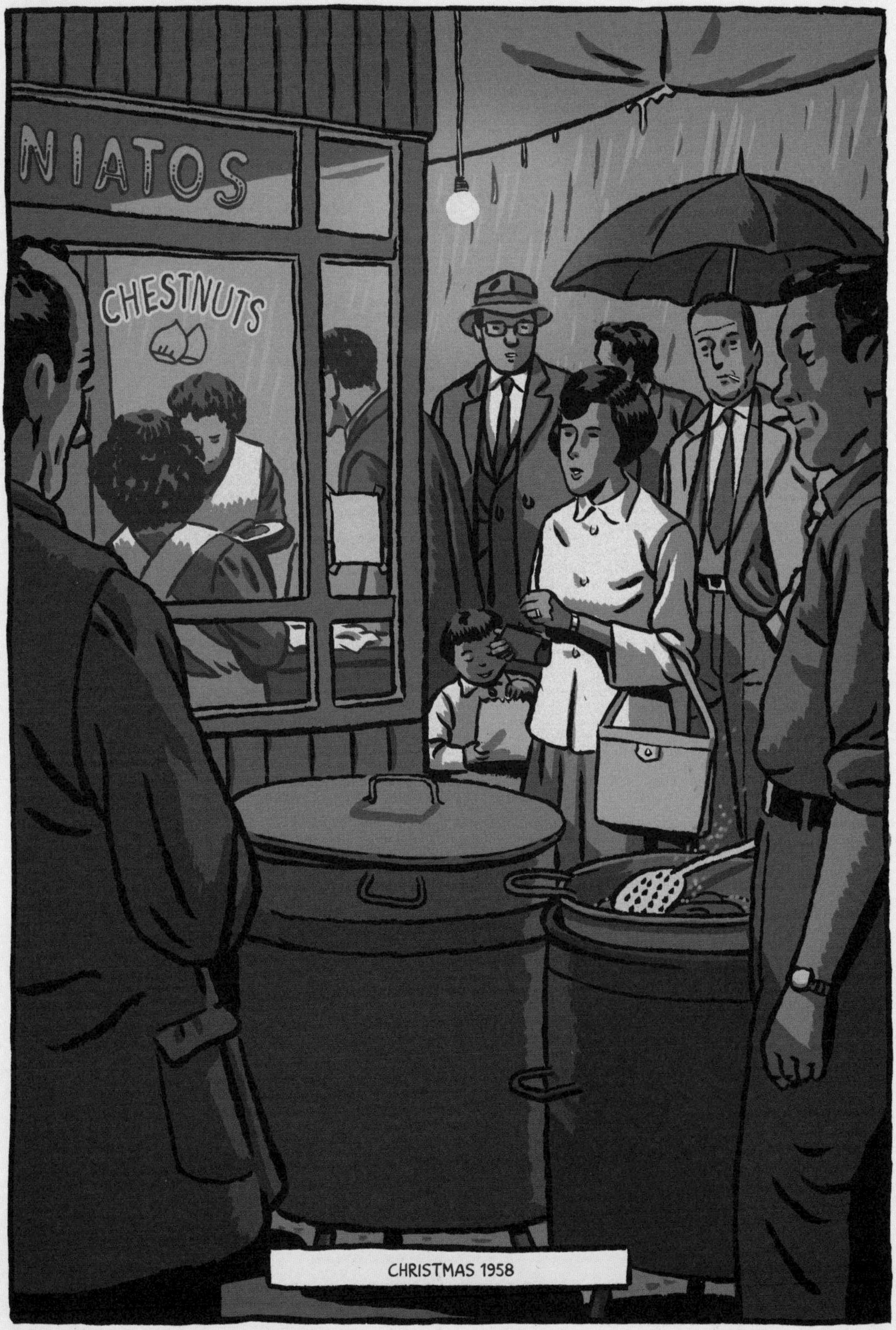
NIATOS
CHESTNUTS
CHRISTMAS 1958

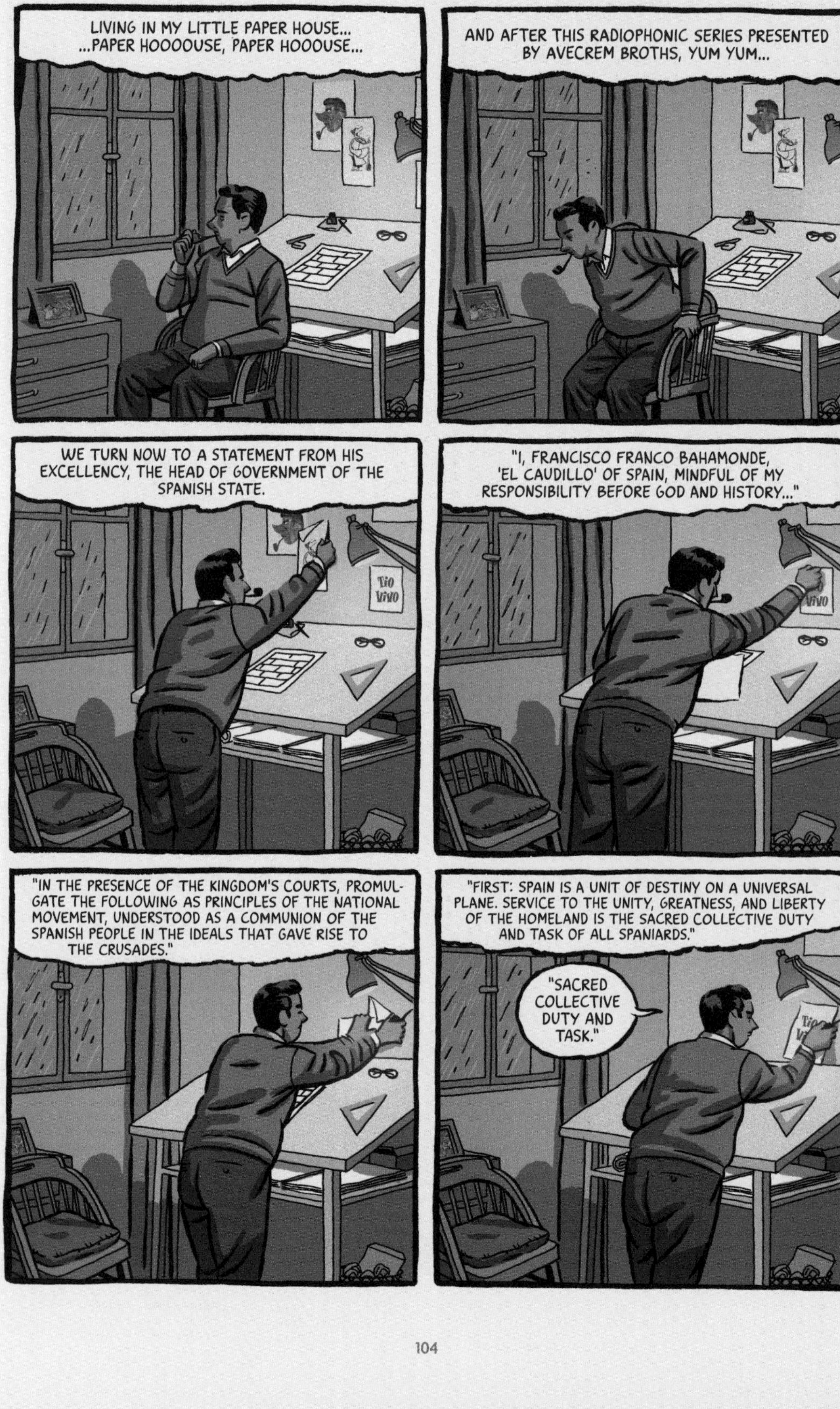
LIVING IN MY LITTLE PAPER HOUSE... ...PAPER HOOOOUSE, PAPER HOOOUSE...
AND AFTER THIS RADIOPHONIC SERIES PRESENTED BY AVECREM BROTHS, YUM YUM...
WE TURN NOW TO A STATEMENT FROM HIS EXCELLENCY, THE HEAD OF GOVERNMENT OF THE SPANISH STATE.
TIO VIVO
"I, FRANCISCO FRANCO BAHAMONDE, 'EL CAUDILLO' OF SPAIN, MINDFUL OF MY RESPONSIBILITY BEFORE GOD AND HISTORY..."
"IN THE PRESENCE OF THE KINGDOM'S COURTS, PROMULGATE THE FOLLOWING AS PRINCIPLES OF THE NATIONAL MOVEMENT, UNDERSTOOD AS A COMMUNION OF THE SPANISH PEOPLE IN THE IDEALS THAT GAVE RISE TO THE CRUSADES."
"FIRST: SPAIN IS A UNIT OF DESTINY ON A UNIVERSAL PLANE. SERVICE TO THE UNITY, GREATNESS, AND LIBERTY OF THE HOMELAND IS THE SACRED COLLECTIVE DUTY AND TASK OF ALL SPANIARDS."
"SACRED COLLECTIVE DUTY AND TASK."

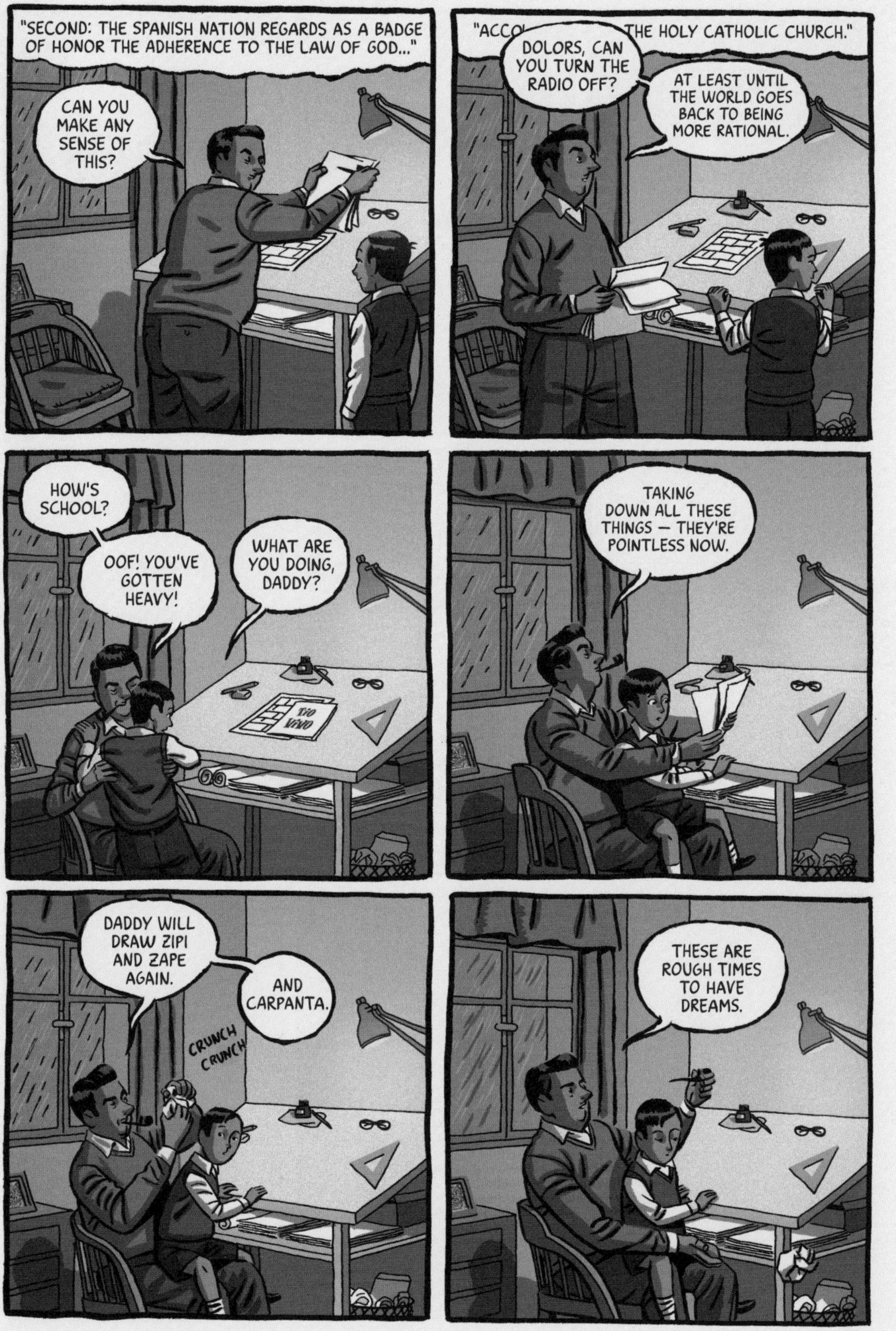
"SECOND: THE SPANISH NATION REGARDS AS A BADGE OF HONOR THE ADHERENCE TO THE LAW OF GOD..."
CAN YOU MAKE ANY SENSE OF THIS?
"ACCO THE HOLY CATHOLIC CHURCH."
DOLORS, CAN YOU TURN THE RADIO OFF?
AT LEAST UNTIL THE WORLD GOES BACK TO BEING MORE RATIONAL.
HOW'S SCHOOL?
OOF! YOU'VE GOTTEN HEAVY!
WHAT ARE YOU DOING, DADDY?
TAKING DOWN ALL THESE THINGS — THEY'RE POINTLESS NOW.
DADDY WILL DRAW ZIPI AND ZAPE AGAIN.
AND CARPANTA.
CRUNCH CRUNCH
THESE ARE ROUGH TIMES TO HAVE DREAMS.

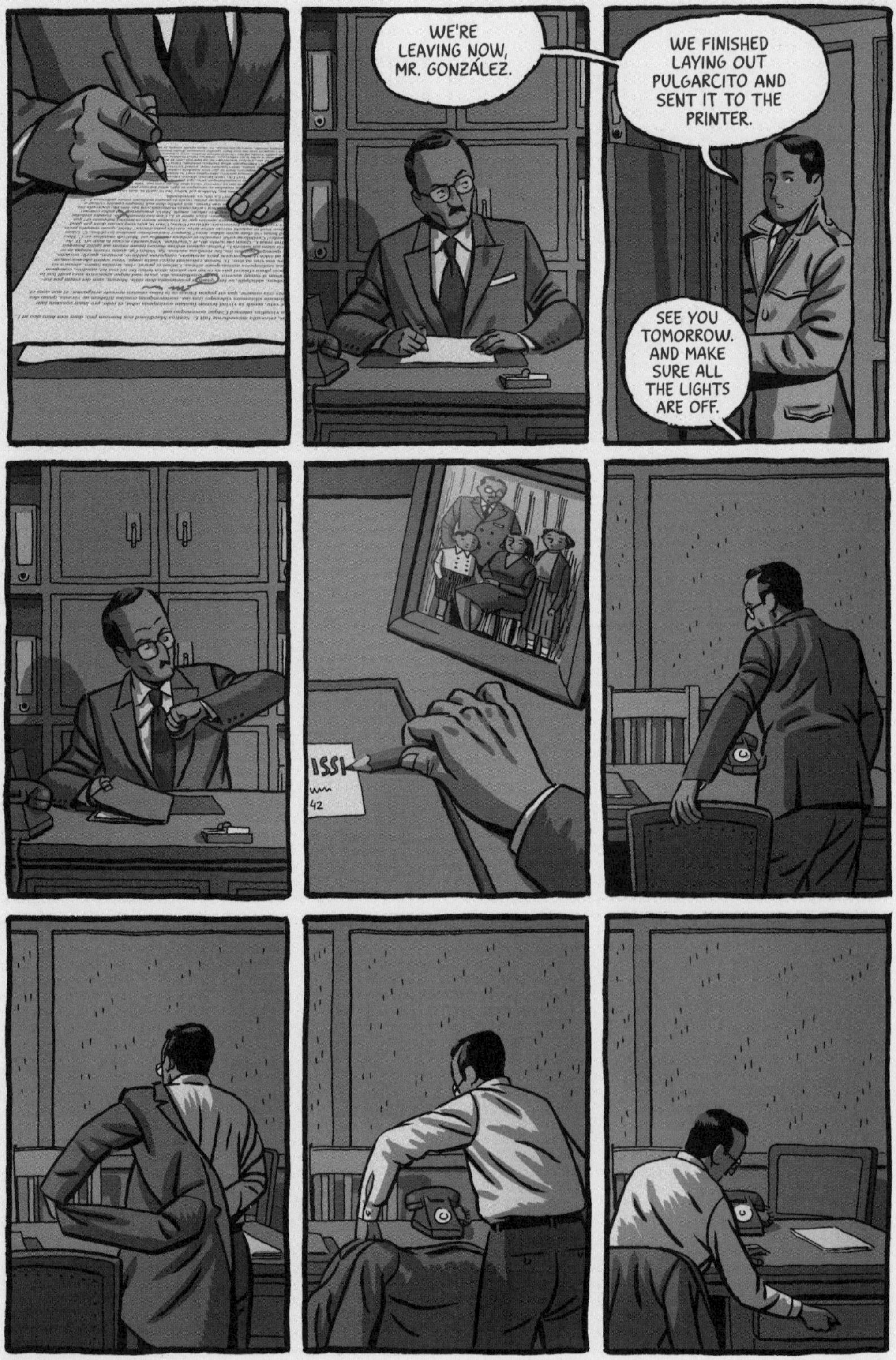
WE'RE LEAVING NOW, MR. GONZÁLEZ.
WE FINISHED LAYING OUT PULGARCITO AND SENT IT TO THE PRINTER.
SEE YOU TOMORROW. AND MAKE SURE ALL THE LIGHTS ARE OFF.

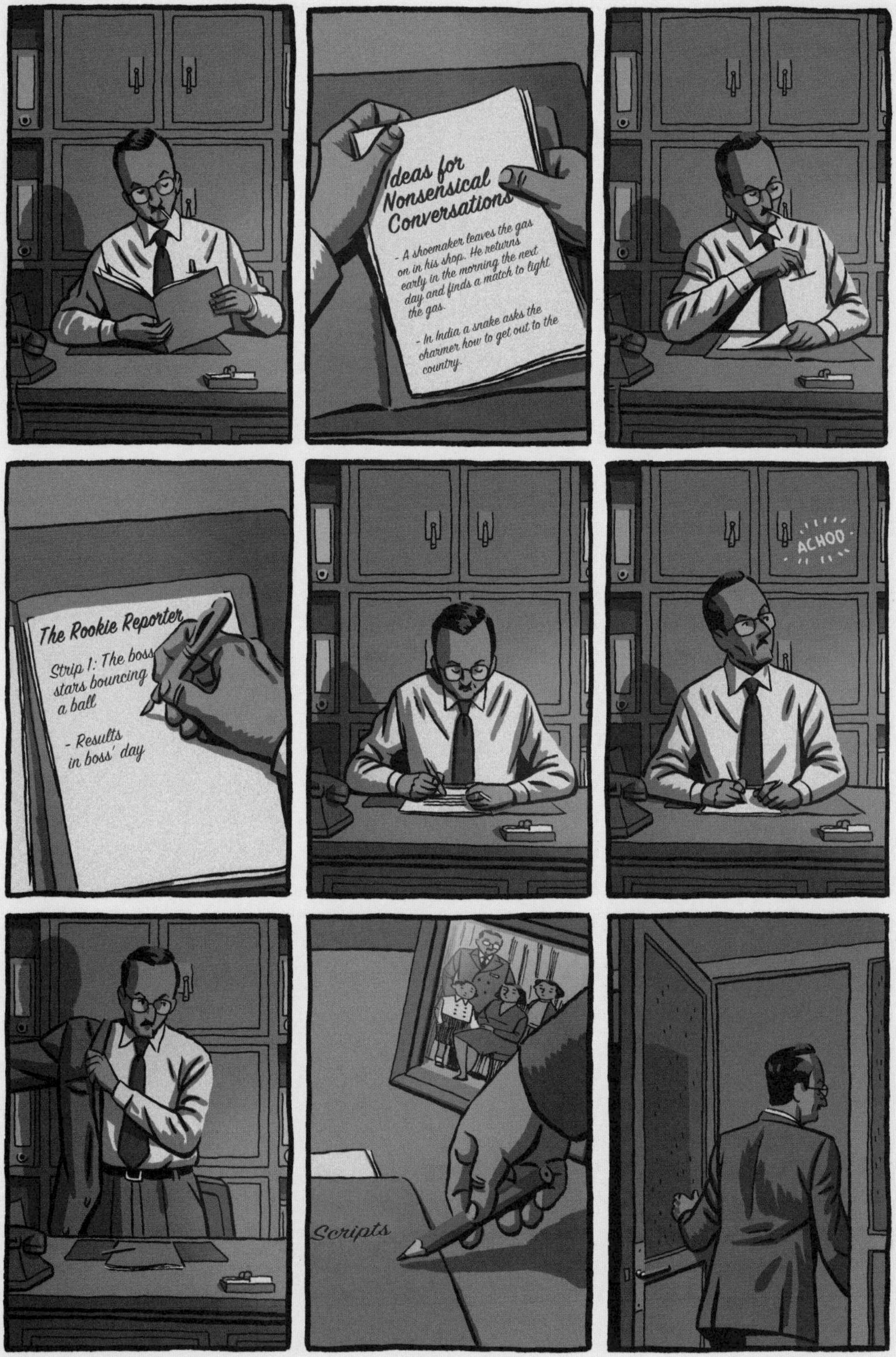
Ideas for Nonsensical Conversations
- A shoemaker leaves the gas on in his shop. He returns early in the morning the next day and finds a match to light the gas.
- In India a snake asks the charmer how to get out to the country.
The Rookie Reporter
Strip 1: The boss stars bouncing a ball
- Results in boss' day
ACHOO
Scripts

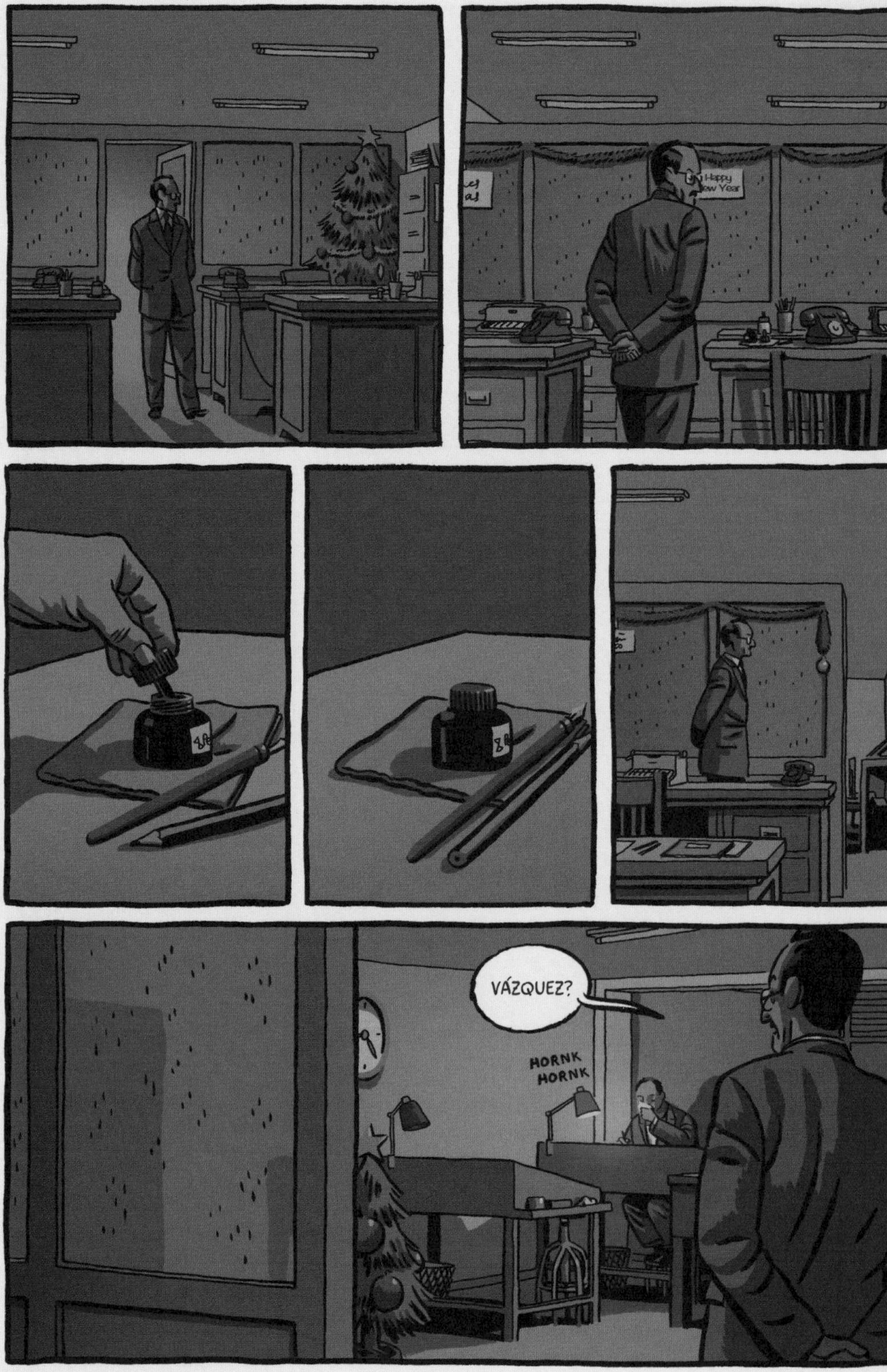
Happy
New Year
VÁZQUEZ?
HORNK
HORNK

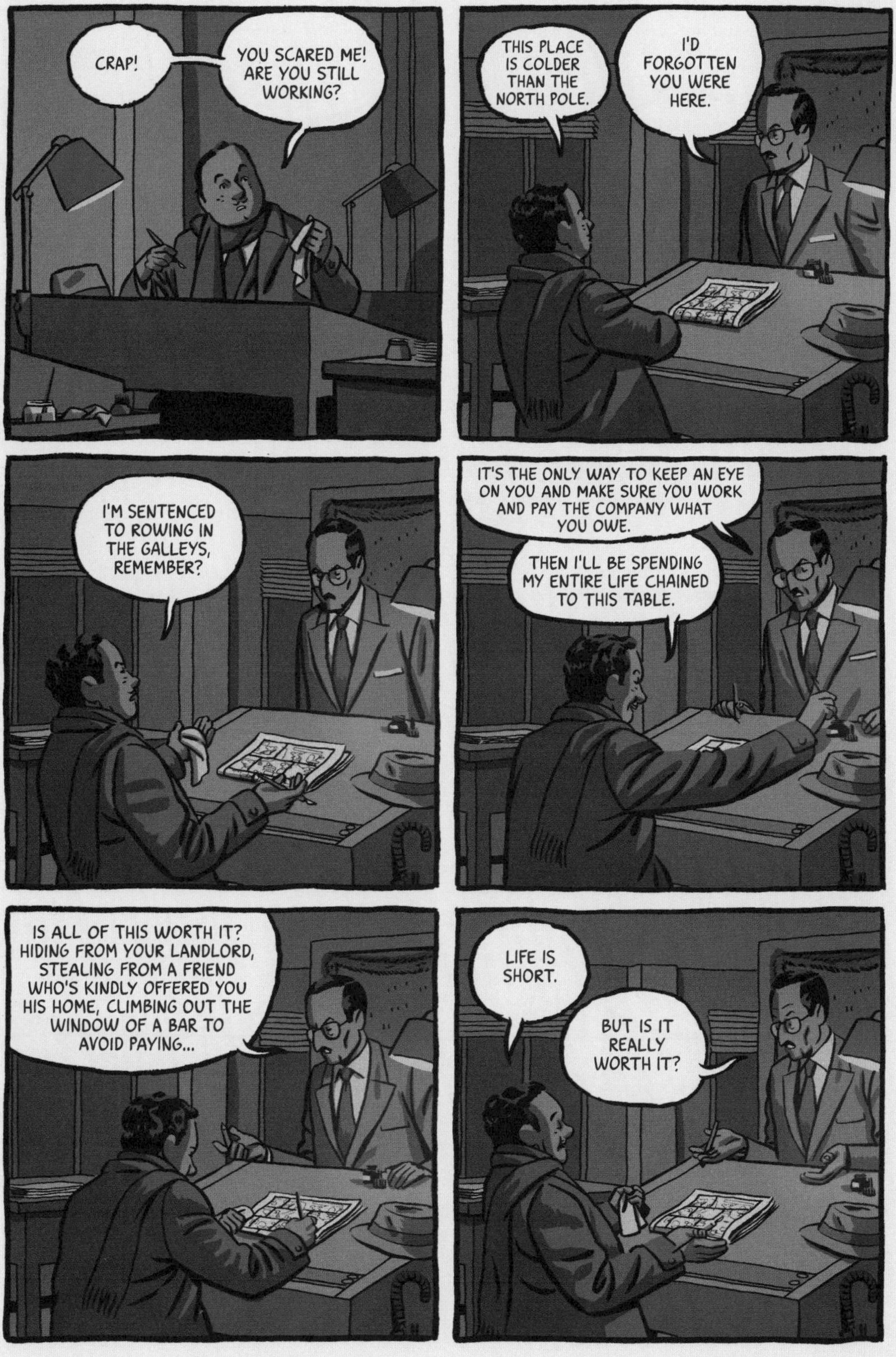
CRAP!
YOU SCARED ME! ARE YOU STILL WORKING?
THIS PLACE IS COLDER THAN THE NORTH POLE.
I'D FORGOTTEN YOU WERE HERE.
I'M SENTENCED TO ROWING IN THE GALLEYS, REMEMBER?
IT'S THE ONLY WAY TO KEEP AN EYE ON YOU AND MAKE SURE YOU WORK AND PAY THE COMPANY WHAT YOU OWE.
THEN I'LL BE SPENDING MY ENTIRE LIFE CHAINED TO THIS TABLE.
IS ALL OF THIS WORTH IT? HIDING FROM YOUR LANDLORD, STEALING FROM A FRIEND WHO'S KINDLY OFFERED YOU HIS HOME, CLIMBING OUT THE WINDOW OF A BAR TO AVOID PAYING...
LIFE IS SHORT.
BUT IS IT REALLY WORTH IT?

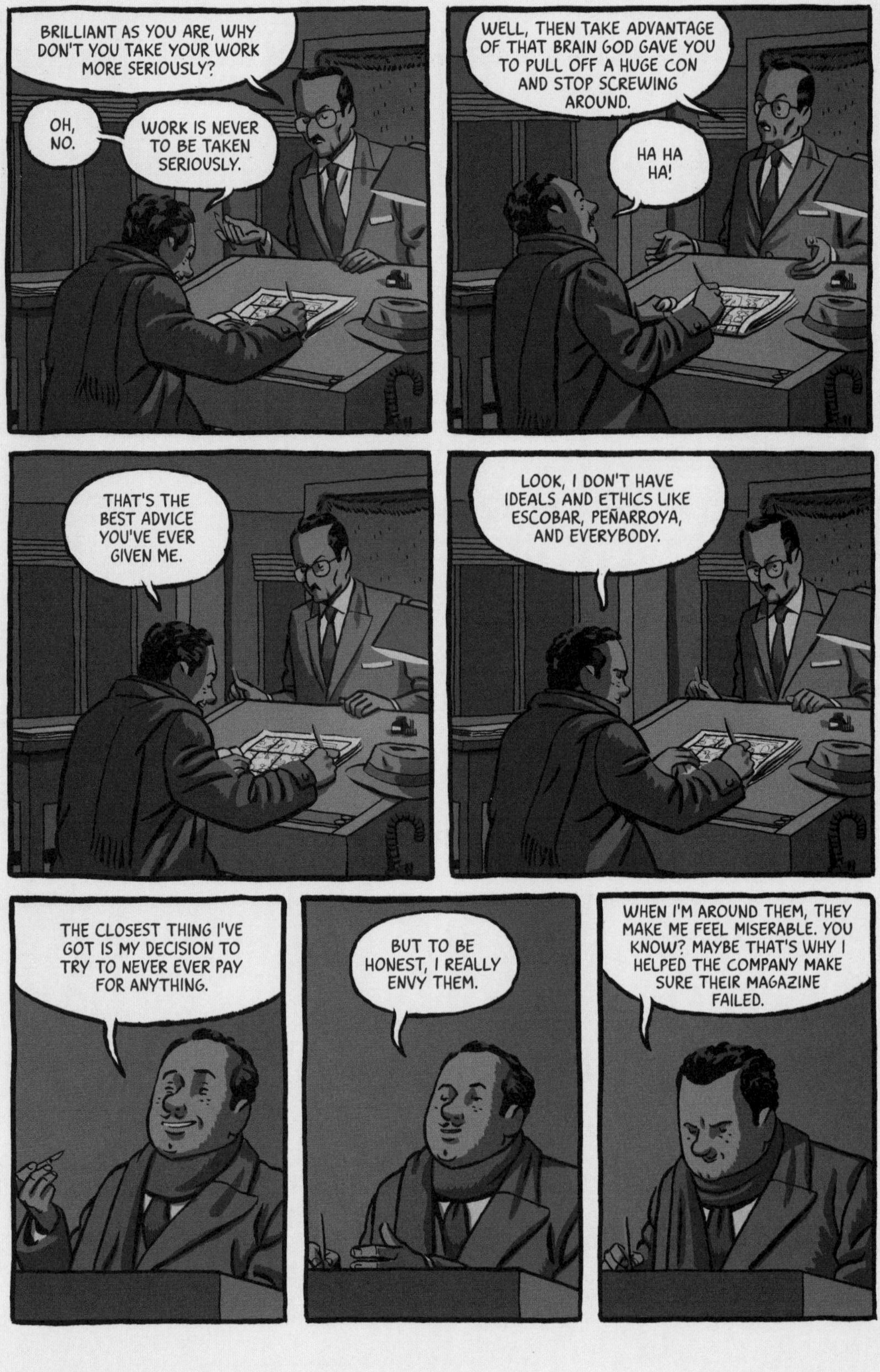
BRILLIANT AS YOU ARE, WHY DON'T YOU TAKE YOUR WORK MORE SERIOUSLY?
OH, NO.
WORK IS NEVER TO BE TAKEN SERIOUSLY.
WELL, THEN TAKE ADVANTAGE OF THAT BRAIN GOD GAVE YOU TO PULL OFF A HUGE CON AND STOP SCREWING AROUND.
HA HA HA!
THAT'S THE BEST ADVICE YOU'VE EVER GIVEN ME.
LOOK, I DON'T HAVE IDEALS AND ETHICS LIKE ESCOBAR, PEÑARROYA, AND EVERYBODY.
THE CLOSEST THING I'VE GOT IS MY DECISION TO TRY TO NEVER EVER PAY FOR ANYTHING.
BUT TO BE HONEST, I REALLY ENVY THEM.
WHEN I'M AROUND THEM, THEY MAKE ME FEEL MISERABLE. YOU KNOW? MAYBE THAT'S WHY I HELPED THE COMPANY MAKE SURE THEIR MAGAZINE FAILED.

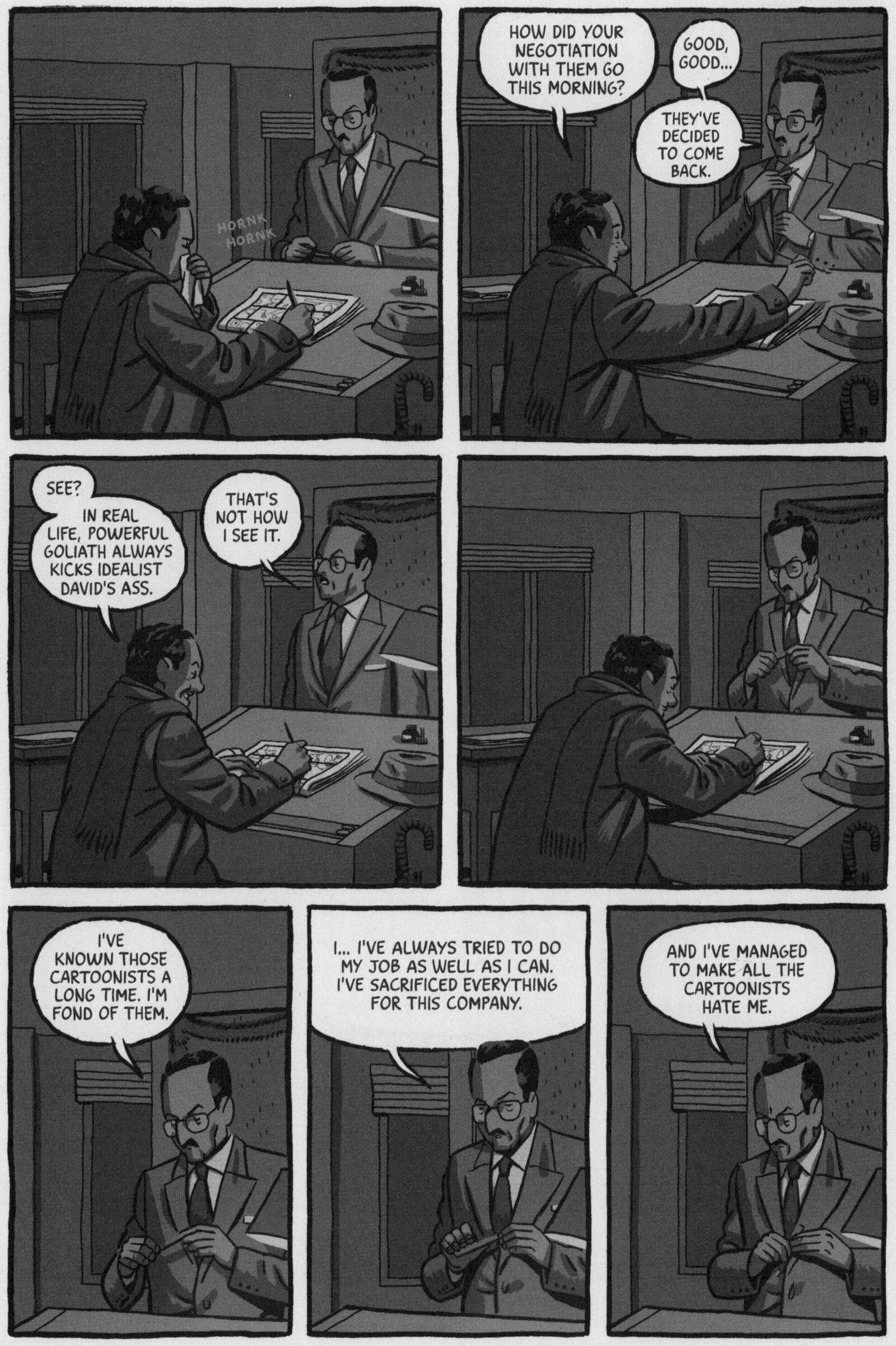
HORNK
HORNK
HOW DID YOUR NEGOTIATION WITH THEM GO THIS MORNING?
GOOD, GOOD...
THEY'VE DECIDED TO COME BACK.
SEE?
IN REAL LIFE, POWERFUL GOLIATH ALWAYS KICKS IDEALIST DAVID'S ASS.
THAT'S NOT HOW I SEE IT.
I'VE KNOWN THOSE CARTOONISTS A LONG TIME. I'M FOND OF THEM.
I... I'VE ALWAYS TRIED TO DO MY JOB AS WELL AS I CAN. I'VE SACRIFICED EVERYTHING FOR THIS COMPANY.
AND I'VE MANAGED TO MAKE ALL THE CARTOONISTS HATE ME.

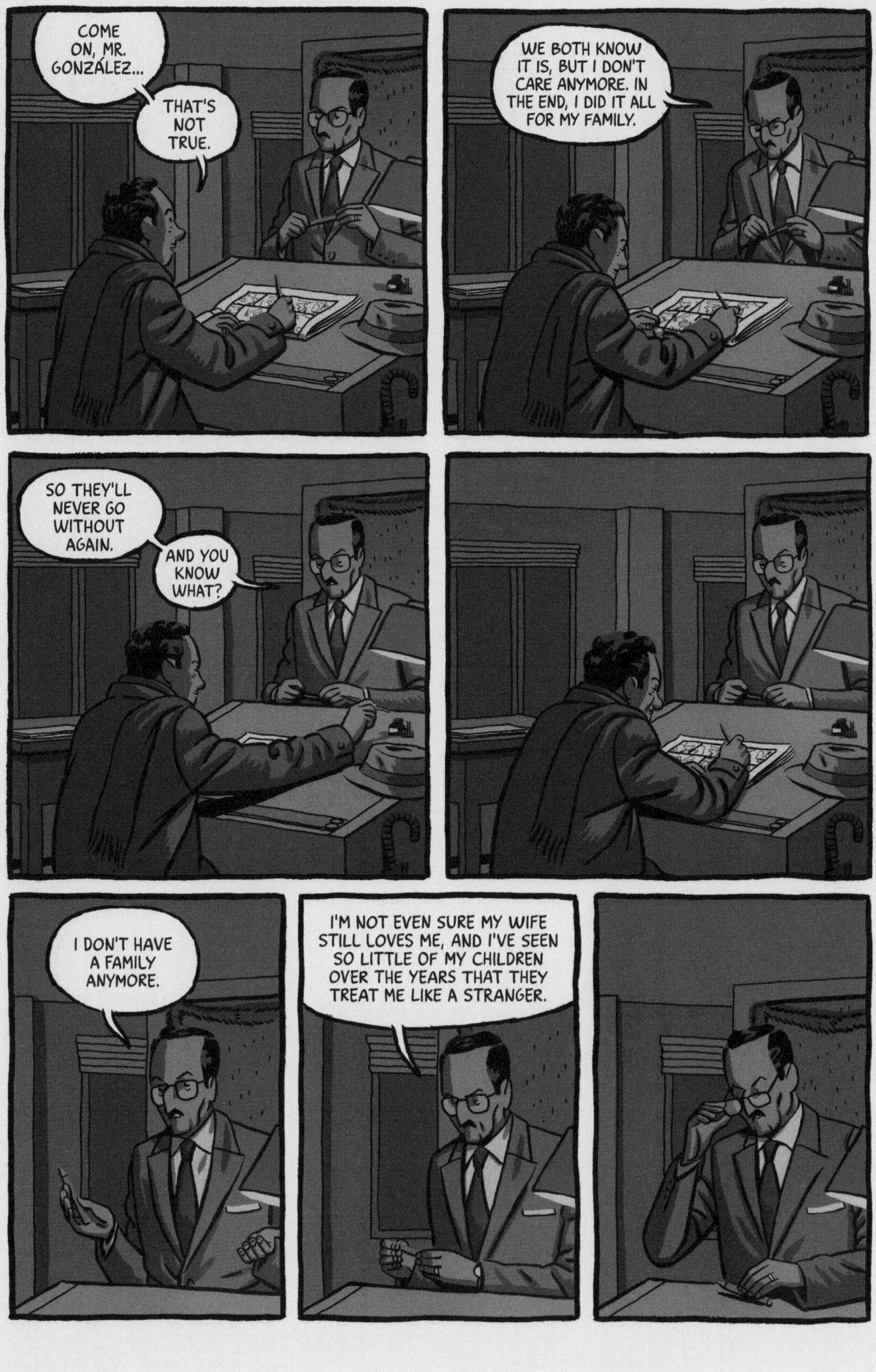
COME ON, MR. GONZÁLEZ...
THAT'S NOT TRUE.
WE BOTH KNOW IT IS, BUT I DON'T CARE ANYMORE. IN THE END, I DID IT ALL FOR MY FAMILY.
SO THEY'LL NEVER GO WITHOUT AGAIN.
AND YOU KNOW WHAT?
I DON'T HAVE A FAMILY ANYMORE.
I'M NOT EVEN SURE MY WIFE STILL LOVES ME, AND I'VE SEEN SO LITTLE OF MY CHILDREN OVER THE YEARS THAT THEY TREAT ME LIKE A STRANGER.

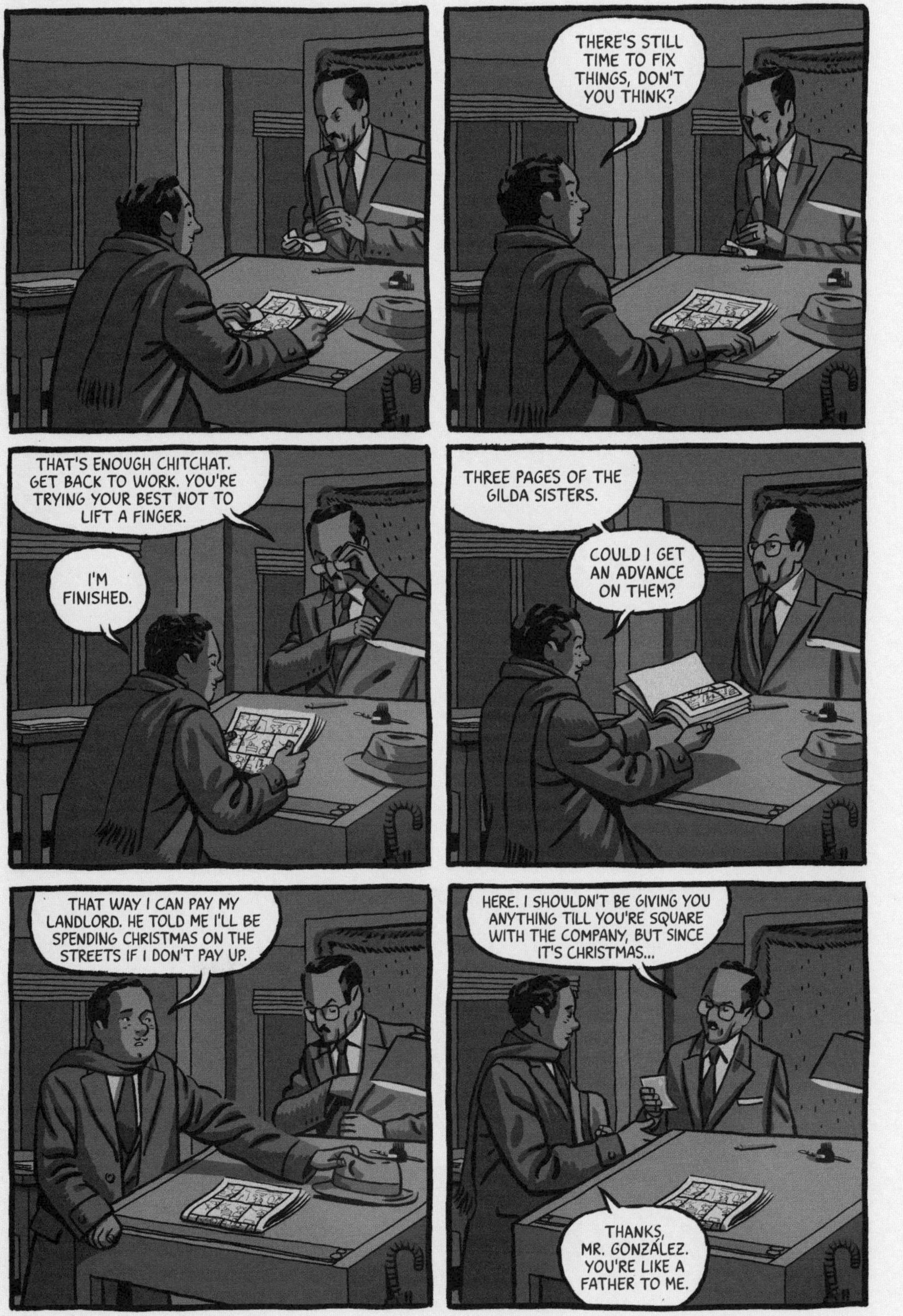
THERE'S STILL TIME TO FIX THINGS, DON'T YOU THINK?
THAT'S ENOUGH CHITCHAT. GET BACK TO WORK. YOU'RE TRYING YOUR BEST NOT TO LIFT A FINGER.
I'M FINISHED.
THREE PAGES OF THE GILDA SISTERS.
COULD I GET AN ADVANCE ON THEM?
THAT WAY I CAN PAY MY LANDLORD. HE TOLD ME I'LL BE SPENDING CHRISTMAS ON THE STREETS IF I DON'T PAY UP.
HERE. I SHOULDN'T BE GIVING YOU ANYTHING TILL YOU'RE SQUARE WITH THE COMPANY, BUT SINCE IT'S CHRISTMAS...
THANKS, MR. GONZÁLEZ. YOU'RE LIKE A FATHER TO ME.

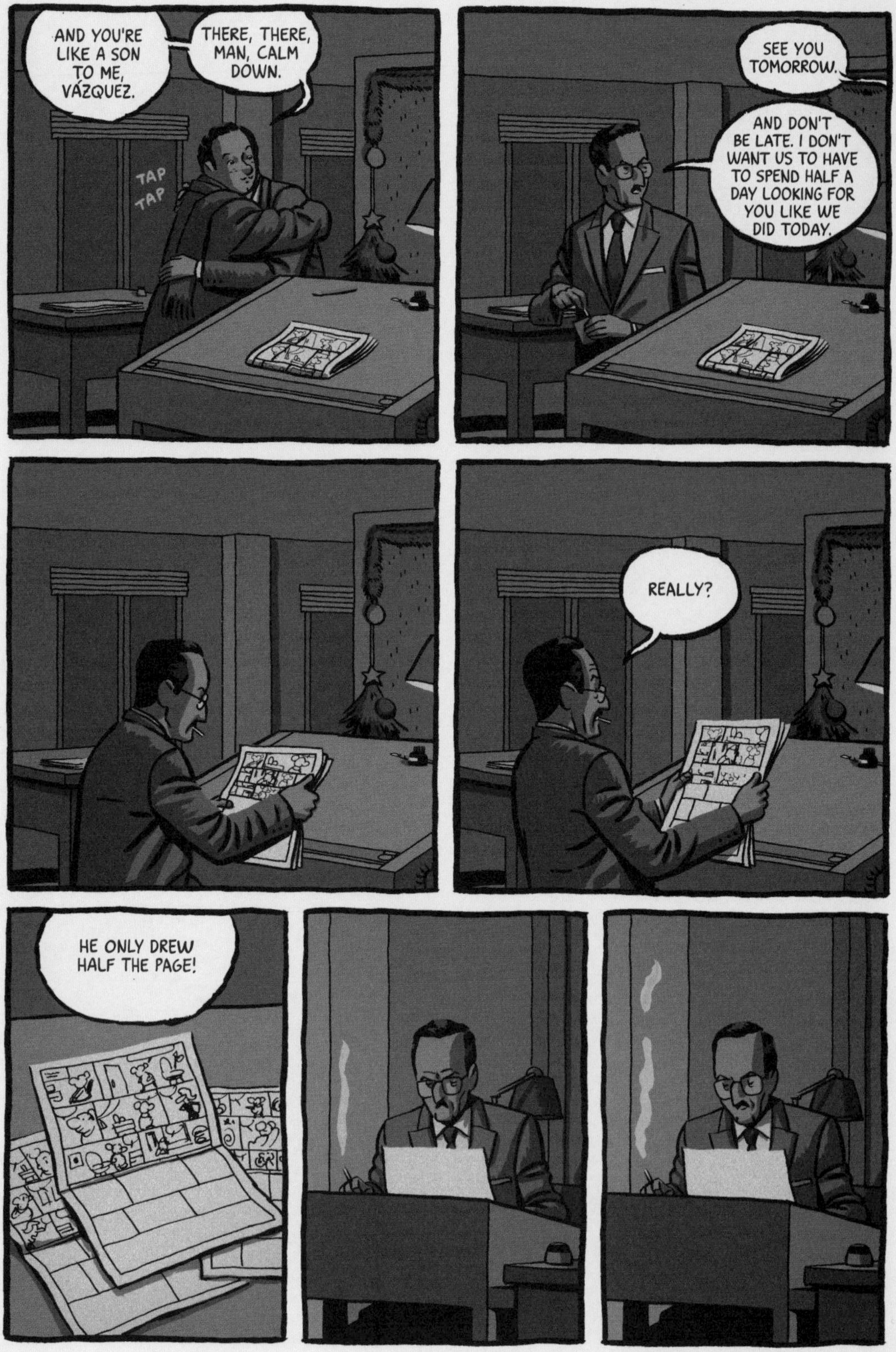
AND YOU'RE LIKE A SON TO ME, VÁZQUEZ.
THERE, THERE, MAN, CALM DOWN.
TAP TAP
SEE YOU TOMORROW.
AND DON'T BE LATE. I DON'T WANT US TO HAVE TO SPEND HALF A DAY LOOKING FOR YOU LIKE WE DID TODAY.
REALLY?
HE ONLY DREW HALF THE PAGE!

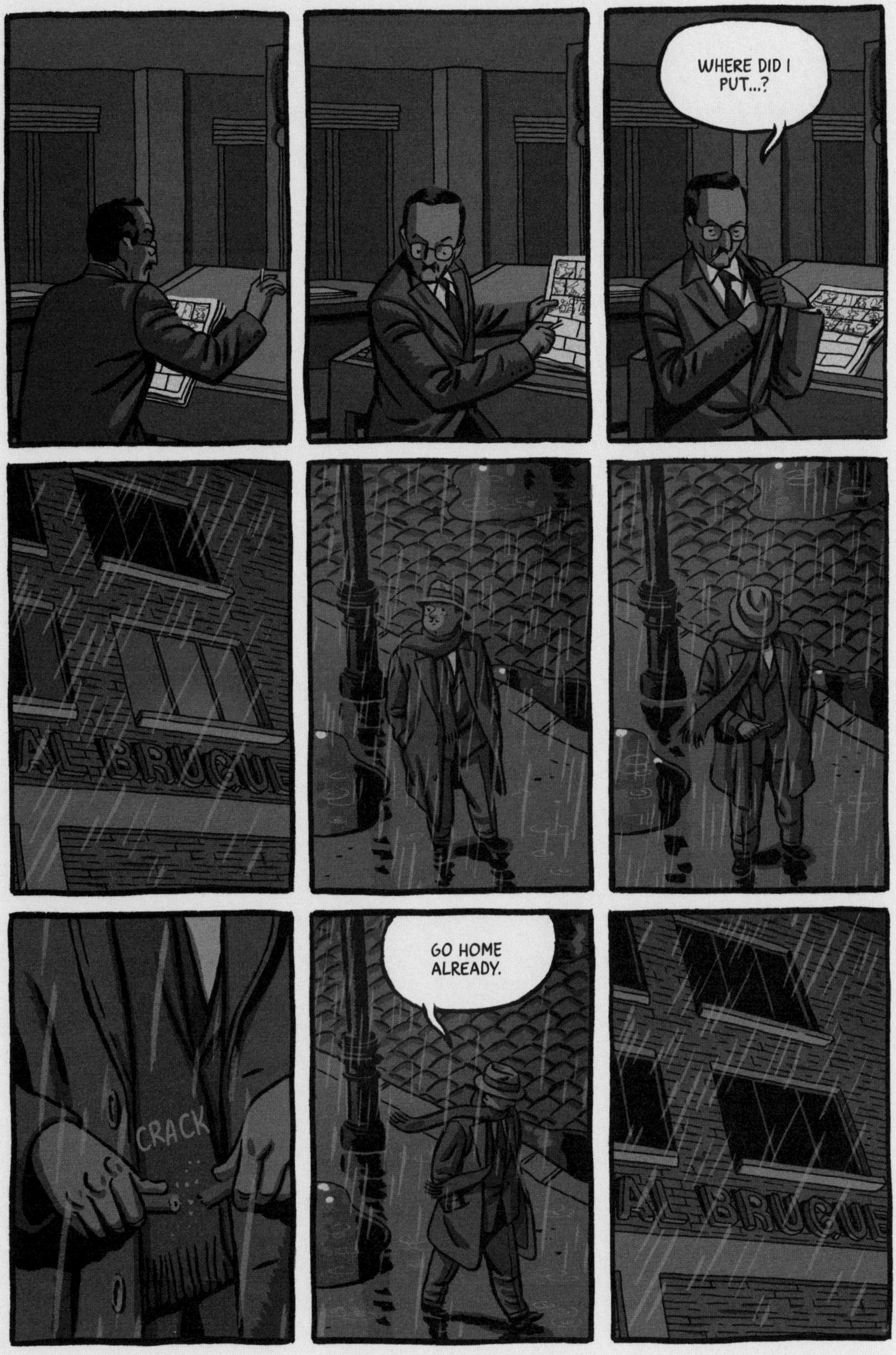
WHERE DID I PUT...?
AL BRUGUE
CRACK
GO HOME ALREADY.
AL BRUGUE

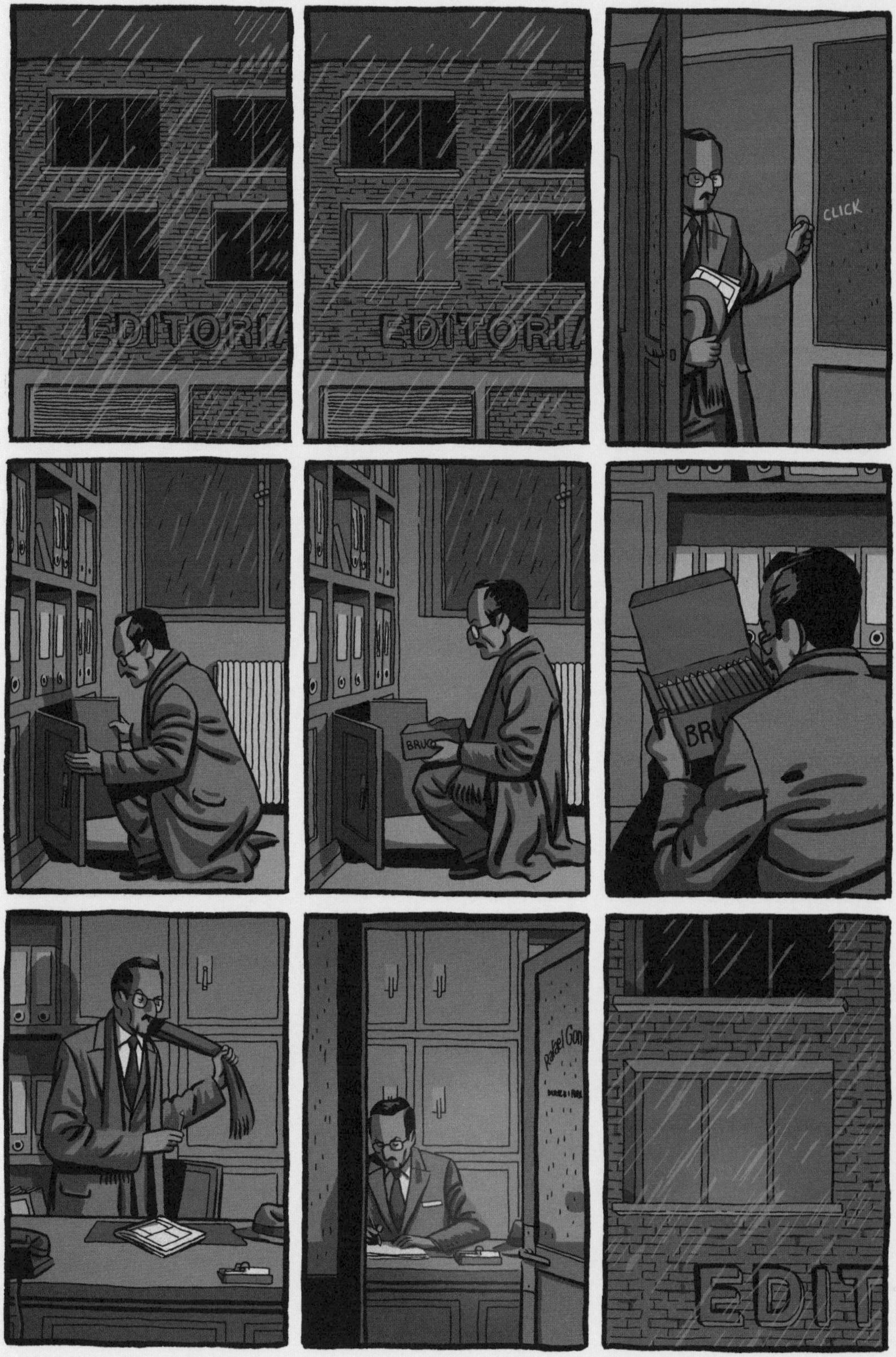
EDITORIA
EDITORIA
CLICK
BRUC
BRU
Rafael Gon
EDIT

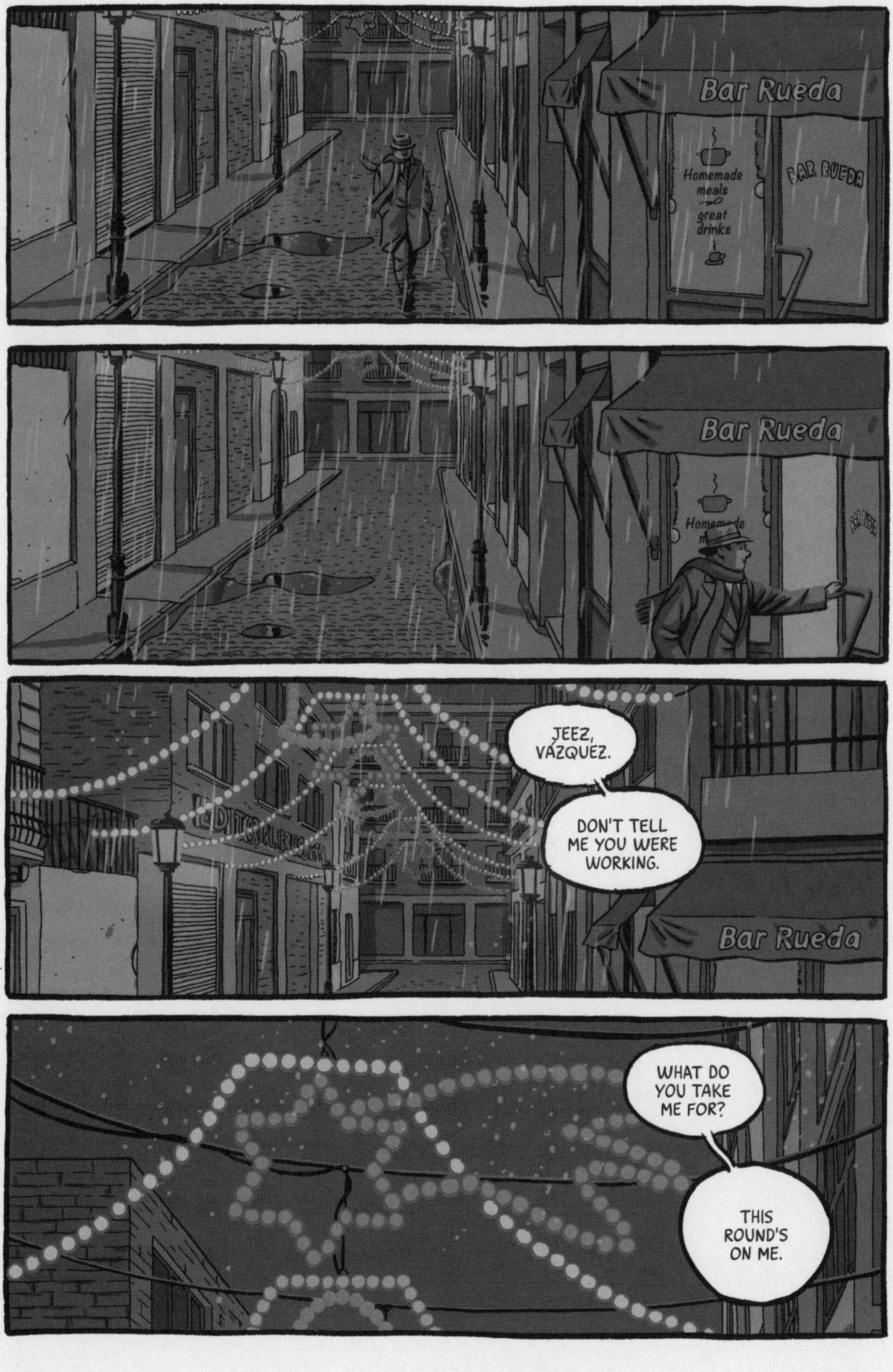
Bar Rueda
Homemade meals great drinks
BAR RUEDA
Bar Rueda
Bar Rueda
JEEZ, VÁZQUEZ.
DON'T TELL ME YOU WERE WORKING.
WHAT DO YOU TAKE ME FOR?
THIS ROUND'S ON ME.

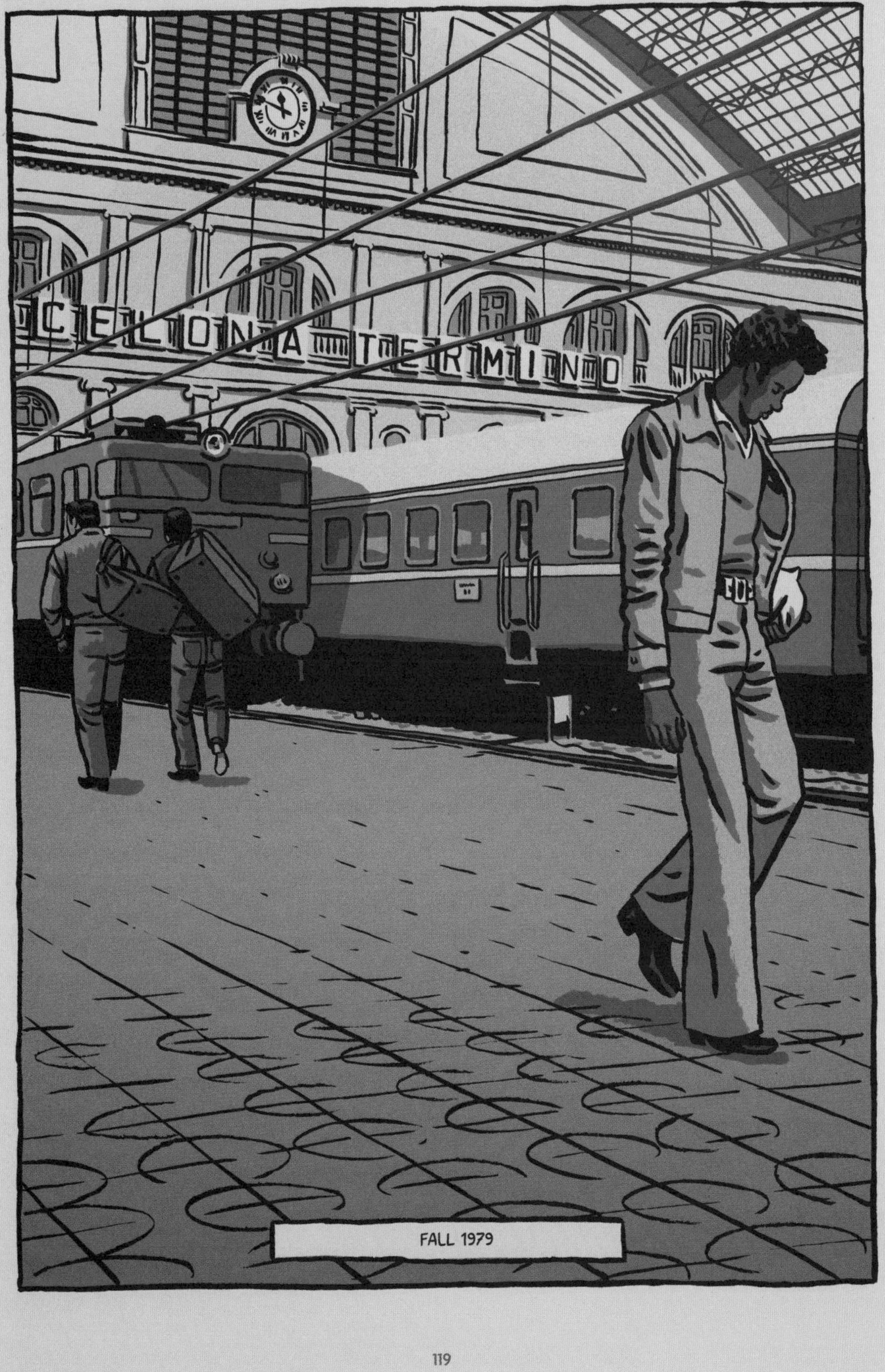
CELONA TERMINO
FALL 1979

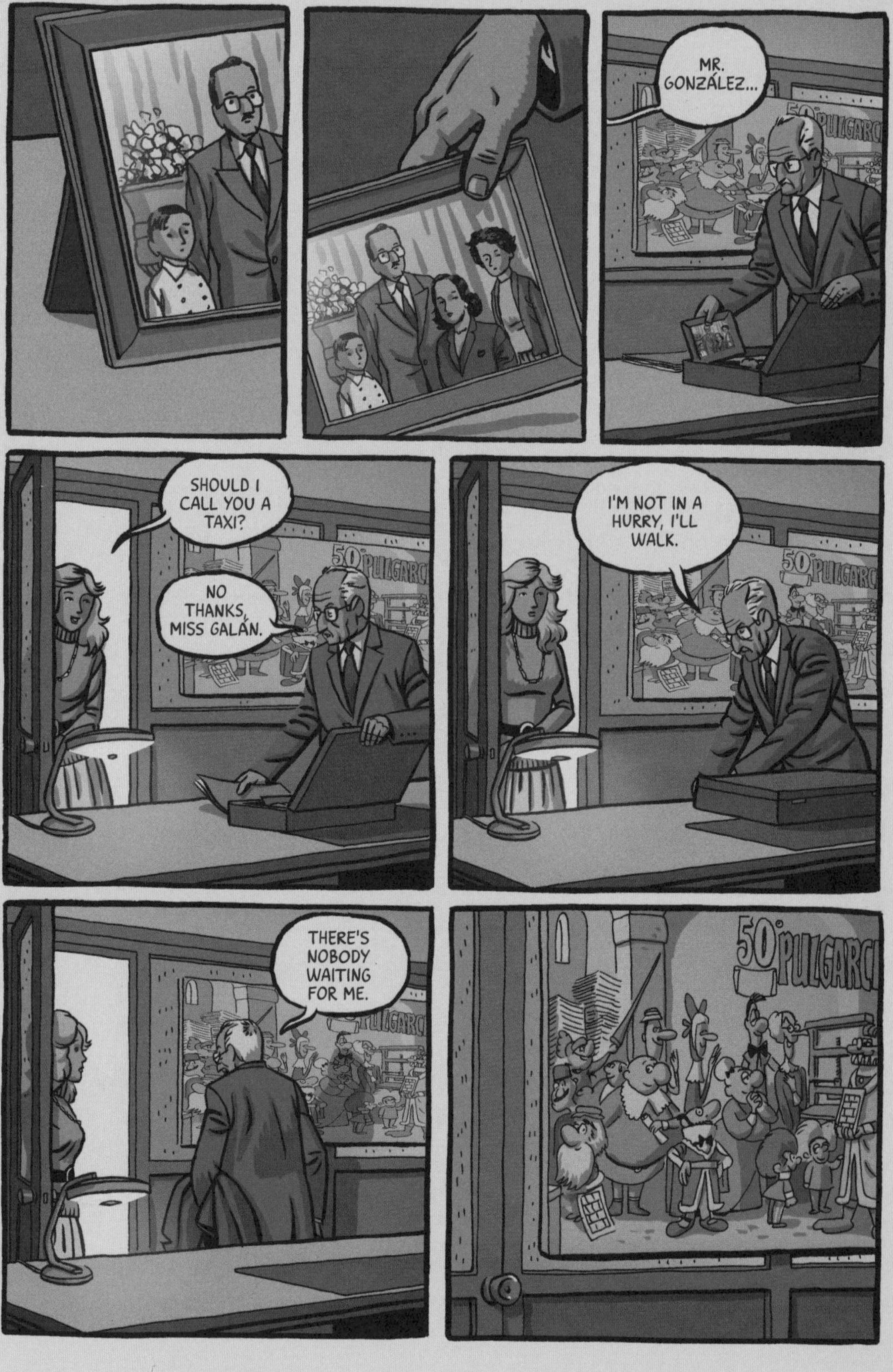
MR. GONZÁLEZ...
SHOULD I CALL YOU A TAXI?
NO THANKS, MISS GALÁN.
I'M NOT IN A HURRY, I'LL WALK.
THERE'S NOBODY WAITING FOR ME.
50 PULGARCITO

The Hope of the Cartoonist

The winters were colder, the summers hotter, the streets grayer. The joy of the defeated had been confiscated. And the defeated included almost all of us.

At the end of the 1950s, we were gradually coming out of a profound economic slump, but everyday life remained humdrum and even grim. Politics wasn't out on the streets — it had been snatched from us with bullets. What remained was an agonizing routine. On the street, the evasive eyes of the vanquished met the arrogant gaze of the victor, the anodyne gaze of the average citizen, and the sharp gaze of the soldier. Life was a question of survival; our dignity had been literally beaten out of us.

But hope remained. Not exactly hope for a better world, because that world remained very far away. A more immediate hope, about the day-to-day. A hope harbored by the proud, the enterprising, the restless.

In Spain in 1957, being a strip cartoonist was a trade. They weren't artists, they were laborers. They charged a fee per page or per strip, being paid by the job, following a set of established and unalterable norms. They gave up their originals and their copyright in exchange for money. They survived. Some of them even did more than that: the ones who started working with foreign publishers and the members of the Bruguera staff, who signed contracts that gave over the ownership of their work in exchange for a sometimes significantly higher annual salary. All of them had to sacrifice family and free time and remain bent over their drawing tables. To survive, to eke out a living.

And in that very same year something happened that shattered the monotony and spread hope. Five extraordinary cartoonists, famous for their characters, tired of giving up what was theirs, ambitious, believed that the comics world could and should recognize their talent and their rights. A wealthy partner gave them a bit of capital, and they organized a revolt. Abandoning Editorial Bruguera and setting up their own company was suicide, but hope, and perhaps desperation, knows no bounds. It is not a coincidence that Carlos Conti, Guillermo Cifré, Josep Escobar, Eugenio Giner, and José Peñarroya were the (self-)appointed ones. They had authored well-known and beloved characters such as arioco, Tribulete, Carpanta, Inspector Dan, and Don Pío. Some of them had been educated in the Spanish Republic, all of them had experienced the Civil War firsthand, and some had even fought for the losing side. They had come into their full selves in a context that lived and breathed hope.

Independence Has Its Price

In 1957, Editorial Bruguera was one of the largest comics publishers in Spain. Back then, its print runs for some of its comic books and magazines were in the hundreds of thousands of copies. These comics included *Roberto Alcázar and Pedrín*, *The Masked Warrior*, *Feats of War*, and the new kid on the block, *Captain Thunder*; the magazines included *Pumby*, *TBO*, *Pulgarcito*, and *El DDT*. There was no lack of work; every week, every fortnight, every month, hundreds of titles came out. Little by little, Bruguera gained power in the marketplace, craftily using its company assets: printing presses, comics, sticker albums, books, and especially the abilities of its technicians and creators. Working for Bruguera was a guarantee: of steady, abundant work, regular pay, a living wage. It was also a guarantee that you'd have to give up rights that, at the time, were denied to all comics artists by every publisher in Spain.

But Cifré, Conti, Escobar, Giner, and Peñarroya took a daring step. They formed DER (Cartoonists and Publishers United) and founded the magazine *Tío Vivo*. It wasn't the first time authors had sought independence as publishers of their work — examples from the same era can be found in countries such as France and the United States — but the Spanish cartoonists were particularly noteworthy: they made their move at a historical moment that did not exactly favor emancipation, in a country without liberties whose citizens were under the yoke of a dictator. And they did it, I sense, buoyed by that hope, that background, that experience, by their eagerness to know that the things they published were their responsibility and theirs alone, for good and for ill. But their calculations were off. In the end, energy and courage weren't enough. The society at large didn't understand freedom. It wasn't sufficient to produce a high-quality magazine, *Tío Vivo*, with a roster of brand-new characters (save Conti's Apolino Tarúguez); it wasn't easy to foil competitors' and distributors' plans; it was no mean feat to juggle producing weekly pages with heading up and managing a publication. Publishing is enormously complicated, full of intricacies. Freedom in a country bereft of that phenomenon doesn't come cheap. And so Cifré, Conti, Escobar, Giner, and Peñarroya were forced to give in. They returned to Bruguera's fold. It was what was expected of them — they were all too good to give up their talent. Giner took a little longer to find professional opportunities in other contexts, working for markets abroad; Cifré, Conti, Escobar, and Peñarroya reclaimed their Bruguera creations and kept making history in Spain's funnies.

Ultimately, the dream lasted only a year. They woke up. Without losing their hope for survival, with their heads held high. They returned to the everyday life at their drawing boards and with their characters, their installments, and their weekly paychecks, their resignation. And through it all, they and their thousands of fellow cartoonists forged the history of the Spanish comic, a history full of light and shadows but absolutely undeniable.

The Winter of the Cartoonist is one of very few works that attempts to recount this history; the history of the cartoonists and their experiences, the history of our nation. Paco Roca has done so with tenderness and respect, but also with realism and consistency. It's not all pretty, but sometimes the truth hurts. Thank you, Paco, for looking back on our legacy and bringing it to the attention and appreciation of a broader public.

–ANTONI GUIRAL

Antoni Guiral is an award-winning Spanish comics editor, critic, and historian. He is the author of 100 Years of Bruguera.

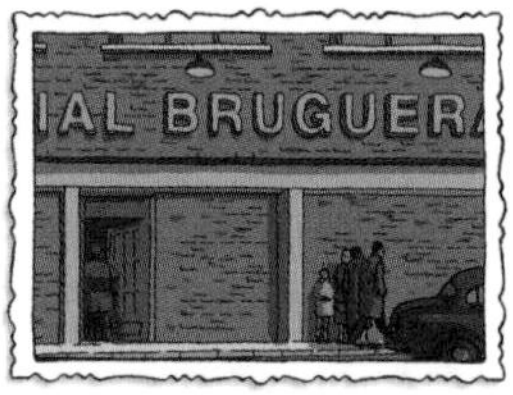
IAL BRUGUER

EDITORIAL BRUGUERA

Founded by Juan Bruguera between 1910 and 1912 under the name El Gato Negro. As Editorial Bruguera (1940–1986), it became one of the foremost publishing companies in Spanish popular culture. It published sticker albums, comics, cut-out dolls, stories, essays, poetry, and novels. It popularized the "pocket book" — popular novels in a small, affordable format — and published collections such as *Pulgarcito; Mortadelo y Filemón, Agencia de Información* (translated into English as *Mort and Phil*); *Colección Historia; Joyas Literarias Juveniles;* and *Bruguera Libro Amigo*.

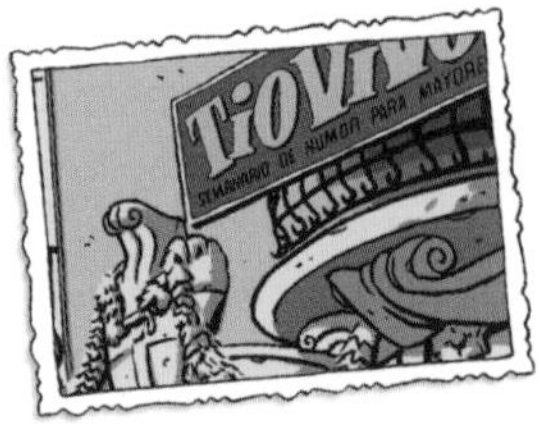

TÍO VIVO

Magazine of comic strips published in 1957 by DER (Cartoonists and Editors United), and jointly directed by Cifré, Conti, Escobar, Eugenio Giner, and Peñarroya — five of Bruguera's most distinguished authors. With their experience, they turned it into a masthead of exceptional visual and content quality. Bruguera's pressure campaign to force the founders to return to the publishing house finally worked in 1958; the magazine continued publication, but in 1960 it was acquired by Bruguera, which started it back up again in 1961 with new numbering.

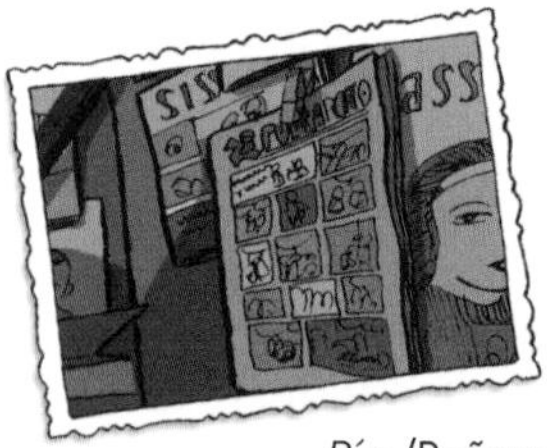

PULGARCITO

Back on the newspaper stands in 1947, after an initial period (1921–1939) being published by El Gato Negro, *Pulgarcito* was one of Bruguera's main humor titles. It birthed series such as *El repórter Tribulete* (Cifré), *Carioco* (Conti), *Zipi y Zape* (Escobar), *El inspector Dan* (González and Giner), *Don Pío* (Peñarroya), *Doña Urraca* (Jorge), *Las hermanas Gilda* (Vázquez), and *Mortadelo y Filemón* (Ibáñez). It was published by Bruguera in various periods until the company closed in 1986.

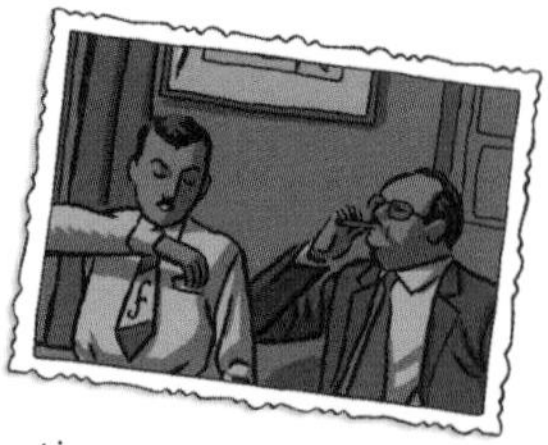

LOS HERMANOS BRUGUERA

Pantaleón Bruguera (1910–1962) and Francisco Bruguera (1912–1990) took over El Gato Negro in 1933, upon the death of their father, Juan Bruguera. Both worked their whole lives to make it a touchstone in the Spanish publishing scene. While Pantaleón took care of the more administrative and financial responsibilities, Francisco transformed the company's artistic structure. The publisher also had interests in graphic design, advertising, distribution, and an international rights agency, Creaciones Editoriales.

RAFAEL GONZÁLEZ

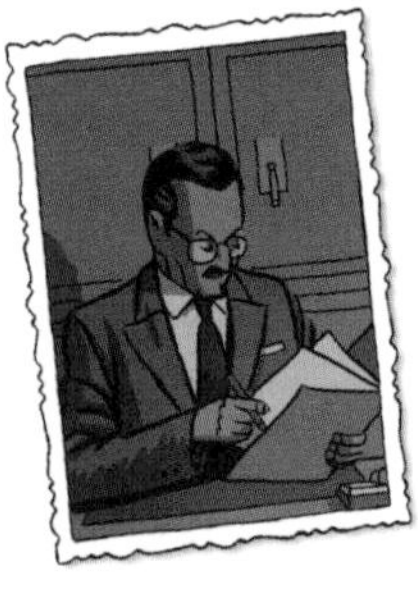

Prohibited from practicing journalism by the Franco regime, Rafael González (1910–1995) fled to France, and upon returning to Spain he eked out a living through a variety of jobs. After writing a number of popular novels, he was hired in 1946 by the Bruguera family to head up the publishing house's editorial side, where he continued to work for the rest of his life. A skilled writer and an energetic man, he was the driving force behind all of the company's comics-related projects, overseeing its content and generating characters and editorial policy.

VÍCTOR MORA

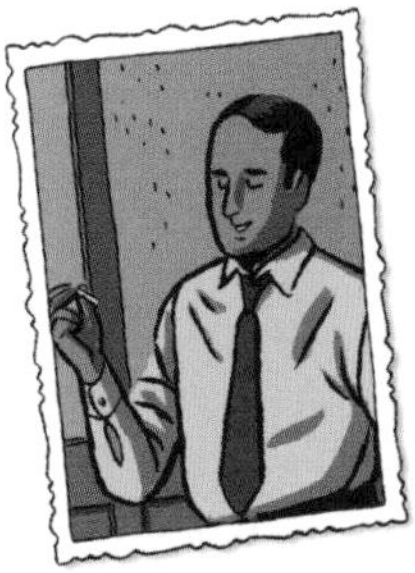

It was Rafael González who dissuaded Víctor Mora (1931–2016) from becoming a comics artist. When he was hired as an editor at Bruguera in 1951, Mora balanced his editorial work with his drive as a script writer, creating celebrated characters such as El Capitán Trueno and El Jabato. He was imprisoned because of his allegiance to the Catalonian communist party, and in 1962 he fled to France, where in addition to writing comics scripts for Franco-Belgian publishers, he started working as a novelist.

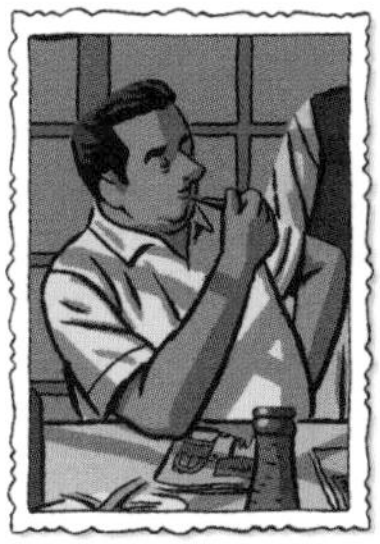

JOSEP ESCOBAR

Josep Escobar (1908–1994) started his professional career as an artist at 14 years old. Because of his commitment to the Spanish Republic before and after the Civil War, he was thrown in prison; after he came out, prohibited from working in the post office, he devoted himself to animated cartoons and comics. A creative and hyperactive artist — he also wrote plays and invented a variety of devices — he created iconic characters for Spanish comics, including *Carpanta* and *Zipi y Zape*. In 1957, he and four of his colleagues from Bruguera set out to attempt editorial self-management with *Tío Vivo*.

CIFRÉ

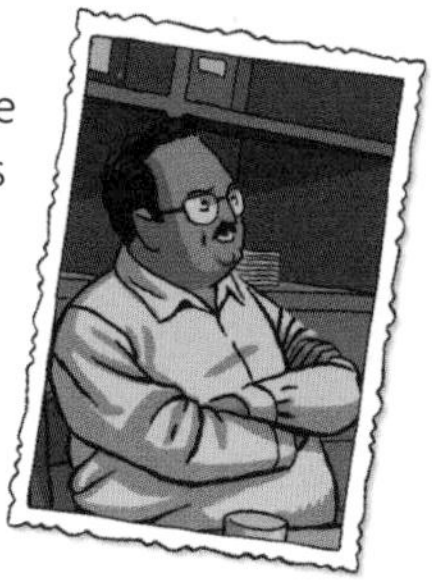

After working as one of Escobar's colleagues in an animation studio in the 1940s, Guillermo Cifré (1922–1962) became one of the Bruguera school's key figures starting in 1945 and continuing until his death. He created characters such as the reporter Tribulete, Don Furcio Buscabollos, and Cucufato Pi, and also employed his gifts as a graphic designer. He had a dynamic style and contributed to the sports press with his humorous personal essays and comic strips featuring his character Don Césped.

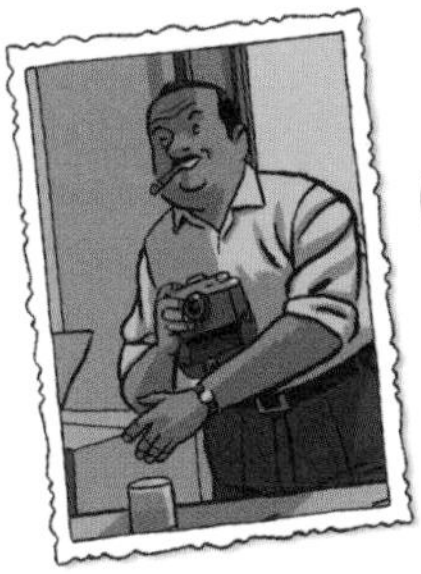

PEÑARROYA

After a stint at the animation studio Dibujos Animados Chamartín, José Peñarroya (1910–1975) took his enormous creativity to Editorial Bruguera, creating characters that were vital to the success of its comics, including Don Pío, Don Berrinche, Gordito Relleno, and Pepe "el Hincha." A prolific, restless creator, he produced work for nearly all of Bruguera's humorous titles, from *Pulgarcito* to *Tío Vivo* to *El DDT* and *Can Can*. He also contributed to the sports magazine *Dicen* and to magazines such as *Tele-Radio* and *Terror Fantastic*.

CONTI

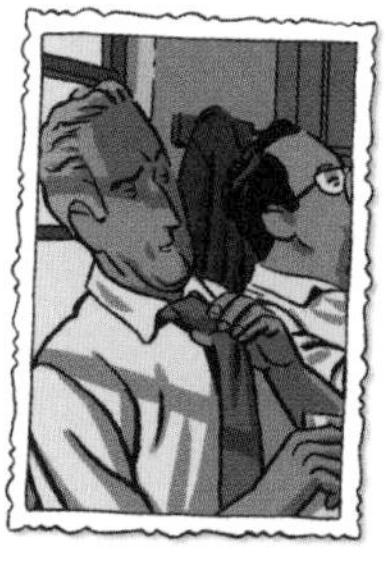

Before his arrival at Bruguera in 1949, Carlos Conti (1916-1975) had been a cartoonist at newspapers such as *La Prensa* — where he published a daily gag strip until his death — and magazines such as *Hola*. He created unique and memorable characters including Carioco, Apolino Tarúguez, and Morfeo Pérez, but also wrote a number of humor columns that appeared in *Can Can*, *El DDT*, and *Tío Vivo*. One of his specialties was the visual joke, and he showed off his talent both at Bruguera and in the humor magazines *Pepe Cola* and *Mata Ratos*.

GINER

Eugenio Giner's (1924–1994) artistic talent was apparent in both his realistic comics and in his more humorous work. In the former, he was the cartoonist for the collection *Adventures and Journeys*, published by Bruguera, as well as *El inspector Dan* — conceived of by Rafael González — one of the most important series among Spanish adventure comics. In 1959, shortly after *Tío Vivo*'s failed attempt at editorial self-management, Giner started working for foreign publishers through a variety of Spanish illustration agencies.

VÁZQUEZ

Manuel Vázquez (1930–1995) is one of Spain's best humor comic strip artists. He spent the lengthy first part of his career at Bruguera, where he created beloved series such as *Las hermanas Gilda, La familia Cebolleta*, and *Anacleto, agente secreto*. A rebellious and even somewhat anarchical writer, he rejected all professional and personal discipline, which affected the continuity of his output but not its quality. A brilliant man, between 1978 and 1995 he was published in magazines aimed at adults in addition to producing a daily strip for the newspaper *El Observador*.

ARMONÍA

Armonía Rodríguez (1929) worked as an editorial coordinator, translator, and script writer at Editorial Bruguera (*Celia, Joyas Literarias Juveniles*). She is also a writer and wrote the scripts for a number of comics aimed at children and illustrated by Pilarín Bayés about democratic institutions.

NADAL

Ángel Nadal (1930–2016) started his career as a comics artist at 14 years of age. From 1948 to 1960 he created for Editorial Bruguera series such as *Casildo Calasparra* and *Pascual, criado leal*. After 1960, he specialized in drawing comics for the British and German markets.

NENÉ

Nené Estivill (1926–2011) published his comics in magazines such as *Camino, La Risa*, and *Jaimito* before developing series such as *La terrible Fifí* and the popular *Agamenón* for Bruguera. He also wrote jokes and humorous comics for publishers in Argentina, Italy, Germany, and the UK.

SEGURA

Robert Segura (1927–2008) was active in the 1950s, drawing for magazines such as *Florita* and *Yumbo* as well as working in an animation studio. Starting in 1957, he worked at Bruguera, bringing to life series such as *Rigoberto Picaporte, Los señores de Alcorcón y el holgazán de Pepón*, and *La panda*.

JORGE

Jorge (Miguel Bernet, 1921–1960) started out as a cartoonist creating adventure comics in collections such as *Aventuras y viajes*, and then shifted to focusing on humor in 1947. He is one of the core figures in the Bruguera school, with series such as *Leovigildo Viruta, Doña Urraca*, and *Doña Filo y sus hermanas*.

RAF

Raf (Joan Rafart, 1928–1997) was one of the young talents brought on by Bruguera in 1957. His energetic, expressive pen produced characters such avas Campeonio, Don Pelmazo, Olegario, and Sir Tim O'Theo. He later worked for foreign markets through agencies, and also dabbled in the world of animation.

IBÁÑEZ

Francisco Ibáñez (1936) started working at Bruguera in 1957 and soon created the series *Mortadelo y Filemón* for *Pulgarcito*. Over the course of his long career at the publishing house, he contributed some of its most popular series, including, in addition to the aforementioned, *13 rúe del Percebe, El botones Sacarino, Rompetechos*, and *Pepe Gotera y Otilio*.

LEDESMA

Francisco González Ledesma (1927–2015) worked at Editorial Bruguera between 1947 and 1964 as an editor, script writer, and lawyer. He took over from his uncle Rafael González as the writer for *El inspector Dan*, and soon became a successful writer under the pseudonym Silver Kane, writing Westerns and detective novels.

Afterword

In a way, this is the book I always wanted to create. It was the series published by Editorial Bruguera that made me start to love comics, and, like so many members of my generation as well as previous and subsequent ones, I grew up with all of their characters: Captain Thunder, Mort, Zipi and Zape, Anacleto... As a child, I wondered what was behind them, what their creators were like, how they worked, and what the publishing house was like, the one to which I, still a little boy, sent my first drawings with the childish dream of becoming a cartoonist like my much-admired Raf, Peñarroya, and Vázquez. Of course, I never received a reply to that letter full of drawings made with Carioca-brand markers, nor did I ever manage to quench my thirst to know more about Bruguera and its cartoonists. Occasionally one of the magazines would include a short interview with a photo of the cartoonists, which I'd read with immense interest, or one of the comics would include a depiction of the Bruguera offices. I would stare intently at those drawings, observing every detail in an effort to understand the inner workings of Editorial Bruguera, which in my imagination was something as marvelous as Willy Wonka's chocolate factory.

You could say that this book has enabled me to fulfill that childhood dream — especially the research element. Piecing the story together through the memories of cartoonists and other people associated with the publishing house while striving to be as faithful as possible to the facts has been the most complicated part of creating this book, but also the most exciting. To write this story, I have needed the help of many people, especially Toni Guiral; without his books on Bruguera and all our phone conversations and the dozens of emails we exchanged, I wouldn't have been able to finish this story. Thanks to Laureano Domínguez, who put me in contact with a number of authors, including Víctor Mora, at whose home in Premià de Dalt I spent a pleasant day with Mora and Armonía. To Julia Galán, Andreu Martín, Jordi Bayona, and Nadal, who shared their memories with me. To Joan Pieras, who, from Andorra, sent me reams of information about Bruguera and some immensely useful newsreels from the Franco-era No-Do. To Jordi Ojeda for tracking down visual documentation of mid-century Barcelona. Thanks to Xavi Franch, who showed me around the Barri del Coll and joined me in investigating Bruguera's various locations over the course of its history. Thanks to the gentleman whose name I do not recall whom Xavi and I met by chance on that day of exploration and who still drank his daily coffee in the same bar where he'd done so all those years ago in the company of the Bruguera cartoonists. To the owner of the stationery shop on the Plaza de Lesseps, where, when she was a little girl, the cartoonists used to buy their brushes and where I bought mine for this book. To Vicente from Imágenes Cómics for giving me old issues of Bruguera publications. To Álvaro Pons and Antonio Martín for their comments on the history of self-publishing. To Óscar Palmer, Quim Pérez, and Mónica for their corrections of my Catalán. To Manuel Bartual for his comments. To Jordi Borrás for tracking down copies and pages of *Pulgarcito* and *Tío Vivo* for me. To Javi Zalbidegoitia for also helping me with documentation and for being a shoulder to cry on in difficult moments while creating this book. To Héloïse for her encouragement. And thanks, too, to Fernando Tarancón, who, years ago, while drinking a beer in Avilés with Koldo, put me on the trail of *Tío Vivo*.

-PACO ROCA